This is an annual. That is to say, it is substantially revised each year, the new edition appearing in January of that year. Those wishing to submit additions, corrections, or suggestions for the 1988 edition should submit them prior to June 1, 1987 using the forms provided in the back of this book. (Letters reaching us after that date will have to wait for the 1989 edition.)

D0958417

What Color Is Your Parachute?

Other Books by Richard N. Bolles

The Three Boxes of Life,
*   And How To Get Out of Them*

Where Do I Go From Here With My Life?
   (co-authored with John C. Crystal)

1987 Edition

What Color Is Your Parachute?

A Practical Manual
for
Job-Hunters
& Career Changers

by

Richard Nelson Bolles

Ten Speed Press

The map drawings for
The New Quick Job-Hunting Map (integrated this year, into chapters 4, 5, and 6)
are by STEVEN M. JOHNSON,
author of *What The World Needs Now*

Copyright © 1987, 1986, 1985, 1984, 1983, 1982, 1981,
1980, 1979, 1978, 1977, 1976, 1975, 1972, 1970
by Richard Nelson Bolles. All rights reserved. No part of this book
may be reproduced in any form, except for brief reviews,
without the written permission of the publisher.
Library of Congress Catalog Card No. 81-50471
ISBN 0-89815-157-0, paper
ISBN 0-89815-158-9, cloth
Published by Ten Speed Press, P.O. Box 7123, Berkeley, California 94707

Type set by Haru Composition, San Francisco, and Wilsted & Taylor, Oakland
Consolidated Printers, Inc., Berkeley, California
Printed in the United States of America

Contents

The Preface, for faithful readers of this book / page xi

Chapter One / page 1
A Job-Hunting We Will Go
A poetic description of the job-hunt as most of us
experience it

Chapter Two / page 9
Rejection Shock
The rules about hiring and firing
The numbers game: what it is, how to play it
Executive search firms
Placing ads; answering newspaper ads
The U.S. Employment Service
College Placement Offices
Registers or Clearinghouses
The effectiveness of job-search methods

Chapter Three / page 41
You Can Do It!
For those who just want "hints": 35 of them
When hints aren't enough: the paths through Job-land
Why career change and creative job-hunting are the same thing
Your keys to success: What, where, and how
Handicaps
Resources for you to draw upon

Chapter Four / page 63
WHAT Skills Do You Most Enjoy Using?
Choosing what your attitude will be
Why should you begin with your skills?

The 40 basic skills you may have
How to analyze your skills with people, information, or things
Special problems. Shortcuts

Chapter Five / page 109

WHERE Do You Want to Use Your Skills?

Why vacancies are not the place to start
How much can you dream?
How to approach the 14,000,000 job markets
Principles for narrowing down the territory
What Special Knowledges do you have, and want to use
   at your next job?
Do you want to work with a product, a service, or information?
At what level in the organization, and at what salary?
What kind of working conditions?
With what kinds of people?
Where, geographically?
Research: the four questions you're trying to answer
Which people can help. Which library books can help
How to figure out the needs of the organization

Chapter Six / page 165

HOW Do You Find the Person Who Has
The Power to Hire You?

Why not the personnel department?
A crash course in resumes
All employers divide into two groups
What an employer's questions are bound to be in the interview
The fears of the employer
The importance of the principle: twenty seconds to two minutes
What questions you should ask in an interview
Salary negotiation: the critical element of timing
The most important thing job-hunters forget after the interview
Checklist when things aren't going well
Does this always work? Luck vs. technique.
How to increase your luck

Appendices

Appendix A / page **213**

BOOKS and Other Resources

Highly Recommended Books, 214

Alternative Patterns of Work, 217

Volunteer Opportunities or Internships, 219

Self-employment or Part-Time Work or Work at Home, 219

Work Dealing with Social Change, 223

Making Your Living by Writing and Getting Published, 224

Working with Arts and Crafts, 224

Getting a Government Job, 225

Overseas Work, 225

The Special Problems of Women, 227

The Special Problems of Minorities, 228

The Special Problems of Handicapped Job-Hunters, 228

The Special Problems of Ex-offenders, 229

The Special Problems of Executives and the Business World, 229

The Special Problems of Couples, 231

The Special Problems of Clergy and Religious, 231

How to Hang On to Your Present Job, 233

Help with Being Fired, Riffed, or Laid Off, 234

Help with Mid-life, Second Careers, or Retirement, 234

Going Back to School or Getting an External Degree, 234

The Special Problems of College Students, 235

Summer Jobs and the Special Problems of High School Students, 236

Getting a Job in Education, 237

Help with Analyzing Your Skills, 238

Help with Interviewing, Salary Negotiations, and Resumes, 238

Help with Places to Live and Job-Hunting in General, 240

If You Are a Career Counselor, or Want to Be, 241

The World of Work Today, 243

Creativity and the Brain, 244

Continued

Appendix B / page 247

Counselors and Other Resources

If You're Thinking of Hiring a Career Counselor to Help You
How to Separate the Sheep from the Goats
A Sampler of Places around the Country Which Counsel Anybody
Resources for Women
Group Support for Those Who Are Unemployed
Directories of Career Counseling Services in Various Cities/States

Appendix C / page 281

Special Problems

The World of Work: A Sampler of Various Jobs
How to Do Job-Hunting While You Are Still Employed
How to Survey a Place Far Away
How to Use the Computer to Aid in Prioritizing

Index / page 304

Author Index / page 320

Miscellanea

If You Want to Be on Our Mailing List and Get
    Our Newsletter / page 323
Life/Work Planning at the Inn of the Seventh Mountain / page 325
Update for the 1988 Edition / page 327

The Preface

FOR FAITHFUL READERS OF THIS BOOK

A new edition of this book comes out every year, in January. Many people, as I have learned, buy each year's new edition. As the beneficiary of this kindness, I am not about to ask why. I just want this year to say a special word to those readers: a word of gratitude, and a word of explanation.

I am deeply grateful every year for your moral support,

and your encouragement. I presume that you buy the book each year because you find the new information useful and helpful, either to yourself or to those around you. But I presume also that you buy the book each year because you trust

—you trust that I am on a journey of personal growth, as you are, and that each year's edition will likely be better than the last. I find that faith immensely touching. I draw great strength from it, as I engage in each year's revision—an otherwise arduous journey of some 200 hours annually.

As you have long since guessed, it is very happenstance as to what I revise each year: it depends very much upon what letters I receive from you all, and it depends upon my annual two-week workshop and what I learn from the students there, and it depends upon the better ways I find to explain things, or the loftier and wiser view that I gain of this whole subject and this whole field.

We are all learners, every one of us. We all sit at the feet of God and at each other's feet, in every experience having the grace to ask, "Yes, but what did I learn from this?"

What I have particularly learned during this past year has been a kind of dichotomous truth: on the one hand, this book has never been more popular. Currently, as I write, it is in its seventh year on the New York Times best-seller list. That is due to the energy of many of you who have so kindly recommended the book to your family and your friends. And I have enjoyed and appreciated that, immensely.

But on the other hand, I have never heard so many people say, "Well, I bought your book and I love your book, but I've never finished it," as has happened during this year past. I have not enjoyed that. In fact, it has troubled me greatly. I mean, maybe *some* authors are content if their book is well-purchased—and never mind what happens after that. But not me. I am an agonizer. I am my own book's severest critic. I not only want it to be bought, I want it to be helpful to the reader. And useful. And digestible. *Not* indigestible.

I quite understand why people have not been able to get through the book. Every year I've kept revising, but revising has been synonymous with adding. The original 1970 edition was 168 pages long. The '86 edition, last year's, was 392 pages long. Good information, all of it, I'm sure; but I certainly understand why people don't want to plow all the way through an almost 400-page book, when they're hanging on the ropes, and job-hunting.

So, I decided that this was the year to bite the bullet, and dramatically streamline the whole thing. "What do you mean by 'dramatically,' dear author?" I'll tell you what I mean. First of all, I dropped out whatever did not seem essential or timely. For example, I dropped the special section which appeared in the '86 edition, on the subject of *Women in the Workplace*. That was a special and timely piece, which took me four years to compile. When published last year, the statistics were up to date. Now, already they are not. I have not time to update it. *Parachute* is the last place where I want an outdated piece to appear; so it went. That's the bad news. The good news is that we've now found a woman to edit and update it, and in a year or so it will be appearing as a separate little booklet.

Next, I removed the *New Quick Job-Hunting Map*. Or at least I removed it from its splended isolation in the back of the book. It is now redistributed in sections, integrated into the mainstream of chapters 4, 5, and 6. The reason I removed it from the Appendices is that the exercises which are to be found in it are so essential, that in my view no conscientious reader, job-hunter, or career-changer should omit doing them. But because readers were not finishing the book, they often never discovered the Map. I thought I should put an end to that. The Map is still available, if you want it, in the form that you knew last year. You can find it in bookstores, or if it is not there you can order it directly from Ten Speed, whose address is on the back of the title page here. Should you find it difficult to write on the smaller pages of this book, then I recommend you order the 8½ x 11-inch size.

Next, I completely rewrote chapters 3, 4, 5, and 6. (There is no chapter 7 anymore.) I tried to find simpler and briefer ways of explaining what the job-hunter or career-changer can do, to increase the effectiveness of their[1] job-hunt. I relegated to the Appendices information which experience has revealed is only of use and interest to a minority among the readers of this book.

1. I want to explain why the word "they" or "them" or "their" is used throughout this book as both a plural and a singular pronoun, rather than just as plural. First of all, I want my writing to be nonsexist. Secondly, I tried for years to use the popular phrases "he or she," "him or her," "his or hers," but my readers wrote to say they found this irritating—and so, in truth, did I. At about that time, Casey Miller and Kate Swift, authors of the classic *The Handbook of Nonsexist Writing* came to my rescue, by suggesting a new approach. In their book, they suggested that the way out was to use "they" as both a plural and a singular pronoun, with both plural and singular verbs. They proceeded to argue—from history—that even as the once solely plural pronoun "you" became in time a pronoun that could be both plural and singular, so in our time the normally plural "they" and all its relatives must begin to be used as both a plural *and a singular* pronoun. The reason for this, they contended, was that in fact the pronoun "they" once was thus treated as both plural and singular in the English language, but this usage changed at a time in English history when agreement *in number* became more important than agreement *in gender*. They argue that it is time now to bring back the earlier usage, because given the sexist consciousness of most writers and readers these days, agreement in gender is now more important than agreement in number. They further argue that this return to an earlier usage has already become quite common out on the street—witness a sign by the ocean which reads "Anyone using this beach after 5 p.m. does so at their own risk." It is only when "they" is used as a singular pronoun in an article or book that grammarians turn pale, and dash off scolding letters to authors—which begin, "Clean up your grammar!" Let me say: I have cleaned it up; my usage is quite deliberate.

Finally, in the Appendices I eliminated the Hotline feature, by which, in the past, readers could write and ask for the name of a career-counselor in their area. With my small staff, and 400,000 readers this year alone, we have fallen as much as four months behind in answering those Hotlines. I have concluded this was setting up false expectations, not to mention letting people down. So, what I have done instead is lengthen the list of counselors in the back of this book. Most of the list that we used to send in response to the Hotlines is now back there. Read it, if you need counsel and help from another during your job-hunt; but read also the preface to that listing. The pocketbook or wallet that you save will be your own.

To conclude the streamlining of this year's edition, I have shortened the list of books in the Appendices, since many readers have written to report that many of the books are out of print before a new edition of *Parachute* even hits the

streets. When a reader has written to say, "Now what?" I have often taken to sending them the sought-after book myself, if I had it in my own personal library at home and was done with it. But with so many readers, there is a limit to what one man can do. It seems better to say, "If there is a particular subject that you need help with, go down to the largest or most helpful bookstore in town and see what they have on that subject. Go also to your local library, and make friends with the helpful reference librarian there."

Observant readers will notice that I have removed prices throughout the book this year, since the saddest (and bitterest) letters I have received have been from readers chagrined to discover that a book or resource which was $4 as we went to press, is $10 or $15 six months later, in a silent testament to rising costs—and greed. As one kind reader said recently, "If prices are rising that fast, making your listings so quickly outdated, why not just omit the price altogether?" Wise and sensible counsel. I have done just that.

Now let me end this year's preface, as I do every year, with my litany of thanks. The litany does not change year by year, because my gratitude does not alter.

I am deeply grateful first of all to every job-hunter or career-changer who has written to express how much this book changed their life. You know, there are men and women everywhere who believe that we all were sent into this world in order to make some special contribution, and do some particular ministry. I am one of those believers, and this book is my ministry, as best I know how to do it, to the bewildered, the lost and the lonely, in the midst of their search for meaningful work. I appreciate all those who write to tell me how this ministry touched their lives. If I did not appreciate it, I would obviously be a fool.

I thank everyone who has written to tell me what special thing worked particularly for them in their job-hunt—that I might share it with you in subsequent editions. I thank all those leaders in this field of career development or job-hunting, who have shared with me their wisdom, their support and their friendship over the years. Most recently—the last ten years—these include Daniel Porot, my dear friend and colleague from Geneva, Switzerland, Arthur Miller in Connecticut, Tom and Ellie Jackson in New York, and Howard Figler in Texas. Further back, but continuing to this day, John Holland in Maryland and Sidney Fine in Washington, D.C., famous vocational psychologists, who taught me much. And furthest back of all, John Crystal, career-counselor and life/work planner extraordinaire, without whom this book would have been only a pale and miserable shadow of what it has otherwise become. John taught me the basic principles which form the titles of chapters 4, 5, and 6; moreover he has been a wonderful friend to me through all of these years. I hope he has a very long life.

I want to record my indebtedness also to the thinking and ideas of all those who were the pioneer writers in this field, including Bernard Haldane and others.

And then, closer to home, my profound and continued thanks to my layout artist, Bev Anderson, who is an irreplaceable genius at her craft; Phil Wood, my publisher and friend, who has been to me everything an author prays a publisher will be—we are friends and allies in a field littered with the bodies of those who became adversaries. My thanks also to Phil's colleagues at Ten Speed who deserve to be named, for their willingness to always go the second mile with me: George Young, Jackie Wan, Cindy Cappa, and many others.

My thanks also to my own wonderful office staff, who labor so long and diligently and hard to lift some of the work off my shoulders: Cindy Bowles (wrong spelling, right person) and Erica Chambre—who ran my Project (the National Career Development Project of United Ministries in Education) from 1975 to 1979, and now has come back to help out once again. My everlasting gratitude.

I would like also, however silly it may sound to some, to publicly acknowledge and thank the Lord God, as I do privately, as it is He who has given me whatever gifts and compassion I possess.

And finally, I want to thank my wife, Carol, for all her encouragement and support. I am sure she is some magical creature of love sent by God from some other planet, and only visiting this one for a time. But I am oh so deeply grateful for that magic and that love, which has transformed both my heart and my life.

R.N.B.
P.O. Box 379

November 1, 1986   Walnut Creek, CA 94597

airy Godmother,
where were you
when I needed you?

Cinderella

CHAPTER ONE

A Job-Hunting
We Will Go

Okay, this is it.
You've been idly thinking about it, off and on, for
some time now, wondering what it would be like.
To be earning your bread in the marketplace.
Or maybe you're already out there,
And the problem is choosing another job — or career —
The old one having run out of gas, as it were.
Anyhow, the moment of truth has arrived.
For one reason or another, you've got to get at it —
Go out, and look for a job, for the first time or the twentieth.
You've heard of course, all the horror stories.
Of ex-executives working as taxi-drivers
Of former college profs with two masters degrees
working as countermen in a delicatessen.
Of women Ph.D.s who can only get a job as a secretary.
Of laid-off auto-workers waiting for the call (back to work)
that never comes.
And you wonder what lies in store for *you*.

Of course, it may be that the problem is all solved.
Maybe some friend or relative has button-holed you
and said, "Why not come and work for me?"
So, your job-hunt ends before it begins.
Or, it may be that you came into your present
career after a full life doing something else, and
You know you're welcome back there, anytime;
Anytime, they said.
And, assuming they meant it,
no problem, right?
So long as that's what you still want to do.
Or maybe you've decided this is the time to
adopt a simpler way of living,
And, so far, it's going well.
But for the vast majority of us,
that isn't how it goes.
We have to find a job, we do,
And no one's making it any easier.
We feel like Don Quixote, mounted, lance in hand; and
the job-hunt is our windmill.

Those who have gone this way before us
   all tell us the very same thing:
      This is how we all go about it, when our job-hunting time has come:
       We procrastinate,
         That's what we do.
           Busy winding things up, we say.
             Or, just waiting until we feel a little less 'burnt-out' and
               more 'up' for the task ahead, we say.
               Actually, if the truth were known,
                we're hoping for that miracle,
                you know the one:
                that if we just sit tight a little longer,
                we won't have to go job-hunting at all, because
                the job will come hunting for us.
               Right in our front door, it will come.
               To show us we are destiny's favorites,
               Or to prove that God truly loves us.
              But, it doesn't, of course, and
            eventually, we realize, with more than a touch of franticness,
          that time and money
       are beginning to run out.

        Time to begin our job-hunt (or career change) in deadly earnest.
       And all of our familiar friends immediately
      are at our elbow, giving advice —
     solicited or unsolicited, as to what it is we should do.
     "Jean or Joe, I've always thought you would make a great teacher."
So we ask who they know
in the academic world,
and, armed with that name,
we go a-calling. Calling, and
 sitting, cooling our heels
  in the ante-room of the Dean's office,
   until we are ushered in, at last:
    "And what can I do for you, Mr. or Ms.?"
     We tell them, of course, that we're job-hunting.
      "And one of my friends thought that you..."
       Oops. We watch the face change,

And we (who *do* know something about body language),
Wait to hear their words catch up with their body.
"You feel I'm 'over-qualified'? I see.
Two hundred applications, you say, already in hand
For five vacancies? I see.
No, of course I understand."
Strike-out. Back to the drawingboard. More advice, from
well-meaning family or friends:
"Jean or Joe, have you tried the employment agencies?"
"Good thinking. Which ones should I try?
The ones that deal with professionals? Where are they?
Okay. Good. Down I'll go."
And down we do go.
Down, down, down, to those agencies.
The ante-room again.
And those other hopeful, haunted faces.
A new twist, however: our first bout
with The Application Form.
"Previous jobs held.
List in reverse chronological order."
Filling all the questions out. Followed by
That interminable wait.
And then, at last, the interviewer,
She of the over-cheerful countenance, and mien —
She talks to us. "Now, let's see, Mr. or Ms.,
What kind of a job are you looking for?"
"Well," we say,
"What do you think I could do?"
She studies, again, the application form;
"It seems to me," she says, "that with your background
—it is a *bit* unusual—
You might do very well in sales."
"Oh, sales," we say. "Why yes," says she, "in fact
I think that I could place you almost immediately.
We'll be in touch with you. Is this your phone?"
We nod, and shake her hand, and that is the
Last time
We ever hear from her.
Words are apparently not always to be believed;
Sometimes they are used just to soften rejection.
Strike out, number two.

Now, our original ballooning hopes that we would quickly land a job
are running into some frigid air,
   So we decide to confess at last
      Our need of help — to some of our more successful friends
        in the business world (if we have such)
      Who *surely* know what we should do, at this point.
       The windmill is tiring us. What would they suggest
        that Don (or Donna) Quixote should do?
        "Well," say they (beaming warmly), "what kind of a job
        are you looking for?"
        Ah, *that*, again! "Well, you know me well, what do you think
        I can do? I'll try almost anything,"
      we say, now that it's four minutes to midnight, as it were.
    "You know, with all the *kinds* of things I've done—"
  we say; "I mean, I've done this and that, and here and there,
It all adds up to a kind of puzzling kaleidoscope; but you see things
That I don't see, so there must be *something* you can suggest!"

"Have you tried the want-ads?" asks our friend.
"Or have you gone to see Bill, and Ed, and John, and Frances and Marty?
Ah, no? Well tell them I sent you."
So, off we go—now newly armed, with new advice.
We study the want-ads. Gad, what misery is hidden in
Those little boxes. Misery in jobs which are built
As little boxes, for the large spirits of men and women.
But, nevertheless we dutifully send our resume, such as it is,
To every box that looks as though
It might not be a box.
And wait for the avalanche of replies, from bright-eyed people
Who, seeing our resume, will surely know
Our worth; even if, at this point, our worth seems increasingly
Questionable in our own eyes.
Avalanche? Not even a rolling stone. (Sorry about that, Bob.) Not a pebble.

Well, time to go see all those people that our friend said we
ought to go see.
You know: Bill, and Ed, and John, and Frances and Marty.
They seem slightly perplexed, as to why we've come,
And in the dark about exactly
Just exactly what it is they are supposed to do for us.
We try to take them off the hook; "I thought, friend of my friend,
Your company might need—of course, my experience *has*
Been limited, but I am willing, and I thought perhaps
that you ..."

The interview drags on, downhill now, all the way
As our host finishes out the courtesy debt,
Not to us but to the friend that sent us; and
then it is time for us to go.
Boy, do we go! over hill and valley and dale,
Talking to everyone who will listen,
Listening to everyone who will talk
With us; and thinking that surely there must be
Someone who knows how to crack this terribly frustrating
job-market;

This job-hunt process seems the loneliest task of our lives.
And we idly wonder: is it this difficult for other people?
Well, friend, the answer is *YES*.

Are other people *this* discouraged, and desperate
And frustrated, and so low in self-esteem after
A spell of job-hunting?
The answer, again —unhappily— is
YES.

YES.

YES.

Well, yes, you do have great big teeth; but, never mind that. You were great to at least grant me this interview.

Little Red Riding Hood

CHAPTER TWO

Rejection Shock

From our youth up, we are taught to hate rejection. At least *most* of us are. I know rejection rolls off some people like water off a duck's back. It doesn't bother them at all. Or at least so it appears. And I know that others actually crave rejection and thrive on it, as ancient warriors went out to meet the dragon. Not so with me. Faced with rejection, I usually go into a corner and whimper a lot. Or jump into bed, curl into the fetal position, and turn the electric blanket up to nine. And so apparently it is with the majority of us. We hate rejection. We'll do *anything* to avoid it—and I mean *anything*.

But then, along comes the job-hunt. Eight times in our lifetime we have to go through this painful process. And, except at its very end, it is *nothing but* a process of rejection, even as I described in the previous chapter. My friend Tom Jackson has aptly captured this, in his depressingly accurate description of a typical job-hunt as consisting of:

NO NO NO NO NO NO NO NO NO NO NO NO NO NO
NO NO NO NO NO NO NO NO NO NO NO NO NO NO
NO NO NO NO NO NO NO NO NO NO NO NO NO NO
NO NO NO NO NO NO NO NO NO NO NO NO YES.

And why does the job-hunting system in this country put us through all this? Because, *the job-hunting system in this country is no system at all.* It is in fact Neanderthal. (Say it again, Sam.)

Year after year, that 'system' condemns each of us to go down the same path, face the same obstacles, make the same mistakes, and face the same rejection.

Moreover, the 'system' is such that often we are given absolutely no warning that we are about to become unemployed. All of a sudden, it is upon us.

And gradually, but only gradually, do we begin to learn what the rules are of this 'system.' And what the rules are, concerning the whole world of work. Slowly and painstakingly we piece them together, and discover finally that there are twelve of them:

1. You will get hired sometimes, for reasons which may have nothing to do with how qualified you are, or aren't. On some unconscious level, you just strike a spark.

2. You will not get hired sometimes, for reasons which may have nothing to do with how qualified you are, or aren't. On some unconscious level, you just don't strike a spark.

3. You will get promoted sometimes, for reasons which may have nothing to do with how well you are doing there.

4. You will not get promoted sometimes, for reasons which may have nothing to do with how well you are doing there.

5. Your employer may treat you well, in accordance with their stated values.

6. Your employer may treat you very badly, in total contradiction of their stated values.

7. Your employer may go on forever, and you may have a job for life, if you want it.

8. Your employer may go out of business, without warning and at a moment's notice, dumping you out on the street.

9. Your employer may stay in business, but you may be abandoned, terminated, fired or otherwise put out on the street, without warning, and at a moment's notice.

10. If you are terminated suddenly, your employer may do everything in the world to help you find other employment.

11. If you are terminated suddenly, your employer may feel that they do not owe you anything. You will feel as though you had been unceremoniously deposited on the rubbage heap.

12. Other employees may promise they will fight to save your job, but you need to be prepared for the fact that when the chips are down, they may actually do nothing to help you.

Our instinctive first reaction to the fact that "this is how things are" is usually anger. Sometimes fierce anger. Sometimes just a kind of cold soul-chilling disillusionment about the workplace and how it treats its people. If we are wise, we learn to let go of that anger and get on with our lives. But many ex-workers, we know, stay locked in to that anger for the remainder of their lives. They can never forgive the world of work for being so different from what they thought it was going to be. Their anger is a burning fire within them, gradually consuming them.

This would not be so, if it were relatively easy to find another job. The anger is perpetuated by the fact that the job-hunting system slowly and systematically strips men and women of their self-esteem, and leaves them feeling devalued and discarded by our society. When it happens to *You,* you go into personal psychological Shock, characterized by a slow or rapid erosion of your self-image, and the conviction that there is something wrong with *you.* This assumes, consequently, all the proportions of a major crisis in your life, where irritability, withdrawal, broken relationships, divorce, and loneliness may become your constant companions; and even suicide is not unthinkable. All because of the job-hunting system in this country, which is actually a 'non-system.'

This 'non-system' has been given a name by personnel experts. They call this non-system "The Numbers Game." That's right, the numbers game.

THE NUMBERS GAME

You can guess where the term came from. It came from the world of gambling, where if you place sufficient bets on enough different numbers, *one* of them is *bound* to pay off, for you. Ah, I see you have grasped immediately what this has to do with job-hunting. Resumes, you say? Ah yes, resumes.

If you're going to use them, you have to play them just like a numbers game: send out just as many as you possibly can. Because, according to a study some time back, only one job offer is tendered and accepted in the whole world of work, for every 1,470 resumes that are floating around out there. Sending 1,469 gets you nowhere. The 1,470th gets a job. Hence, "the numbers game."

It's terrible. But you probably should try to understand it, in all its parts.

HOW TO USE THE NUMBERS GAME, INSTEAD OF BEING USED BY IT

The reason why you ought to understand it is that you may want to use *some* parts of it to *supplement* your main job-hunt, as outlined in chapters 4 through 6.

A study of *The Job Hunt* by Harold L. Sheppard and A. Harvey Belitsky[1] revealed that the greater the number of auxiliary avenues used by the job-hunter, the greater the job-finding success. It makes sense, therefore, to know *all* the avenues that are open to you, how they work and what their limitations are, so that you can choose *which* avenue or avenues you want to use, and *how* you want to use them. You will then be in the driver's seat about these matters, as you should be.

The parts of this game most commonly alluded to in books, articles, and elsewhere are:

- mailing out your resume
- contacting executive search firms
- answering newspaper ads
- placing newspaper ads
- going to private employment (or placement) agencies
- going to the federal/state employment agency
- contacting college placement firms
- using executive registers or other forms of clearinghouses
- making personal contacts through friends, personal referrals and so forth.

We will look at the virtues, and defects, of each of these now, in rapid succession; to see why they usually don't work—

---

1. In their book, *The Job Hunt: Job-Seeking Behavior of Unemployed Workers in a Local Economy.*

and how you might get around their limitations. I will quote some statistics as I go along, in order to *illustrate* the afore-mentioned defects.[1] So, on with our exciting story.

HEADHUNTERS, OTHERWISE KNOWN AS RECRUITERS OR EXECUTIVE SEARCH FIRMS

If you play the numbers game, and especially if you pay someone to guide you through it, you will be told to send your resume to Executive Search firms. And what, pray tell, are *they*? Well, they are recruiting firms that are retained by employers. The very existence of this thriving industry testifies to the fact that employers are as baffled by our country's Neanderthal job-hunting 'system' as we are. <u>Employers don't know how to find decent employees, any more than we know how to find decent employers.</u> So, what do employers want executive recruiting firms to do? They want these firms to *hire away* from other firms or employers, executives, sales-people, technicians, or whatever, who are already employed, and rising. (In the old days, these firms searched only for executives—hence their now-outdated title.) Anyway, you will

---

1. You will note that some of these statistics are not, ahem, *current*—to put it gently. That's because the most recent study about this-or-that part of the numbers game was done some years ago, and after seeing the depressing findings, no one has thought it useful to repeat that study since that time.

realize these head-hunting firms are aware of, and trying to fill, known vacancies. That's why, in any decent scatter-gun sending out of your resume, you are advised—by any number of experts—to be sure and include Recruiters. Not surprisingly, there are even a number of enterprising souls who make a living by selling lists of such firms.

You can get lists of such firms from:

1. The American Management Association, Inc., 135 W. 50th St., New York, NY 10020, has a list entitled *Executive Employment Guide.*

2. The Association of Executive Recruiting Consultants, 151 Railroad Ave., Greenwich, CT 06830, has its own list of sixty top recruiters.

EXECUTIVE RECRUITERS

Name: Executive recruitment consultants, executive recruiters, executive search firms, executive development specialists, management consultants, recruiters.

Nicknames: Head-hunters, body snatchers, flesh pedlers, talent scouts.

Number: Some 12,000 professionals, currently.

Volume of business: They had combined billings of more than $2 billion a year.

Number of vacancies handled by a firm: Each staff member can only handle 6 to 8 searches at a time (as a rule)[1]; so, *multiply* number of staff that a firm has (if known) times six. Majority of firms are one to two

staff (hence, are handling 5 to 10 current openings); a few are four to five staff (20 to 25 openings are being searched for); and the largest have staffs handling 80 to 100 openings.

---

1. L. A. Butler, *Move In and Move Up,* pp. 160-61.

3. Directory of Executive Recruiters, published by Consultant News, Templeton Rd., Fitzwilliam, NH 03447. Published yearly. Lists several hundred firms and the industries served.

The question is: do you *want* these lists, i.e., are they going to do you any good?

Well, let's say you decide to send recruiters your resume (unsolicited—they didn't ask you to send it, you just sent it). The average Executive Search firm may get as many as 100 to 300 such resumes, or "broadcast letters"[1] a week. And, as we see above, the majority of such firms may be handling five to ten *current openings,* for which they are looking for executives who are presently employed and rising.

Well okay, that Executive Recruiter is sitting there with 100 to 300 resumes in his or her hands, at the end of that week— yours (and mine) among them. You know what's about to happen to that stack of People-in-the-Form-of-Paper. That old Elimination, Winnowing, or Screening Process again. Your chances of surviving? Well, the first to get eliminated will be those who a) are not presently executives, or b) are not presently employed as such, or c) are not presently rising in their firm.

That's why even in a good business year, many experts say to the unemployed: *Forget it!* I do think it is necessary, however, to point out that things are changing in the Recruiting field. For one thing, some firms now call themselves Recruiters

1. A term coined by Carl Boll, in his book, *Executive Jobs Unlimited.*

when yesterday they would have been called Employment Agencies. These new Recruiters do indeed represent employers; but they are hungry for the names of job-hunters, and in many cases will interview a job-hunter who comes into the office unannounced or mails them a resume. I have known so-called Recruiters who truly extended themselves on behalf of very inexperienced job-hunters. So, were I job-hunting this year, I think I would get one of the aforementioned Directories, look up the firms that specialize in my particular kind of job or field, and go take a crack at them. I wouldn't have done that when *Parachute* first came out in 1970. But times do change!

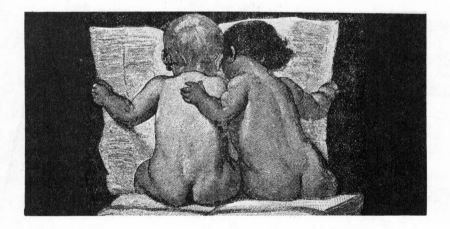

ANSWERING NEWSPAPER ADS

Experts will advise you, for the sake of thoroughness, to study the job advertisements in your newspaper *daily* and to study *all of them, from A to Z*—because ads are alphabetized by job title; and there are some very strange and unpredictable job titles floating around. Then you are advised that if you see an ad for which you might qualify, even three-quarters, send off:

  a) your resume, OR
  b) your resume and a covering letter, OR
  c) just a covering letter.

NEWSPAPER ADS

Where found:
1. In the business section of the Sunday *New York Times* and the education section; also in Sunday editions of the *Chicago Tribune* and the *Los Angeles Times*.
2. In the business section (often found with the sports section) of your daily paper; also daily *Wall Street Journal* (especially Tuesday and Wednesday's editions).
3. In the classified section of your daily paper (and Sunday's, too).

Jobs advertised: Usually those which have a clear-cut title, well-defined specifications, and for which either many job-hunters can qualify, or very few.

Number of resumes received by employer as result of the ad: 20 to 1,000, commonly.
Time it takes resumes to come in: 48 to 96 hours. Third day is usually the peak day, after ad is placed.
Number of resumes NOT screened out: Only 2 to 5 out of every 100 (normally) survive. In other words, 95 to 98 out of every 100 answers *are* screened out.

In short, what they're telling you is that you're playing the Numbers Game, when you answer ads. And the odds are stacked against you just about as badly as when you send out your resume scatter-gun fashion. How badly? (Better sit down.) A study conducted in two sample cities revealed, and I quote, that "85% of the employers in San Francisco, and 75% in Salt Lake City, did not hire any employees through want ads" in a typical year. Yes, that said *any* employees, *during the whole year.*[1] Well, then why are ads *run*? For the fascinating answer to that, read "Blind Ad Man's Bluff" in David Noer's *How to Beat The Employment Game.*[2]

Of course, you may be one who still likes to cover all bets, and if so, you will want to know how *your* resume can be the one that gets through the Screening Process. (Let's be honest: answering ads *has* paid off, for *some* job-hunters.)

Most of the experts say, *if* you're going to play this game:

1. All you're trying to do, in answering the ad, is to avoid getting screened out, and to be invited in for an interview. Period. So, quote the ad's specifications, and tailor your resume or case history letter (if you prefer *that* to a resume)— so that *you* fit their specifications as closely as possible.

2. Omit all else from your response (so there is no further excuse for Screening you out). Volunteer *nothing* else. Period.

3. *If* the ad requested salary requirements, some experts say ignore the request; others say, state a salary range (of as much as three to ten thousand dollars variation) adding the words "depending on the nature and scope of duties and

responsibilities," or words to that effect. If the ad does not mention salary requirements, *don't you either.* Why give an excuse for getting your response Screened Out?

---

1. Olympus Research Corporation, *A Study to Test the Feasibility of Determining Whether Classified Ads in Daily Newspapers Are an Accurate Reflection of Local Labor Markets and of Significance to Employers and Job Seekers.* 1973. From: Olympus Research Corporation, 1670 East 1300 South, Salt Lake City, UT 84105.

2. Ten Speed Press, Box 7123, Berkeley, CA 94707. Or at your local library.

THINGS TO BEWARE OF
IN NEWSPAPER ADS

BLIND ADS
(no company
name, just a
box number).
These, accord-
ing to some
insiders, are
particularly
unrewarding
to the job-
hunter's time.

FAKE ADS
(positions
advertised
which don't
exist)—
usually run
by placement
firms or others,
in order to
fatten their
"resume bank"
for future
clout with
employers.

PHONE NUMBERS
in ads: don't
use them except
to set up an
appointment.
Period. ("I can't
talk right now.
I'm calling from
the office.")
Beware of say-
ing more. Avoid
getting screened
out prematurely
over the tele-
phone.

THOSE PHRASES
which need lots of
translating, like:
"Energetic self-
starter wanted"
(= You'll be working
on commission)
"Good organizational
skills" (= You'll be
handling the filing)
"Make an investment
in your future"
(= This is a franchise
or pyramid scheme)
"Much client contact"
(= You handle the phone,
or make 'cold calls' on clients)
"Planning and coordi-
nating" (= You book the
boss's travel arrangements)
"Opportunity of a
lifetime" (= No where
else will you find such a
low salary and so much work)
"Management training
position" (= You'll be
a salesperson with a wide
territory)
"Varied, interesting
travel" (= You'll be a
salesperson with a wide
territory)

PLACING ADS YOURSELF

Sometimes job-hunters try to make their availability known, by placing ads themselves in newspapers or journals.

PLACING ADS

<u>Name of ads (commonly)</u>: Positions wanted (by the job-hunter, that is).

<u>Found in</u>: *Wall Street Journal*, professional journals and in trade association publications.

<u>Effectiveness</u>: Very effective in getting responses from employment agencies, peddlers, salesmen, and vultures who prey on job-hunters. Practically worthless in getting responses from prospective employers, who rarely read these ads. But it *has* worked for some.

<u>Recommendation</u>: If you take odds seriously, you'd better forget it. Unless, just to cover all bets, you want to place some ads in professional journals appropriate to your field. Study other people's formats first, though.

<u>Cost</u>: Varies.

ASKING PRIVATE EMPLOYMENT AGENCIES FOR HELP

The two places that every job-hunter knows instinctively to turn to when looking for a job is want ads and employment agencies. The latter, in particular, seem very attractive when one is "up against it." We all like to think that *somewhere* out there is *someone* who knows just exactly where jobs are to be found. Unhappily *no one* in this country knows where all the jobs are. The best that anyone can offer to us is some clues about where it is that *some* jobs are to be found. In any event, places which know where some jobs are to be found are called private employment agencies. The Yellow Pages of your phone book will give you their names. Now let's see what we know about agencies in general:

ASKING PRIVATE EMPLOYMENT
AGENCIES FOR HELP

PRIVATE EMPLOYMENT AGENCIES

Number: Nobody knows, since new ones are born, and old ones die, every week. There are probably at least 8,000 private employment or placement agencies in the U.S. Maybe a lot more.

Specialization: Many specialize in executives, financial, data processing, or other specialties.

Fees: Employer; or job-hunter may pay *but only when and if hired.* Fees vary from state to state. Tax deductible. In New York, for example, a fee cannot exceed 60% of one month's salary, i.e., a $15,000-a-year job will cost you $750. The fee may be paid in weekly installments of 10% (e.g., $75 on a $750 total). In 80% of executives' cases, it is the employer who pays the fee.

Contract: The application form filled out by the job-hunter at an agency *is* the contract.

Exclusive handling: Don't give it, even if they ask for it. If you find a job independently of them, you may still have to pay them a fee.

Nature of business: Primarily a volume business, requiring rapid turnover of clientele, with genuine attention given only to the most-marketable job-hunters, in what one insider has called "a short-term matching game."

Effectiveness: Some time back, a spokesman for the Federal Trade Commission announced that the average placement rate for employment agencies was only

PRIVATE EMPLOYMENT
AGENCIES continued

5% of those who walked in the door. (That means a 95% failure rate, right?)

Loyalty: Agency's loyalty in the very nature of things must lie with those who pay the bills (which in most cases is the employer), and those who represent repeat business (again, employers).

Evaluation: An agency, with its dependency on rapid-turnover volume business, usually has no time to deal with *any* problems (like, career-transitions). *Possible exception for you to investigate*: a new, or suddenly expanding agency, which needs job-hunters badly if it is ever to get employers' business.

ASKING THE
FEDERAL-STATE
EMPLOYMENT SERVICE
FOR HELP

UNITED STATES
EMPLOYMENT SERVICE

Number: 2,600 offices in the country. USES (often called "Job Service") has been greatly reduced in staff and budget over the years.

Services: Most state offices of USES not only serve entry level workers, but also have services for professionals. Washington, D.C. had most innovative one. Middle management (and up) job-hunters still tend to avoid it.

Nationwide network: In any city (as a rule) you can inquire about job opportunities in other states or cities, for a particular field. Also see Job Bank (page 28).

Openings: Nine million non-agricultural job vacancies were listed with USES in 1979. Today, who knows?

UNITED STATES EMPLOYMENT SERVICE
continued

Placements: Of the 15+ million registering with USES back in 1979, approximately 30% were placed in jobs. Almost half of these were blue-collar jobs, and another quarter were white-collar jobs. A survey of one area raised some question about the quality of placement, moreover, when it was discovered that 57% of those placed in that geographical area by USES were not working at their jobs anymore, just 30 days later. (That would reduce the placement rate to 17%, *at best;* an 83% failure rate. It's probably closer to 13.7% placement, hence an 86.3% failure rate.) Things haven't changed much since then.

COLLEGE PLACEMENT CENTERS

COLLEGE PLACEMENT OFFICES

Where located: Most of the 3,280 institutions of higher education in this country have some kind of placement function, however informal.

Helpfulness: Some are very good, because they understand that job-hunting will be a repetitive activity throughout the lives of their students; hence they try to teach an empowering process of self-directed job-hunting. Other offices, however, still think they have done their job if they have helped "each student find a job upon graduation," through the use of recruiters, bulletin board listings, and the like; i.e., if they help their students with this one job-hunt this one time.

"CATHY" by Cathy Guisewite
© Copyright 1981. Reprinted with permission of Universal Press Syndicate. All rights reserved.

COLLEGE PLACEMENT OFFICES continued

Directory: A directory of these offices is published, and is available for perusal in most Placement Offices. It is called the *Directory of Career Planning and Placement Offices,* and is published by the College Placement Council, Inc., Box 2263, Bethlehem, PA 18001. This directory is not a complete listing of all such offices in the country. The Career Planning and Placement Office (c/o Office of Counseling and Testing) at Western Nevada Community College, for example, has asked us to point out that they exist, even though they are not in this directory. (7000 Sullivan Ln., Reno, NV 89505. 702-673-4666.)

If you are not only a college graduate but also a hopeless romantic, you will have a vision of blissful cooperation existing between all of these placement offices across the country. So that if you are a graduate of an East Coast college, let us say, and subsequently you move to California, and want help with career planning, you should in theory be able to walk into the placement office on any California campus, and be helped by that office (a non-altruistic service based on the likelihood that a graduate of that California campus is, at the same moment, walking into the placement office of your East Coast college—and thus, to coin a phrase, "one hand is washing another"). Some places do do this. But, alas and alack, dear graduate, in most cases it doesn't work like that. You will be told, sometimes with genuine regret, that *by official policy,* this particular placement office on this particular campus is only allowed to aid its own students and alumni. One Slight Ray of Hope: on a number of campuses, there are career counselors who think this policy is absolutely asinine, so if you walk into the Career Planning office on that campus, *are lucky enough to get one of Those Counselors,* and you don't mention whether or not you went to that college—the counselor will never ask, and will proceed to help you just as though you were a real person.

This restriction (to their own students and graduates) is less likely to be found at Community Colleges than it is at four-year institutions. So if you run into a dead end, try a Community College near you.

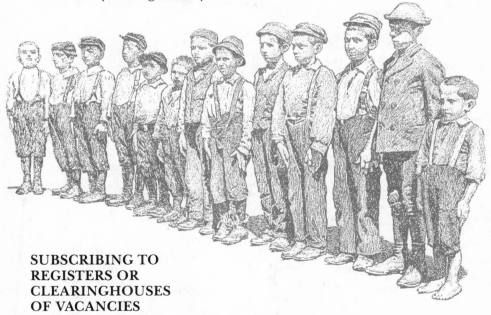

SUBSCRIBING TO REGISTERS OR CLEARINGHOUSES OF VACANCIES

These are attempts to set up "job exchanges" or a kind of bulletin board where employer and job-hunter can meet. The private clearinghouses commonly handle both employer and job-hunter listings, charging each.

REGISTERS OR CLEARING-HOUSE OPERATIONS

Types: Federal and private; general and specialized fields; listing either future projected openings, or present ones; listing employers' vacancies, or job-hunters' resumes (in brief), or both.

Cost to job-hunter: Ranges from free, to $75 or more.

Effectiveness: A register may have as many as 13,000 clients registered with it (if it is a private operation), and (let us say) 500 openings at one time, from employer clients. Some registers will let employers know of every client who is eligible; others will pick out the few best ones. You must figure out what the odds for you as job-hunter are. A newer register *may* do more for you than an older one.

This is a very popular idea, and new entrants in the field are appearing constantly. On the following cards, we list some examples:

REGISTERS ETC.
continued

General clearinghouse listing present vacancies: The State Employment Offices in 48 states, covering more than 300 separate labor market areas, have set up a computerized (in most cities) *job bank* to provide daily listings of job openings in that city. If every employer cooperated and listed every opening they had, each day, it would be a great concept. Unhappily, employers prefer to fill many jobs above $11,000 in more personal, informal ways. So the Job Bank remains a rather limited resource for such jobs. *Can be a helpful research instrument*, however. A summary of the job orders placed by employers at Job Banks during the

previous month used to be published under the title
of "Occupations in Demand at Job Service Offices."
It is apparently no longer available.

A clearinghouse of newspaper ads: The idea of someone
reading on your behalf the classified sections of a lot
of newspapers in this country, and publishing a summary thereof on a weekly basis (or so), is not a new
idea—but it is apparently growing increasingly popular. Problem: how old the ads may be by the time you
the subscriber read them. That answer will turn out
to be the sum of the following times: a) the time it
took for the hometown paper, in which the ad first
appeared, to be sent to the town in which the clearinghouse operates; plus b) the time the clearinghouse

"WHILE YOU'RE WAITING FOR YOUR SHIP
TO COME IN, WHY DON'T YOU DO SOME
MAINTENANCE WORK ON THE PIER ?"

REGISTERS ETC.
continued

held on to the ad—especially if it just missed "last week's" edition of the clearinghouse Report; plus c) the time it took, after insertion in the Report, before the Report came 'off the press'; plus d) the time it took for the clearinghouse's Report to get across the country to you (discount this last, if you live in the clearinghouse's backyard; otherwise give this Large Weight, especially if it is not sent First Class/Airmail—or have you forgotten about our beloved Postal Service?); plus e) the time it takes to get your response from your town to the town in which the ad appeared. You'll recall from page 18 that most classified ads receive more than enough responses

within 96 hours of the ad's first appearing; how likely an employer is to wait for you to send in your response many days, or even weeks, later, is something you must evaluate for yourself—and weigh that against the cost of the service. If you want it, there are several places offering this service. Among the most reliable: the *Wall Street Journal* publishes a weekly compilation of "career-advancement positions" from its four regional editions. Available on some newsstands, or order from: National Business Employment Weekly, 420 Lexington Ave., New York, NY 10170.
212-808-6792.

REGISTERS ETC.
continued

<u>Register for teachers</u>: The NESC Jobs Newsletters are published by the National Education Service Center, 221A E. Main St., Riverton, WY 82501. 307-856-0170. Between April and August, this weekly series of Newsletters lists about 58,000 job openings annually. Each week's edition contains only new listings, none repeated. The newsletters are published year round, with fewer listings in the months August to April. You select one or more of fourteen different job categories, and receive listings of jobs in those categories only.

REGISTERS, ETC.
continued

Register for government jobs: *Federal Career Opportunities*, published biweekly by Federal Research Service, Inc., 370 Maple Ave. W., Box 1059, Vienna, VA 22180. 703-281-0200. Each issue is 64 pages, and lists 3,200+ currently available federal jobs, in both the U.S. and overseas.

Registers in the church: Intercristo is a national Christian organization that lists over 35,000 jobs, covering 4,600 vocational categories, available within about 2,000 Christian organizations in the U.S. or overseas. Their service is called Christian Placement Network. In 1986, 15,000 people used Intercristo; one out of every fifteen job-hunters who used this service found a job thereby. Their address is 19303 Fremont Ave. N., Seattle, WA 98133, and their toll-free phone number is 800-426-1342. Dick Staub, Executive Director.

Register for the blind: Job Opportunities for the Blind, 1800 Johnson St., Baltimore, MD 21230. 301-659-9314, or 1-800-638-7518. Exists to inform blind applicants about positions that are open with public and private employers throughout the country. Maintains a computerized listing. Also, they have cassette instructions on *everything* for the blind job-seeker. Operated by the National Federation of the Blind in partnership with the U.S. Department of Labor.

OTHER REGISTERS OR
CLEARINGHOUSES:

Is a thing a register or not? If job listings exist all by themselves, they tend to be legitimately called "registers." If they
exist within the framework of a journal or magazine which
also contains other material, they tend to be called "ads."
There is a list of such journals; see Feingold, S. Norman, and
Hansard-Winkler, Glenda Ann, *900,000 Plus Jobs Annually:
Published sources of employment listings.* Garrett Park Press,
Garrett Park, MD 20896. Lists more than 900 journals which
carry employment want ads. The following list straddles both
sides:[1]

For Internships and Jobs with Nonprofit Organizations: *Community Jobs,* published by the Community Careers Resource
Center, 1520 16th St. NW, Washington, DC 20036. Phone 202-
387-7702.

For Jobs Overseas: *International Employment Hotline.* Monthly
issues profile international employment opportunities. International Employment Hotline, Box 6170, McLean, VA 22106.

For Jobs in Criminal Justice: The *NELS Monthly Bulletin,*
National Employment Listing Service, Criminal Justice Center, Sam Houston State Univ., Huntsville, TX 77341, 713-294-
1692. A nonprofit service providing information on current
job opportunities in the criminal justice and social services
fields.

For Jobs with Youth or Children: The Child Care Personnel
Clearinghouse, Box 548, Hampton, VA 23669, publishes a
biannual list called *Help Kids.* You *must* enclose $1 for postage
and handling, in order to get it, however.

**For Jobs with Museums, Historical Agencies, and Arts Organ-
izations in the Northeastern U.S.:** *NCES* (Northeast Cultural
Employment Services) *JOBSLETTER.* Published by N.C.E.S.,
Box 1080, Portland, ME 04104. Published weekly. Send self-
addressed, stamped business envelope for further information
and current subscription rates.

---

1. My thanks to my friend, John William Zehring, former Director of Career Planning and Placement at Earlham College, for help with this list.

"Same career, change of career, same career... change of..."

For Jobs Outdoors: Environmental Opportunities, Box 670, Walpole, NH 03608, publishes a monthly listing of environmental jobs, internships and positions-wanted notices under the same name. Each issue contains 24 to 40 full-time positions in a variety of disciplines. The Natural Science for Youth Foundation, 16 Holmes St., Mystic, CT 06355, publishes a bimonthly job-listing, called *Opportunities*. Colorado Outward Bound School, 945 Pennsylvania St., Denver, CO 80203, publishes a nationwide "Jobs Clearing House" list.

One final word about registers: the very term "register" can be misleading. The vision: one central place where you can go, and find listed every vacancy in a particular field of endeavor. *But, sorry, Virginia; there ain't no such animal.* All you'll find by going to any of these places is *A Selected List* of some of the vacancies. A smorgasbord, if you will.

So far as finding *jobs for people* is concerned, these clearinghouses and agencies (like employment agencies) really end up finding *people for jobs.* (Think about it!) Heart of gold though they *may* have, these agencies serve employers better than they serve the job-hunter.

And yet there are always *ways* of using such registers to gain valuable information for the job-hunter and to suggest places where you may wish to *start* researching your ideal job (more in chapter 4). So at the least, you *may* want to consult the Federal job bank (if there is one in your city), and perhaps a relatively inexpensive Register (if there is one in your particular field), as *auxiliaries* to the main thrust of your job-search.

OTHER IDEAS

OTHER IDEAS

<u>Your resume in a book</u>: Some organizations circulate small booklets which are essentially mass distribution of people's resumes in concise form. Forty-Plus Clubs do this, through their *Executive Manpower Directory*. So do some of the executive registry places. Evaluation as to its worth to you as job-hunter: well, it's a gamble, just like everything else in this Numbers Game system. A real gamble, if you are trying to start a new career. You have to boil your resume down to a very few words, normally. And then decide if you stand out. If not, forget it.
If yes, well . . . maybe.

OTHER IDEAS

<u>Off-beat methods</u>: Mailing strange boxes to company presidents, with strange messages (or your resume) inside; using sandwich board signs and parading up and down in front of a company; sit-ins at a president's office, when you are simply determined to work for *that* company, association, or whatever. You name it—and if it's kooky, *it's been tried.* Sometimes it has paid off. Kookiness is generally ill-advised, however. $64,000 question every employer must weigh: if you're like this *before* you're hired, what will they have to live with *afterward?*

To summarize the effectiveness of all the preceding methods in a table (you do like tables, don't you?), we may look at the results of a survey the Bureau of the Census made. The survey, made in 1972 and published in the *Occupational Outlook Quarterly* in the winter of 1976, was of 10 million jobseekers. Unhappily, this ten-year-old study is valid still:

USE AND EFFECTIVENESS
OF JOB SEARCH METHODS

Percent Of Total Jobseekers Using the Method	Method	Effectiveness Rate*
66.0%	Applied directly to employer	47.7%
50.8	Asked friends about jobs where they work	22.1
41.8	Asked friends about jobs elsewhere	11.9
28.4	Asked relatives about jobs where they work	19.3
27.3	Asked relatives about jobs elsewhere	7.4
45.9	Answered local newspaper ads	23.9
11.7	Answered nonlocal newspaper ads	10.0
21.0	Private employment agency	24.2
33.5	State employment service	13.7
12.5	School placement office	21.4
15.3	Civil Service test	12.5
10.4	Asked teacher or professor	12.1
1.6	Placed ad in local newspaper	12.9
.5	Placed ad in nonlocal newspaper	**
4.9	Answered ads in professional or trade journals	7.3
6.0	Union hiring hall	22.2
5.6	Contacted local organization	12.7
.6	Placed ads in professional or trade journals	**
1.4	Went to place where employers come to pick up people	8.2
11.8	Other	39.7

*A percentage obtained by dividing the number of jobseekers who found work using the method, by the total number of jobseekers who used the method, whether successfully or not.
**Base less than 75,000.

Well, anyway, Mr. or Ms. Job-Hunter, this just about covers the favorite job-hunting system of this country *at its best.* (Except personal contacts, which we give special treatment—chapter 5.):

The Numbers Game.

If it works for you, right off, *great!* But if it doesn't, you may be interested in *the other plan*—you know, the one they had saved up for you, in case all of this didn't work? Small problem: with most of the personnel experts in our country, *there is no other plan.*

And that is that.

PRAY, as though everything
depended on God;
then work, as though everything
depended on You.

CHAPTER THREE

You Can
Do It!

Well, you've gotten the picture by now, I am sure. We all start out in life thinking that if we are tragically thrown out of work, someone out there will come to our rescue, steer us in the right direction, and hook us up with a proper job. Voila! Our troubles will be short-lived. We are, of course, unclear about who that someone will be: a union, or the government, or private agencies, or newspapers—but we believe it will be *someone*. Alas, when our time comes, and we are completely out of work, instead of someone coming to save us, there is only the sound of silence.

In religion, there is a Savior. But not in job-hunting. Many unemployed people have sat at home, waiting for God to prove that He loves them, by causing a job to walk in the door. It doesn't happen. The previous chapter surely drove home to you this solemn truth: You *have to* take over the management of your own job-hunt or career-change, if it is to be successful. No one else here on earth is going to have such concern for how it turns out, as you do. No one else is going to be willing to lavish so much time on it, as you will. No one else will be so persistent, as you will. No one else has so exact a picture of what kind of job you are looking for, as you do.

If your job-hunt were a movie script, and we were casting the lead, we would have to choose You, as the best qualified for the part. By a long shot.

So let us assume you are currently looking for work. That's why you're reading this book. What can we tell you, about how to take charge of your job-hunt?

Well, it all depends on how much time you're willing to put in on it, and how systematic you want to be, about it all. Many job-hunters do not want a system. They do not want to forge through all the chapters of this book. They do not want to spend hour after hour of self-searching exercises. They do not want to put blood, sweat and tears into their job-hunt. Rather they want essentially to throw themselves on the river of job-hunting, and see where it carries them. They want, well, just a few hints. That's all. They figure if someone will tell them just a few things they should be aware of, or a few things they could do differently, that should be enough to get them through.

Okay, here are:

THIRTY-FIVE HINTS
FOR TODAY'S JOB-HUNTER

(Can be read in the time it takes to
eat a burger at a fast-food outlet.)

1. You must be ready to go job-hunting *anytime*, for no matter how good a job you have been doing at your present workplace, that job may vanish—Poof!—tomorrow, due to circumstances entirely beyond your control.

2. If you have been unjustly let go, your first great need is to let go of your righteous anger at how different the world of work is from what you thought it would be; otherwise, that anger will cripple your job-hunting efforts. You will reek of it to every employer you go see, even as a drunk reeks of his strong drink.

3. No one owes you a job; you have to fight to win a job.

4. The major difference between successful and unsuccessful job-hunters, by and large, is the way that they go about their job-hunt—and *not* some factor "out there," such as a depressed labor market.

5. If you want your job-hunt to succeed, make a list of what you would do if you had to make your job-hunt fail. Yes, I said fail. Put the factor that would most surely make your job-hunt fail, at the top of your list, then the next one, and so forth. (One man's surest factor was "Sit at home.") In a second column, state the opposite of each factor (for example, "Get out of the house every single day") and you will then have a list of what you must do in your job-hunt in order to make it succeed.

6. Do not expect that you will necessarily be able to find exactly the same kind of work that you used to be doing. Be prepared to define some other lines of work that you can do, and would enjoy doing.

7. Take the label ("I am a . . . .") off yourself. You are a person who . . . .

TRAVELS WITH FARLEY by Phil Frank (c) 1982 Field Enterprises, Inc. Courtesy of Field Newspaper Syndicate

8. The more time you spend on figuring out what makes you stand out from nineteen other people who can do what you do, the better your chances.

9. Forget "what's available out there." Go after, with hammer and tongs, the job you really want the most.

10. If a thing turns you on, you'll be good at it; if it doesn't, you won't. (Courtesy of David Maister)

11. Figure out whether you're best with People, or with Things, or with Information.

12. In trying to change careers or go into a new field (for you), don't look for the rules or generalizations. Look for the exceptions to the rules. The rule is: "In order to do this work you have to have a master's degree and ten years' experience at it." You search for the exception: "Yes, but do you know of anyone that is in the field who hasn't got all those credentials? And where might I find him or her?"

13. Go after organizations with twenty or less employees. That's where two-thirds of all new jobs are. You will want to see the boss, not "the personnel department." (Only 15% of all organizations, mostly large organizations, even have personnel departments.)

14. Two-thirds of all job-hunters spend five hours or less a week, on their job-hunt; determine to spend six times that much.

15. Job-hunters visit an average of six employers a month; determine to see at least two a day.

16. The greater the number of job-hunting avenues you use, the greater the likelihood that you will find a job. As we saw in the previous chapter, there are twelve different job-hunting avenues out there: (1) mailing out your resume; (2) contacting executive recruiters; (3) answering ads in local papers, and nonlocal papers, and professional or trade journals; (4) going to private employment agencies; (5) going to federal/state job services; (6) contacting college placement offices; (7) using executive registers or some form of clearinghouse; (8) asking relatives, friends, teachers, professors, and other personal

referrals about jobs where they work; (9) applying directly to employers, face-to-face; (10) applying through Civil Service; (11) going to a union hiring hall or other places where employers go to find people; (12) working through a group job-search program. The average job-hunter uses 1.6 of these twelve methods.

17. Expect that your job-hunt is going to take some time. The average job-hunt lasts between six and eighteen weeks, depending on the state of the economy. Be prepared for the eighteen weeks or longer. Experienced outplacement people say that your job-hunt will probably take one month for every $10,000 of salary that you are seeking.

18. Look as sharp as you can *at all times* while you are out of work. Be neat, clean, well-dressed whenever you are outside your home; you never know who will see you—and possibly recommend you to someone who is hiring.

19. Go after many different organizations, instead of just one or two.

20. Go face-to-face with employers, whenever possible, rather than sending paper—such as a resume.

21. The major issue you face with employers is not what skills you have, but how you use them: whether you just "keep busy" or try to actually solve problems, thus increasing your effectiveness and the organization's effectiveness, too.

22. Whatever you produce, be sure it is something you are proud of. A University of Michigan study found that one out of four American workers felt so ashamed of the quality of the products they were producing, that they would not buy them themselves.

23. The manner in which you do your job-hunt and the manner in which you would do the job you are seeking—are *not* assumed by most employers to be two unrelated subjects, but one and the same. A slipshod, half-hearted job-hunt is taken as a warning that you would do a slipshod, half-hearted job, were they foolish enough to ever hire you.

24. There are not two things which will get you a job—Training or Experience—but three: Training, or Experience,

or a Demonstration of your Skills right before the employer's eyes. If there is any way that you can show an employer what you are capable of doing—through pictures, samples of things you have made or produced, or whatever—do it, during the interview.

25. If you and the employer really hit it off, but they cannot at that time afford to hire you, you might consider offering to do volunteer work there for a week or two, so they see firsthand how good you are at what you do.

26. Don't be wearied by rejection. We saw Tom Jackson's model of the typical job-hunt as NO NO NO NO NO NO etc. But remember you only need one YES—and the more NOs you get out of the way, the closer you are to that YES.

27. Every job-hunter is handicapped. The only question is: What is the handicap, and does it show?

28. Treat every employer with courtesy, even if it seems certain they can offer you no job there; they may be able to refer you to someone else next week, *if* you made a good impression.

29. Don't assume *anything*. ("But I just assumed that . . . .")

30. Send short handwritten thank-you notes that very night, to everyone you talked to that day in your job-hunting activities: secretaries, receptionists, thanking them for seeing or helping you.

31. Be gently persistent, and be willing to go back to places that interested you, to see if their "no jobs" situation has changed.

32. Once you know what kind of work you are looking for, tell *everyone* what it is; have as many other eyes and ears out there looking on your behalf, as possible.

33. When calling on an employer, ask for twenty minutes only, and don't stay one minute longer.

34. Whenever you are speaking to an employer, don't "hold forth" all by yourself for longer than two minutes, at any one time. Talk one-half the time, listen one-half the time.

35. Organizations only hire winners; go to that organization and to the interview as "a resource person," not as "a job beggar."

"Let's put it this way—if you can find a village without an idiot, you've got yourself a job."

WHEN HINTS AREN'T ENOUGH

Now, the hints may be *all* that you need. One or two of these may strike just the right chord in you, give you just the idea that you need, to go out and do a smashing job on your job-hunt.

But, we can't leave it at that. If the hints work for you, fine. But what if they don't? Then, you're going to need something more. You're going to need a more systematic way of getting at your job-hunt.

This is particularly true if you're thinking of changing careers. You don't have to go back to college and get retrained, in order to change careers. But you *do* have to sit down and do some thorough homework on yourself, and some thorough research about what's going on out there in the marketplace.

So, let's step out and take a look at all your options—systematically. Let's get an overview of THE MANY PATHS THROUGH JOB-LAND.

PART-TIME WORK

FULL-TIME WORK

A COMPOSITE CAREER (2, 3 OR MORE PART-TIME CAREERS)

ONE CAREER

WORKING FOR SOMEONE ELSE ←

→ WORKING FOR YOURSELF

DOING VOLUNTARY WORK OR AN INTERNSHIP

GOING BACK TO SCHOOL FOR LEGITIMATE RETRAINING

Jobs in this country last an average of 3.6 years. That sounds like we have to go job-hunting every 3.6 years. But that's only speaking of averages.

In actual fact, a particular job that you have may last longer than 3.6 years—especially as you grow older. So, surveys reveal the number of times you will have to go job-hunting in your entire lifetime will likely be eight times.

When it is time for you to go job-hunting, there are many roads you can take. They are shown on the map above.

STEVEN M. JOHNSON

TO PUT THE MAP INTO WORDS

These are the choices you face each time you are unemployed:

(1) ☐ Should I make a career change? OR
☐ Should I stay in the same field/career?

(2) If I choose to stay in the same field/career:
☐ Should I move to a different organization, though staying in the same type of job? OR
☐ Should I stay in the same organization where I am now?

(3) If the same organization:
☐ Should I stay in the very same job as I am now in? OR
☐ Should I move to a different department or different job there?

(4) If I make a career change:
☐ Should I change careers by going back to school for retraining? OR
☐ Should I change careers without going back to school?

(5) If I change careers without further schooling:
☐ Should I look for a new career in which I work for someone else? OR
☐ Should I look for a new career in which I work for myself?

(6) If I look for a new career in which I work for someone else:
☐ Should I seek a job at decent or even high pay? OR
☐ Should I seek for a volunteer job at first, or even an internship?

(7) If I look for a new career in which I work for myself:
☐ Should I seek a career made up of just one job? OR
☐ Should I seek a composite career, made up of several (2-5) different jobs/careers?

(8) And, once I have answered all the above questions, *what* is it I should do?

You need to work your way through these decisions. It may at first sight seem to you that each pair of decisions requires a different pathway. This is not true.

They are all approached by the same pathway—a basic "trunk" road that precedes them all.

This "trunk" road has three sections to it, and you MUST travel all three sections—no matter which road through Job Land you are currently leaning toward. The three sections you MUST cover, are:

1. **WHAT.** This has to do with your skills. You need to inventory and identify what skills you have that you most enjoy using. These are called transferable skills, because they are transferable to any field/career that you choose, regardless of where you first picked them up.

2. **WHERE.** This has to do with jobs as environments. Think of yourself as a flower. You know that a flower which blooms in the desert will not do well at 10,000 feet up—and vice versa. Every flower has an environment where it does best. So with you. You are like a flower. You need to decide where you want to use your skills, where you would thrive, and do your most effective work.

3. **HOW.** You need to decide how to get where you want to go. This has to do with finding out the names of the jobs you would be most interested in, AND the names of organizations (in your preferred geographical area) which have such jobs to offer, AND the names of the people or person there who actually has the power to hire you.

And, how you can best approach that person to show him or her how your skills can help them with their problems. How, if you were hired there, you would not be part of the problem, but part of the solution.

Now, to be sure, these three basic sections of your job-hunting or career-changing road will be traveled in a slightly different way, depending on your goals. If you ultimately become sure that you want to go into business for yourself, then the HOW will consist in identifying all the people who have already done something like the thing you are thinking of, so that you can go interview them and profit from their learnings and mistakes before you set out on your own. And the HOW may consist in identifying the potential customers or clients who would use your services or buy your product.

But, adaptation aside, you WILL need to travel all three sections of this basic trunk road, regardless of where you plan to end up. The only exception to this rule, is if you plan on staying at the same job and in the same organization where you presently are; and you are using this Map only to get a better picture of your strengths. In this case, you will omit the HOW picture—but will still need to travel the WHAT and WHERE sections of the road. For even if

you plan on remaining where you are—as it is already the "ideal" job for you—you will still function much better there if you know more intimately what your skills or strengths are, and where you like to use them.

(As one satisfied worker put it, "The skills inventory is something I do every two or three years. Each time I do it, I find out more specific things about what I do well. This information tells me what to watch for in the world—what kind of tasks I can volunteer for and do very well at. I know more about the *kind* of thing I want to be, do, be surrounded by. I am now sensitized and ready to recognize them when they swim by.")

THE RULE:
TAKE NO SHORTCUTS

Aside from this special case of staying right where you are, you WILL need to travel all three sections of the road, WHAT, WHERE and HOW.

If you only do the homework on the WHAT, you will be like a cart without any horse to pull it. It just stands helplessly beside the road.

"WHAT" furnishes you with the cart; "WHERE" furnishes the horse to pull it; and "HOW" furnishes the road along which your cart and horse travel, to your chosen destination.

Handicaps

Most of us think that when we go job-hunting, we need a special road, just for us. You probably think you have some special handicap in the job-hunt, that requires special handling. Here is a list of some of these handicaps—an expansion of a list originally put together by Daniel Porot, the job-hunting expert of Europe.

You may check off the ones which apply to you:

☐ I am just graduating
☐ I just graduated
☐ I graduated too long ago
☐ I am a woman
☐ I am a self-made man
☐ I am too young
☐ I am too old
☐ I have a prison record
☐ I have a psychiatric history
☐ I have never held a job before
☐ I have only had one employer
☐ I am a foreigner
☐ I have not had enough education
☐ I have had too much education
☐ I am too much of a generalist
☐ I am too much of a specialist
☐ I am a clergyperson
☐ I am Hispanic
☐ I am Black
☐ I am just coming out of the military
☐ I have a physical handicap

☐ I have a mental handicap
☐ I have only worked for large employers
☐ I have only worked for small employers
☐ I am too shy
☐ I am too assertive
☐ I come from a very different kind of background
☐ I come from another industry
☐ I come from another planet

If you checked off any of these, this makes you a handicapped job-hunter or career-changer. Most of us are so handicapped. The true meaning of the above comprehensive list is that there are about three weeks of your life when you're employable. That is, if handicaps cannot be overcome.

But of course they can be overcome. There are, after all, two kinds of employers (or clients or customers) out there:

those who will be put off by your handicap, and therefore won't hire you; AND

those who are NOT put off by your handicap, and therefore will hire you if you are qualified for the job.

You are not interested in the former kind of employer, client or customer. No matter how many of them there are. You are only looking for those employers who are NOT put off by your handicap, and therefore will hire you if you are qualified for the job.

The most important thing for you to know is that your best chance of bridging whatever handicap you have or think you have is CAREFUL PREPARATION ON YOUR PART.

The employers, clients, customers who will not care about your handicap will be most impressed if you approach them, not as a job-beggar, but as a resource person. Preparation such as this Map will change you from a job-beggar into A Resource Person.

In this sense, the trunk road, about which we have been talking,—the WHAT, WHERE, and HOW—is a bridge over whatever handicap you may have.

What It Takes
To Find A Job

What will it take for you to successfully get over that bridge? What will it take for you to do the WHAT, WHERE and HOW most effectively?

You want, of course, to hear that the answer is a bunch of sure-fire techniques, which we are about to teach you in this Map.

Alas, there are no techniques which will *guarantee* that you will find a job, if only you follow them faithfully.

Any true job-hunting veteran will tell you in all honesty that it takes three things to find a job:

a. Techniques. There are things others can teach you, and they will increase your effectiveness and improve your chances. You need to take these very seriously. But, by themselves, these are not enough.

b. Art. As in the phrase: "There's a real art to the way she does that." We refer here to the special stamp that each person's individuality puts on what they do. A certain amount of the job-hunt others cannot teach you. You bring your own unique art to the job-hunt, as you do to everything else you do. It's that extra pizazz, enthusiasm, energy that is uniquely yours, which must be present, before you can be successful at the job-hunt. We cannot clone you. Genuine individuality always marks every successful job-hunt.

c. Luck. Following certain techniques faithfully, and combining them with your own individual art in the way you do it, will not in and of themselves get you the job. There is always a certain amount of luck involved in any successful job-hunt. You have to be the right person in the right place at the right time.

These factors have varying importance, depending on which part of the job-hunt you are dealing with.

Your own individual way of doing things, your "art," is most important during the WHAT. This is because skill identification is more of an art, than a science. We can give you the basic rules, but a lot of it you have to do in your own individual way.

Techniques become more important during the WHERE and the HOW: those parts of the job-hunt can more easily be defined.

And Luck becomes most important during the HOW part of your job-hunt. So, if you like diagrams, your job-hunt will come out looking something like this:

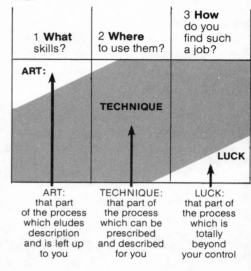

1 **What** skills?	2 **Where** to use them?	3 **How** do you find such a job?
ART:	**TECHNIQUE**	**LUCK**

ART: that part of the process which eludes description and is left up to you	TECHNIQUE: that part of the process which can be prescribed and described for you	LUCK: that part of the process which is totally beyond your control

What Can a Systematic Approach Give You? Obviously, it cannot give you good luck, or give you individuality. You must already possess that individuality, and you must have Lady Luck smile on you, for your job-hunt to succeed. BUT, by using the Systematic Approach in the next three chapters, the amount of luck you will need is greatly reduced. "Luck favors the prepared mind," as someone has observed. This Systematic Approach, if followed faithfully, WILL give you a thoroughly prepared mind.

The remainder of this book will be devoted to describing those techniques *in detail*. Chapter 4 is devoted to WHAT. Chapter 5 to WHERE. Chapter 6 to HOW.

RESOURCES FOR
YOU TO DRAW ON

You will naturally want to know what or who there is to help you, as you go through this process of the job-hunt or career-change. Here are the types of resources you can draw on:

I. *Yourself*. Doing the homework for yourself, tackling the exercises in chapters 4, 5, and 6, and reading and re-reading these chapters is to be preferred above all other resources, for any number of reasons. First of all, knowledge which you gain for yourself is more ingrained than knowledge that is simply handed to you by others. Secondly, the job-hunt process rightly understood is itself a preparation for, and training in, skills you will need to exercise once you get the job; to deprive yourself of the opportunity to get valuable practice in these skills during the job-hunting process, is to make it just that much more difficult for yourself on the job. Thirdly, even if you pay money (and a whole lot of it) to one kind of professional agency or another, there is no guarantee that they will do the process any better than, or even as well as, you would do it yourself.

M O R A L
Every investment of your money is a gamble unless you have first tried to do it on your own, know what you did find out, what you did not find out, and therefore what kind of help you now need from others.

II. *Books and other visual or audio materials*. If there's a particular phase where you get bogged down, a particular technique that confuses you, a particular obstacle you want help in getting around, then check out Appendix A—where such things are listed, by subject. I would urge you, however, to read all the way through chapters 4, 5, and 6 *first*, to get an overview. I get letters from readers which say, "I've only read part of your book so far, but I want to know what you have to suggest about . . ." And, of course, they refer to a subject that *is* covered in the chapters they haven't yet read. So, do *read* before you write. And if, after you read this book, there's something that's perplexing you, *do* check out the different subjects and books that are listed in Appendix A. That's why they are there.

III. *Free professional help*. When people get bogged down in their job-hunt, they often rush off to pay some career counselor to help them. Well, that's okay; but sometimes, if you'll just stop to analyze exactly what you need at that particular moment, you might discover there is professional help for you that is available *at no cost*. Examples of where such free help is to be found:

- the reference librarian, at your local library or college library;
- career counseling offices at your nearby community college;
- job-clinics at your local chamber of commerce, federal/state employment agency, advertising council, and the like;

- local federally funded "job clubs," for specific popula-
tions, such as WIN recipients, etc. Your local federal/
state employment office often knows their locations and
times of meeting; funding comes, in most cases, from the
Job Training Partnership Act of the Federal Government;
- self-directed job-support groups that meet in local
churches or synagogues, in many communities.

There is a section in Appendix B at the back of this book
that lists a few of these, and tells you how to find others.
In some cases, the help isn't, strictly speaking, totally free.
But the dues charged are so small, that for all intents and
purposes we may classify them as free.

The likelihood that such help is available in your community increases if you are from certain *disadvantaged* groups, as
low income, or welfare recipients, or youth, or displaced
workers, or those laid off permanently. Ask around.

IV. *Professional help for a fee.* Now here, a lot depends on what
kind of help you need or want. Is it aptitude/skills testing?
The grand-daddy of all such firms is Johnson O'Connor, nee
Human Engineering Laboratory, located in some of our prin-
cipal cities in the U.S. You can write them at 347 Beacon St.,
Boston, MA 02116, for a list of their offices. There are other
such firms around the country—such as Rockport Institute in
Washington, D.C. (2025 I St. NW, Ste. 203). Many colleges
and universities will give you vocational testing, for somewhat
more modest fees. You do need to ask whether it is *aptitude*
testing or merely *interests* testing. I have more to say about
that in the next chapter. The distinction is important.

If you want help with the overall process of job-hunting,
Appendix B in the back of this book has a Sampler that lists
some of the career counseling offices to be found around the
country. Your yellow pages will also have a list of these in
your area, under the headings of "Aptitude and Employment
Testing," "Career Counseling," "Executive Consultants," "Management Consultants," "Personnel Consultants," and "Vocational Consultants." You will have to pick your way with great
care through those woods. Just when you think you've gotten
safely to grandmother's house, you may find there is a wolf
there. Appendix B has an introductory section which I would

urge you read no less than three times before you ever venture forth to press your money and your job-hunt into somebody else's hands.

Some professional groups have their own counseling centers. For example, if you are a clergyperson, you will want to look at the church career development centers which have sprung up all over the country. A list of them is to be found under "The Special Problems of Clergy," section 15 in Appendix A, page 231.

V. *Your family or friends.* I believe as a general rule—there *are* exceptions—you ought to try never to go through the job-hunt *all by yourself alone.* Co-opt *somebody*—your partner or mate, a grown-up son or daughter who lives nearby, your best friend, someone you know well from your church or synagogue—to be your weekly *support person.*

PRACTICAL EXERCISE
(SO YOU DON'T GO IT ALONE)

Choose a support-person for your job-hunt. Ask them if they're willing to help you. Assuming they say yes, put down in both your appointment books a regular weekly date when they will *guarantee* to meet with you, check you out on what you've done *already,* and be very stern with you if you've done little or nothing since your previous week's meeting. The more a gentle but firm taskmaster this confidante is, the better. Tell them that it is at least a 20,000 hour, $500,000 project. Or whatever. It's also responsible, concerned, committed *Stewardship.*

Where did we get 20,000 hours? Well, a forty-hour-a-week job, done for fifty weeks a year, adds up to 2,000 hours annually. So, how long are you going to be doing this new job or new career that you are looking for? How many years do you plan to stay in the world of work? Ten years? That means 20,000 hours. Longer than that? Even more hours. So, it's *at least* a 20,000-hour project.

Why $500,000? Well, figure it out for yourself. Say, you hope to start this new job or new career of yours at $20,000 a year. Even if you are forty years old, you still have thirty good years of work left in you. So, let us say that over that period of thirty years you get enough raises to make your annual salary somewhere between $25,000 and $30,000. Multiply this by thirty years, and you get a total earnings of something in the neighborhood of more than half a million dollars. If you've got more years ahead of you, or a higher potential salarywise, you're talking about even more money. So it's *at least* a $500,000 project that you're working on, with this job-hunt of yours as the doorway.

That should get you going!

There is no expedient
to which a man will not
resort to avoid the real
labor of thinking.
—Sir Joshua Reynolds

CHAPTER FOUR

The Systematic Approach To The Job-Hunt and Career-Change:

PART I

What
Skills Do You Most Enjoy Using?

Well, let us begin by getting motivated.

There is a vast world of work out there, where 111 million people are employed in this country alone—*many of whom* are bored out of their minds. All day long. Not for nothing is their motto TGIF—"Thank God It's Friday." They *live* for the weekends, when they can go do what they really want to do.

There are already more than enough of such poor souls. The world does not need you or me to add to their number. What the world does need is more people who know what they really want to do, and who do it at their place of work—as their chosen work. The world needs more people who feel true enthusiasm for their work. People who have taken the time to think—and to think out what they uniquely can do, and what they uniquely have to offer to the world.

This is, of course, where you come in. IF you are willing to sit down and do this task of identifying your skills. Is it hard work? Well, it can be. Is it fun? Well, it can be. It all depends on you.

I remind you of some words of Victor Frankl:

"We who lived in concentration camps can remember the men who walked through the huts comforting others, giving away their last piece of bread. They may have been few in number, but they offer sufficient proof that everything can be taken from a man but one thing: the last of the human freedoms —to choose one's attitude in any given set of circumstances, to choose one's own way."

And so it is, that in tackling this homework for your job-hunt or your career-change, you have the last of the human freedoms—the freedom to choose what your attitude will be about all this.

You can choose to see it as a lot of drudgery and hard work, which you would never do were it not for the difficult labor market that you face.

Or, you can choose to see it as *fun*—an exploration of the inner world of yourself, where you unwrap your skills with joy as a child unwraps his or her gifts at Christmastime. You can choose to prize this process as a means of gaining more of a sense of control over your life and over your destiny, under God. You are also gaining the weapons to protect yourself. For, at job-hunting time you are very vulnerable, and therefore very much at risk of being manipulated by others: be they those who might make money off your plight, or be they future employers, or even well-meaning loved ones or friends.

Not long ago, I overheard two college students talking, in Central Park in New York City. We'll call them Jim and Mike. In half a minute of conversation they perfectly illustrated what I am saying:

Jim: Hey, what are you majoring in?

Fred: Physics.

Jim: Physics? Man, you shouldn't major in physics. Computer science is the thing these days.

Fred: Naw, I like physics.

Jim: Man, physics doesn't pay much.

Fred: Really?

Jim: Switch to computer science.
Fred: Okay, I'll look into it tomorrow.

Upon such little conversations do huge life-decisions depend. This is why it is so important to do your homework, on identifying your favorite and strongest skills. Settle it in your mind right now:

As you set about your job-hunt, you have got to know what it is you want—or else someone is going to sell you a bill of goods somewhere along the line that can do irreparable damage to your self-esteem, your sense of worth, and your stewardship of the talents that God gave you.

Okay, let us begin.

WHY DO YOU BEGIN WITH YOUR SKILLS?

You begin the systematic approach to your job-hunt by first of all identifying your skills. The reason for this is that skills are the most basic unit—the atoms—of your life in the world of work. You can see this from the accompanying diagram.

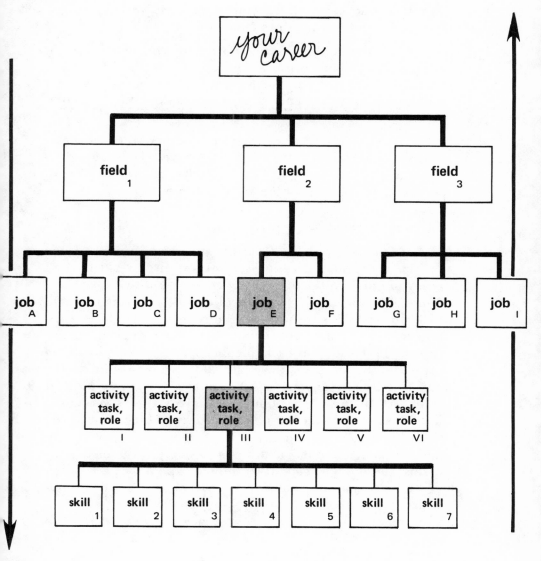

I'm not much for definitions, but if *you* prefer definitions they are relatively easy to come by—once you have seen this diagram:

• A CAREER is your total life in the world of work. Careers are often, in everyday conversation, spoken of as though they were synonymous with "FIELDS of knowledge" or "majors"— so that when we mean to say "field change" we often content ourselves instead with the less precise phrase "career-change." But in the end it really doesn't matter.

• A JOB is defined by what is above it and below it. Above it is "field," and below it are "TASKS" and "skills." Thus it is that a job is a particular kind of work in a particular field, where you set your hand to particular tasks using particular skills.

• As for SKILLS, you can of course call them by other names— and many prefer to: gifts, talents, aptitudes. The name does not matter. Whatever you call them, they are the essence of what you have to contribute to the world of work.

DEFINITION OF "SKILLS"

Now, many people just "freeze" when they hear the word "skills." It begins with high school job-hunters: "I haven't really got any skills," they say. It continues with college students: "I've spent four years in college. I haven't had time to pick up any skills." And it lasts through the middle years, especially when a person is thinking of changing his or her career: "I'll have to go back to college, and get retrained, because otherwise I won't have any skills in my new field." Or: "Well, if I claim any skills, I'll start at a very entry kind of level." All of this fright about the word "skills" is very common, and stems from a total misunderstanding of what the word means. A misunderstanding that is shared, we might add, by altogether too many employers, personnel departments, and other so-called "vocational experts."

By understanding the word, you will automatically put yourself way ahead of most job-hunters. And, especially if you are weighing a change of career, you can save yourself much waste of time on the (currently popular) folly called "going back to school for retraining."

So, herewith our crash-course on skills:

According to the *Bible* of career counseling—the fourth edition of the *Dictionary of Occupational Titles* (U.S. Government Printing Office, Washington, D.C., 1977)—skills break down, first of all, into three groups according to whether or not they are being used with Data (Information), or People or Things. (See diagram.) Thus broken down, and arranged in a hierarchy of less complex skills at the bottom to more complex skills at the top, they come out looking like inverted pyramids.

14 Skills With People, primarily, though they also involve information and things

[14. Working With Animals]
13. Training
12. Counseling (holistic)
11. Advising, Consulting
10. Treating
9. Founding, Leading
8. Negotiating, Deciding
7. Managing, Supervising
6. Performing, Amusing
5. Persuading
4. Communicating
3. Sensing, Feeling
2. Serving
1. Taking Instructions

15 Skills With Information or Data, primarily, though they also involve things

29. Achieving
28. Expediting
27. Planning, Developing
26. Designing
25. Creating, Synthesizing
24. Improving, Adapting
23. Visualizing
22. Evaluating
21. Organizing
20. Analyzing
19. Researching
18. Computing
17. Copying, Storing & Retrieving
16. Comparing
15. Observing

11 Skills With Things, primarily, though they may also involve information

40. Repairing
39. Setting Up
38. Precision Working
37. Operating (vehicles)
36. Operating (equipment)
35. Using (tools)
34. Minding
33. Feeding, Emptying
32. Working With The Earth Or Nature
31. Being Athletic
30. Handling (objects)

INCREASINGLY DISCRETIONARY

INCREASINGLY PRESCRIBED

Before we get to your skill identification, let us note . . .

FIVE LITTLE KNOWN FACTS ABOUT SKILLS

1. The skills are ranked in a hierarchy, one above the other, and each skill, as you go up the ladder (or The Pyramids, here), typically includes or involves most or all of those skills which are listed below it. We can see this clearly, just by looking at the skills that are used with PEOPLE (see following box). This particular list of definitions, incidentally, is taken from the third edition (1965) of the *Dictionary of Occupational Titles,* Vol. II, pp. 649-50, as modified and adapted by my wonderful friend, Dr. Sidney A. Fine. You will note that the list differs slightly from the one in the previous pictorial, and elsewhere in this chapter.

At your public library, on pp. 1369-71 in the 1977 edition of the D.O.T., as the *Dictionary of Occupational Titles* is called, you can find similar lists for Data and Things.

2. As you note the increasing complexity of the higher skills, you will of course—in keeping with the modest nature for which you are widely known—be tempted to identify your skills down near the bottom of The Inverted Pyramids—"just to be on the safe side." "Mustn't claim too much," and all that sort of rubbish.

3. But, in fact, it is in your own best interest to claim the highest skills that you legitimately can. Because, the higher the skill that you have, the more creativity you will be permitted in your future job or new career. You will be free to carve out the job so that it truly fits you. On the other hand, the lower the skill you claim, the more you will have to follow instructions in that future job and do what your supervisors tell you to do. The lower the skill you claim, the more you will have to fit in.

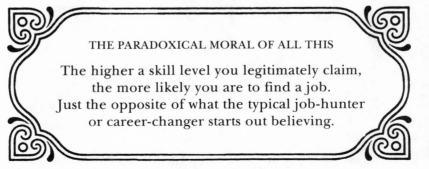

THE PARADOXICAL MORAL OF ALL THIS

The higher a skill level you legitimately claim,
the more likely you are to find a job.
Just the opposite of what the typical job-hunter
or career-changer starts out believing.

WORKING WITH PEOPLE
Increasing Levels of Skill
Beginning With
The Most Elementary Definition

TAKING INSTRUCTIONS — HELPING
Attends to the work assignment, instructions, or orders of supervisor. No immediate response or verbal exchange is required unless clarification of instruction is needed.

SERVING
Attends to the needs or requests of people or animals, or to the expressed or implicit wishes of people. Immediate response is involved.

EXCHANGING INFORMATION
Talks to, converses with, and/or signals people to convey or obtain information, or to clarify and work out details of an assignment, within the framework of well-established procedures.

COACHING
Befriends and encourages individuals on a personal, caring basis by approximating a peer- or family-type relationship either in a one-to-one or small group situation, and gives instruction, advice, and personal assistance concerning activities of daily living, the use of various institutional services, and participation in groups.

PERSUADING
Influences others in favor of a product, service, or point of view by talks or demonstrations.

DIVERTING   Amuses others.

CONSULTING
Serves as a source of technical information and gives such information or provides ideas to define, clarify, enlarge upon, or sharpen procedures, capabilities, or product specifications.

INSTRUCTING
Teaches subject matter to others, or trains others, including animals, through explanation, demonstration, practice, and test.

TREATING
Acts on or interacts with individuals or small groups of people or animals who need help (as in sickness) to carry out specialized therapeutic or adjustment procedures. Systematically observes results of treatment within the framework of total personal behavior because unique individual reactions to prescriptions (chemical, behavioral, physician's) may not fall within the range of prediction. Motivates, supports, and instructs individuals to accept or cooperate with therapeutic adjustment procedures, when necessary.

continued next page

INCREASING LEVELS OF SKILL continued

SUPERVISING
Determines and/or interprets work procedure for a group of
workers, assigns specific duties to them (particularly those which
are prescribed), maintains harmonious relations among them,
evaluates performance (both prescribed and discretionary), and
promotes efficiency and other organizational values. Makes decisions on procedural and technical levels.

NEGOTIATING
Exchanges ideas, information, and opinions with others on a
formal basis to formulate policies and programs on an initiating
basis (e.g., contracts) and/or arrives at resolutions of problems
growing out of administration of existing policies and programs,
usually after a bargaining process.

MENTORING
Deals with individuals in terms of their overall life adjustment
behavior in order to advise, counsel, and/or guide them with
regard to problems that may be resolved by legal, scientific,
clinical, spiritual and/or other professional principles. Advises
clients on implications of diagnostic or similar categories, courses
of action open to deal with a problem, and merits of one strategy
over another.

---

4. The higher the level of skills that you can honestly and
legitimately claim for yourself, on the basis of your past performance, the less likely it is that the jobs which use such
skills will be advertised through normal channels. And because they are not advertised through normal channels, you
will need to use unorthodox methods to find out about them.

5. On the other hand, the harder the jobs are to find out
about, the less people there will be to compete with you for

that job. And in fact, if you succeed, as you are likely to do, in uncovering an unmet need within the organizations of your choice, there is an excellent chance that they will create for you a job that did not even exist before you walked in. This means you will be competing with no one, since you will be the sole applicant for that newly created job.

What Skills You Have and Most Enjoy Using

The easiest way to get into the subject of your skills is to just dive in. Imagine, if you will, that this diagram below is the aerial view of a room in which a Party is taking place (the view is taken from the next floor up). At this Party, for some unknown reason, people with similar interests or skills have gathered together with one another, in the same corner of the room. As there are basically six such groups, it is fortunate the room has six corners:

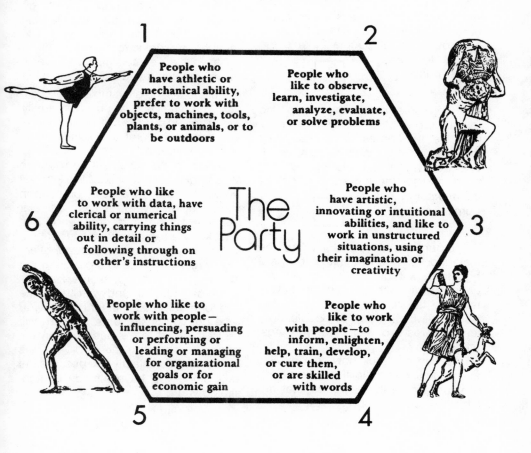

1 People who have athletic or mechanical ability, prefer to work with objects, machines, tools, plants, or animals, or to be outdoors

2 People who like to observe, learn, investigate, analyze, evaluate, or solve problems

6 People who like to work with data, have clerical or numerical ability, carrying things out in detail or following through on other's instructions

The Party

3 People who have artistic, innovating or intuitional abilities, and like to work in unstructured situations, using their imagination or creativity

5 People who like to work with people — influencing, persuading or performing or leading or managing for organizational goals or for economic gain

4 People who like to work with people — to inform, enlighten, help, train, develop, or cure them, or are skilled with words

It is a party that is to go on, all through the night. You are told that you must choose to be with one of the groups in one of the corners of the room.

a) Which corner of the room would you instinctively be drawn to, as "your kind of people"—whom you would most *enjoy* being with, for the longest time? Leave aside any question of shyness; maybe they will do all the talking, and you can just listen, with rapt attention. Write the *number* for that corner here: □

b) Suppose for some reason *that* group left the party, without you. (They have gone to another party, crosstown. How inconsiderate!) Of the groups which *still remain* at *this* Party, which group would you *now* be most drawn to, as "your kind of people"? Write the *number* for their corner here: □

c) For some reason, this group also leaves for another party crosstown. (Hey, get the address of *that* party.) Of the groups which now remain, which one would you enjoy being with the most, and for the longest time? Write the *number* of that corner here: □

Incidentally, if you don't like the metaphor of a Party, think of this as a bookstore, with different book sections; or a job fair, with different employers ready to talk to you, or whatever. The issue is: which group of people, subjects, interests, or skills, are you most attracted to?

You can go back now, if you wish, and underline specific skills within each of your favorite three groups, that are the skills you like the very best.

There, you have done what we call "elementary skill identification"—and in less than three minutes. This was just to give you a quick "feel" for the exercise. The principle on which this exercise was based, is that *we are instinctively attracted to people who are doing what we would like to do. And we would like to do those things which we already do well, and enjoy.*

That's all.

Now that you've taken your first step on the bridge of WHAT skills you have and most enjoy using, let's really roll up our sleeves, and get to work.

You Are Going To Go On A 'Verb Hunt'

The skills you are now going to go hunting for, are called "transferable skills" or "functional skills." In order to find them, it is going to be necessary for you to write out some simple statements about something you did in the past.

Here is a simple example: "(I) *organized* a committee in our community, which raised $15,000 to help a family that had been burnt out of their home on Christmas Eve."

Hidden in that statement, and all such statements about your past, is a key *skill* word. It is always a verb, or a noun made out of a verb. In this particular example, it is the word "organized." That is a skill. We can of course later put the skill in various forms: *organized,* effectively *organizes,* able *to organize,* good at *organizing,* or adept at *organization.*

We can play around with the tense and form of it, later. But for now, as you write out your statements, the verb will be in the past tense, such as "organized." The skill is in the verb. And it is convincing. For, clearly you possess the skill, since you have already demonstrated you do.

Notice that in the above example the word "I" is in parentheses. It's fine where it is, in this statement about the past. But when it comes time for you to polish and shine your skill identifications later, you will then want to wipe out the "I." It is normally *omitted* in any final definition of your skill, such as a letter or resume or 'qualifications brief.' You will be listing a number of skills at that time, and the word "I" in front of each one is totally unnecessary. After all, if it's your statement, we know who did it. You won't need to keep telling us "I."

In skill identification, first and last, it is not the noun but the *verb* that is important. That is why you may think of this part of your job-hunt—the WHAT phase —as essentially "a verb hunt."

You Need Some Stories— Seven, To Be Exact

We can't just go hunting for *verbs* by themselves. Though, you can always try that approach. You will almost certainly discover, however, that the verbs are best found in stories. So, you need to write out some stories about your past. Ultimately, you are going to need seven such stories. These stories need to be:

1. *Brief.* A paragraph or two, at most.

2. *Experiences in which You are the chief actor or actress.* Telling us a story about something done *to* you, like being given an award or something, will NOT do. It must be something YOU did. Then it's all right if there's an award, at the end.

3. *Experiences in which You accomplished something.* There must have been:

a. Some kind of problem you needed to solve.

b. Some kind of action that you took, in order to solve it.

c. Some concrete results that could be seen, or even better, measured.

4. *Experiences in which you were truly enjoying yourself.* You can dredge up Skills from anything you have ever done, anyplace. *But* what you are looking for are the Skills you used *when you were enjoying yourself, accomplishing something.*

5. *Taken from any period of your life, and from any part of your life: work OR leisure OR learning.*

6. *Told step-by-step, in detail.*

You Need Seven Sheets Of Paper

For this exercise, you will eventually need seven blank sheets of notebook paper: one sheet for each story/job/role.

But, you start out with just one sheet, for you begin by writing just one story.

Do that NOW, please.

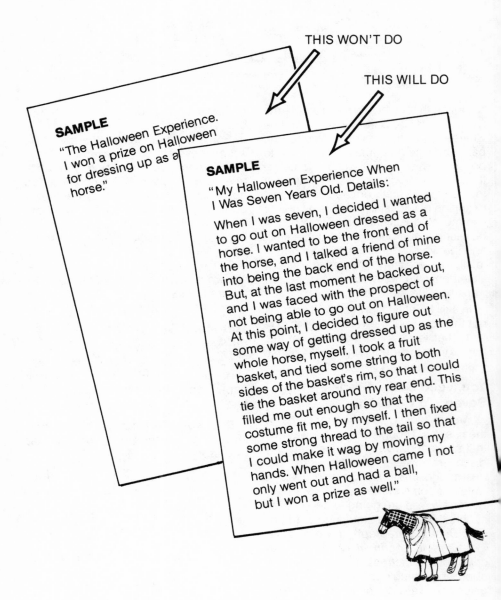

THIS WON'T DO

THIS WILL DO

SAMPLE

"The Halloween Experience.
I won a prize on Halloween
for dressing up as a
horse."

SAMPLE

"My Halloween Experience When
I Was Seven Years Old. Details:

When I was seven, I decided I wanted
to go out on Halloween dressed as a
horse. I wanted to be the front end of
the horse, and I talked a friend of mine
into being the back end of the horse.
But, at the last moment he backed out,
and I was faced with the prospect of
not being able to go out on Halloween.
At this point, I decided to figure out
some way of getting dressed up as the
whole horse, myself. I took a fruit
basket, and tied some string to both
sides of the basket's rim, so that I could
tie the basket around my rear end. This
filled me out enough so that the
costume fit me, by myself. I then fixed
some strong thread to the tail so that
I could make it wag by moving my
hands. When Halloween came I not
only went out and had a ball,
but I won a prize as well."

If you *absolutely* can't think of any experiences you've had where you enjoyed yourself, and accomplished something, then try this: Describe the seven most enjoyable *jobs* that you've had; or seven *roles* you've had so far in your life, such as: wife, mother, cook, homemaker, volunteer in the community, citizen, dress-maker, student, etc. Tell us something you did or accomplished, in each role.

You Need A List (Of Skills)

Once you have the story written, you will want to go back over it and identify the skills that you used in that story (in the doing of it, not the telling of it). Here we run into a problem. Not every verb is a skill. And sometimes the verb you want, is only implied in the story.

So, what are you do to? Try to name the skills, off the top of your head? Most of us have poor luck when we try to do this. We know what we did, but we run out of words to describe it. Therefore, sooner or later—usually sooner—we cry out for a list. We need a list.

You Need People, Or Data Or Things

How many skill verbs should be on the list? Well, the answer could be "thousands." After all, there are at least 12,000 different jobs in this world. There are 8,000 alternate titles for those 12,000 jobs. So, there are at least 20,000 different job titles you can choose from; and heaven only knows how many skills lie beneath those titles. *Too* many! We need some way to simplify the list. *Fortunately,* there is such a way.

As we saw earlier, all jobs deal with three things. And only three. So, ulti-mately all transferable skills deal with only three things, too.

Your skills are either:
skills with **People**, or
skills with **Information**,
sometimes called **Data**, or
skills with **Things**.

You have all three, in varying degrees. The question is, what are the particular skills that you have with each? *And,* which of these do you enjoy the most? That is what you now need to explore.

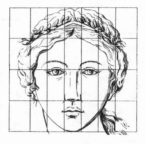

Basically there are only 13 things you can do with People (plus one additional group, for work with animals). And there are only 15 things you can do with Information, or Data. And there are only 11 things you can do with Things. Every other skill identification is a variation, or a sub-particle of these 40:

If you want some definitions of PEOPLE, INFORMATION/DATA, and THINGS, here goes:

• PEOPLE may mean all kinds of people, or very specific kinds of people—defined by age, culture, background, kinds of problems they face, etc. PEOPLE also includes animals, and beings from other orders of Reality.

• INFORMATION/DATA may mean information, knowledge, data, ideas, facts, figures, statistics, etc. Information is present in every job.

• THINGS may mean physical objects, instruments, tools, machinery, equipment, vehicles, materials, and desk-top items such as pencils, paper clips, telephones, stamps, etc.

14 Skills With People,
primarily, though they also involve information and things

/\

[14. Working With Animals]
13. Training
12. Counseling (holistic)
11. Advising, Consulting
10. Treating
9. Founding, Leading
8. Negotiating, Deciding
7. Managing, Supervising
6. Performing, Amusing
5. Persuading
4. Communicating
3. Sensing, Feeling
2. Serving
1. Taking Instructions

11 Skills With Things,
primarily, though they may also involve information

/\

40. Repairing
39. Setting Up
38. Precision Working
37. Operating (vehicles)
36. Operating (equipment)
35. Using (tools)
34. Minding
33. Feeding, Emptying
32. Working With The Earth Or Nature
31. Being Athletic
30. Handling (objects)

Using the first story we asked you to write, above, you now need to run that story down the list of *possible* skills with PEOPLE, INFORMATION, and then THINGS. Since your possible skills are in all three categories, the Road now divides into three branches, at least temporarily:

15 Skills With Information or Data,
primarily, though they also involve things

/\

29. Achieving
28. Expediting
27. Planning, Developing
26. Designing
25. Creating, Synthesizing
24. Improving, Adapting
23. Visualizing
22. Evaluating
21. Organizing
20. Analyzing
19. Researching
18. Computing
17. Copying, Storing & Retrieving
16. Comparing
15. Observing

- first, the road through skills with PEOPLE, and then
- the road through skills with INFORMATION/DATA, and then
- the road through skills with THINGS.

YOUR FUNCTIONAL / TRANSFERABLE SKILLS INVENTORY

I N S T R U C T I O N S

1.   Get story. Take the story you have just written. It should be on a separate sheet of paper. Give the story some brief title.

2.   Get list. Turn to the next page   You will see that the road flows by (on the left-hand side) a list of Skills you may have with People.

3.   Read the list, one by one. Put your story's title at the bottom of the page where it says "#1." Then, read over the first People Skill, its definition, and all the skill verbs immediately under it.

4.   Color in. If you feel that in the story in question you used that skill, or any of its variations, *color in* with pen or pencil the appropriate rectangle/square in column #1. For example:

1. TAKING INSTRUCTIONS		

/1 /2 /3 /

1. TAKING INSTRUCTIONS
Giving attention to instructions, and then carrying out the prescribed action.
Representing; following through; executing; enforcing regulations; rendering support services.

5.   Copy words that apply. *If* you colored in this rectangle/square, it means you feel *some* skill verbs there, apply to you in this story. Choose the ones most meaningful to you, and copy them into the box with the heading, "I am skilled at . . ." Leave plenty of room in that box, as during the succeeding six stories that you will be analyzing eventually, you may want to copy other words for those six.

6.   Adapt the words so they are yours. There is nothing sacred about the skill words on the left-hand side of the page. If you can think of a better way to say what your skill is, *do not hesitate* to put the skill into your own words. Use the *Bank* of Additional Skill-Verbs (to the right of the page) for helpful suggestions.

7.   Work your way on down the page. As you read each skill in turn, do not ask yourself "Do I have this skill?" That is not the issue. The issue is: "Did I use this skill, or any of its variations, in *this* story?" If you can hardly bear to pass by a box, because you *know* you have that skill—even though it was not used in *this* story—think hard of some achievement of yours from the past, where you *did* use that skill. Jot down a reminder to yourself, to use that as your next story. You will be writing seven such stories eventually, remember. Now you know what one to write next. And maybe, before you're through going down this entire list with your first story, you'll get some terrific ideas for the other six.

8.   Turn to page 86.   That has to do with Skills you may have with Information. Follow the same procedure.

9.   Turn to page 92.   That has to do with Skills you may have with Things. Follow the same procedure.

10. You are done with your first story. You have matched it against the 40 major skills that exist in the world of work, and plucked out those that describe you *in that story.* You have also probably gotten an idea of an even better story you could have chosen. Never mind. Just make that one your next story.

11. Write your second story, now. Don't write it *until* now. You see why. As a result of running your first story all the way through this Skills List, you doubt-less got a better idea of *what to write, and how* to write it. Take your second story through the same process as the first, now, beginning with writing its title down at the bottom where it says #2, on all three pages.

12. Etc. When you are done analyzing the second story, then write your third. Run it through the same process. Then your fourth. Etc. Etc. Etc. until you are done with all seven.

Skills you may have with
People

Basically thirteen skills, with one additional one that
deals with animals

	1	2	3	4	5	6	7

1. TAKING INSTRUCTIONS
Giving attention to instructions, and then carrying out the prescribed action.
Representing; following through; executing; enforcing regulations; rendering support services.

2. SERVING
Answering implicit or explicit wishes or needs of others.
Preparing (something for someone); helping; hostessing; waiting on (tables); nursing; protecting.

3. SENSING, FEELING
Apprehending through intuition, showing sensitivity to others, especially to their feelings.
Intuiting; being sensitive and responsive to the feelings of others; empathizing; showing warmth; keen ability to put self in someone else's shoes; having keen sense of taste; having keen sense of smell.

4. COMMUNICATING
Signaling, speaking or listening to others so as to convey or receive information.
Listening; receiving information; learning; questioning; interviewing; exchanging information; signaling; telling; talking; writing; informing; giving instructions; speechwriting; playwriting.

5. PERSUADING
Moving people by means of demonstration or argument toward a course of action.
Influencing; inspiring; convincing; motivating; moving; developing rapport or trust; recruiting talent or leadership; demonstrating (a product); selling tangibles or intangibles; publicizing; promoting; fund-raising; writing proposals; arranging financing.

6. PERFORMING, AMUSING
Getting up before a group of people, and performing in a manner that illuminates, gives pleasure, or both.
Exhibiting showmanship; amusing; making people laugh; acting; dramatizing; modeling; singing; dancing; playing music; giving poetry readings; making oral presentations; exceptional speaking ability; thinking quickly on one's feet; writing with humor, fun, and flair.

*Some title for each of
your life stories / achievements* ⟶

1   2   3   4   5   6   7

am skilled at

Additional Skill-Verbs Bank: Expert at getting things done; ability to follow detailed instructions; ability to implement decisions; unusual ability to represent others.

Additional Skill-Verbs Bank: Attending to; rendering services to; ministering to; caring for the handicapped; skilled at public relations; dealing patiently with difficult people.

Additional Skill-Verbs Bank: Developing warmth over the telephone; creating an atmosphere of acceptance; ability to shape atmosphere of a place so that it is warm, pleasant and comfortable; refusing to put people into slots or categories; treating others as equals, without regard to education, authority or position.

Additional Skill-Verbs Bank: Skilled at striking up conversations with strangers; talks easily with all kinds of people; adept at gathering information from people by talking to them; listening intently and accurately; ability to hear and answer questions perceptively; adept at two-way dialogue; expressing with clarity; verbalizing cogently; responding.

Additional Skill-Verbs Bank: Expert in reasoning persuasively; influencing the ideas and attitudes of others; making distinctive visual presentations; selling a program or course of action to decision-makers; obtaining agreement after the fact; building customer loyalty; promotional writing; creating imaginative advertising and publicity programs.

Additional Skill-Verbs Bank: Having strong theatrical sense; understudying; addressing large or small groups confidently; very responsive to audiences' moods or ideas; distracting; diverting; provoking laughter; relating seemingly disparate ideas by means of words or actions; employing humor in describing one's experiences; exceptionally good at facial expressions or body language to express thoughts or feelings eloquently; using voice tone and rhythm as unusually effective tool of communication; giving radio or TV presentations.

Possible skills with People *(CONTINUED)*

	1	2	3	4	5	6	7
7. MANAGING, SUPERVISING *Monitoring individual behavior and coordinating with others',* *for the systematic achieving of some organizational objective.* Determining goals; interpreting goals; promoting harmonious relations & efficiency; encouraging people; coordinating; managing; overseeing; heading; administering; directing public affairs; directing (production of); controlling (a project).							
8. NEGOTIATING, DECIDING *Arriving at an individual or jointly agreed-upon decision,* *usually through discussion and compromise.* Exchanging information; discussing; conferring; working well in a hostile environment; treating people fairly; mediating; arbitrating; bargaining; umpiring; adjudicating; renegotiating; compromising; reconciling; resolving; charting mergers; making policy.							
9. FOUNDING, LEADING *Enlisting and synergizing others toward a corporate objective.* Initiating; originating; founding; instituting; establishing; charting; financing; determining goals, objectives and procedures; recognizing and utilizing the skills of others; enlisting; displaying charisma; inspiring trust; evoking loyalty; organizing diverse people into a group; unifying; synergizing; team-building; sharing responsibility; delegating authority; contracting; taking manageable risks; conducting (music).							
10. TREATING *Acting to improve a physical, mental, emotional or spiritual problem* *of others, by using a specified technique or substance.* Caring for; improving; altering; rehabilitating; having true therapeutic abilities; prescribing; counseling; praying over; curing.							
11. ADVISING, CONSULTING *Giving expert advice or recommendations,* *based on an area of expertise one possesses.* Reading avidly; continually gathering information with respect to a particular problem or area of expertise; offering services; giving expert advice; consulting; trouble-shooting; recommending; referring.							
12. (HOLISTIC) COUNSELING *Dealing with a person's problems in the context of their total self,* *to identify and resolve them through self-directed action.* Advising; counseling; mentoring; facilitating personal growth and development of others; helping people identify their problems, needs, and solutions; interpreting dreams; solving problems; raising people's self-esteem.							

1 2 3 4 5 6 7

I am skilled at	
	Additional Skill-Verbs Bank: Devising systematic approach to goal setting; monitoring behavior through watching, critical evaluation, and feedback; adept at planning and staging ceremonies; planning, organizing and staging of theatrical productions; conducting (music).
	Additional Skill-Verbs Bank: Collaborating with colleagues skillfully; handling prima donnas tactfully and well; handling super-difficult people in situations, without stress; getting diverse groups to work together; expert at liaison roles; adept at conflict management; accepting of differing opinions; arriving at jointly agreed-upon decision or policy or program or solution; promoting and bringing about major policy changes.
	Additional Skill-Verbs Bank: Unusual ability to work self-directedly, without supervision; perceptive in identifying and assessing the potential of others; attracting skilled, competent, and creative people; willing to experiment with new approaches; instinctively understands political realities; recognizing when more information is needed before a decision can be reached; skilled at chairing meetings; deft at directing creative talent; adept at calling in other experts or helpers as needed.
	Additional Skill-Verbs Bank: Making and using contacts effectively; finding and getting things not easy to find; acting as resource broker; giving professional advice; giving insight concerning—
	Additional Skill-Verbs Bank: Helping people make their own discoveries; clarifying values and goals of others; putting things in perspective; adept at confronting others with touchy or difficult personal matters.

Possible skills with People *(CONCLUDED)*

	1	2	3	4	5	6	7

13. TRAINING
Giving new information or ideas to people, through lecture, demonstration, or practice.

Knowing (something); causing an individual or group to know (something); lecturing; fostering a stimulating learning environment; instilling in people a love of the subject being taught; explaining difficult or complex concepts or ideas; giving examples; demonstrating; showing; translating; detailing; modeling desired behavior; group-facilitating; helping others to express their views; helping others to experience (something); empowering.

[14. WORKING WITH ANIMALS]
In general this involves using, with special refinement, the same skills as in the preceding thirteen categories; specifically:
Serving; sensing; communicating; persuading; performing; managing; negotiating; leading; treating; training.

	1	2	3	4	5	6	7

I am skilled at	
	Additional Skill-Verbs Bank: Designing educational events; organizing and administering in-house training events; showing others how to take advantage of a resource; explaining; instructing; enlightening; patient teaching; guiding; tutoring; coaching; using visual communications as teaching aids; interpreting; inventing down-to-earth illustrations for abstract principles or ideas; translating jargon into relevant and meaningful terms, to diverse audiences; speaking a foreign language fluently; teaching a foreign language; skilled at planning and carrying out well-run seminars, workshops or meetings; directing the production of (as, a play).

Additional Skill-Verbs Bank: Ranching; farming; animal training.

Skills you may have with
Information

Basically fifteen skills

	1	2	3	4	5	6	7

15. OBSERVING
Studying the behavior of people, animals or things,
or the details of a particular phenomenon or place.
Paying careful attention to; being very observant; studying;
concentrating; keeping track of details; focusing on minutiae.

16. COMPARING
Examining two or more people or things,
to discover similarities and dissimilarities.
Comparing; checking; making comparisons; proofreading;
discovering similarities or dissimilarities; perceiving identities
or divergences; developing a standard or model.

17. COPYING, STORING, AND RETRIEVING
Making an imitation in the mind or on various materials.
Entering (data); keeping records; addressing; posting; copying;
transcribing; recording; memorizing; classifying expertly; protecting;
keeping confidential; filing in a way to facilitate retrieval;
remembering; retrieving; extracting; reproducing; imitating;
reviewing; restoring; giving out information patiently and accurately.

18. COMPUTING
Dealing with numbers, performing simple or complex arithmetic.
Counting; taking inventory; calculating; solving statistical problems;
auditing; keeping accurate financial records; reporting; maintaining
fiscal controls; budgeting; projecting; purchasing; operating a
computer competently with spreadsheets and statistics (and, by
extension, with all computer applications: word processing, data-
bases, graphics, and telecommunications).

19. RESEARCHING
Finding and reporting on, things not easy to find.
Investigating; detecting; surveying; inventorying; interviewing;
identifying; finding; gathering; collecting; assembling; compiling;
composing; collating; tabulating; classifying; ascertaining;
determining; proving; disproving; reporting.

20. ANALYZING
Breaking a principle or thing into its constituent parts,
or basic elements.
Examining; visualizing; reasoning; finding the basic units;
dissecting; extracting; selecting; testing; evaluating; perceiving
and defining cause-and-effect relations; proving; interpreting.

Your life stories/achievements ➜

1	2	3	4	5	6	7

I am skilled at	
	Additional Skill-Verbs Bank: Being keenly aware of surroundings; being highly observant of people or data or things; studies other people's behavior perceptively.
	Additional Skill-Verbs Bank: Keeping superior minutes of meetings; having a keen and accurate memory for detail; recalling people and their preferences accurately; retentive memory for rules and procedures; expert at remembering numbers and statistics accurately, and for a long period; having exceedingly accurate melody recognition; exhibiting keen tonal memory; accurately reproducing sounds or tones (e.g., a foreign language, spoken without accent); keeping confidences; keeping secrets; encrypting.
	Additional Skill-Verbs Bank: Performing rapid and accurate manipulation of numbers, in one's head or on paper; preparing financial reports; estimating; ordering; acquiring.
	Additional Skill-Verbs Bank: Relentlessly curious; reading ceaselessly; adept at finding information by interviewing people; discovering; getting; obtaining; reporting accurately; briefing; acting as a resource broker.
	Additional Skill-Verbs Bank: Debating; figuring out; critiquing.

Possible skills with Information *(CONTINUED)*

	1	*2*	*3*	*4*	*5*	*6*	*7*
21. ORGANIZING *Giving a definite structure and working order to things.* Forming into a whole with connected and interdependent parts; collating; formulating; defining; classifying materials; arranging according to a prescribed plan or evolving schema; expertly systematizing.							
22. EVALUATING *Making judgments about people, information, or things.* Diagnosing; inspecting; checking; testing; perceiving common denominators; weighing; appraising; assessing; deciding; judging; screening out people; discriminating what is important from what is unimportant; discarding the unimportant; editing; simplifying; summarizing; consolidating.							
23. VISUALIZING *Able to conceive shapes or sounds, perceiving their patterns and structures, and to enable others to see them too.* Having form perception; imagining; able to visualize shapes; perceiving patterns and structures; skilled at symbol formation; creating poetic images; visualizing concepts; possessing accurate spatial memory; easily remembering faces; having an uncommonly fine sense of rhythm; estimating (e.g., speed); illustrating; photographing; sketching; drawing; coloring; painting; designing; drafting; mapping.							
24. IMPROVING, ADAPTING *Taking what others have developed,* *and applying it to new situations, often in a new form.* Adjusting; improvising; expanding; improving; arranging (as, music); redesigning; updating; applying.							
25. CREATING, SYNTHESIZING *Transforming apparently unrelated things or ideas,* *by forming them into a new cohesive whole.* Relating; combining; integrating; unifying; producing a clear, coherent unity; intuiting; inventing; innovating; conceptualizing; hypothesizing; discovering; conceiving new interpretations, concepts and approaches; formulating; programming; projecting; forecasting.							
26. DESIGNING *Fashioning or shaping things.* Creating (things); designing in wood or other media; experimenting; fashioning; shaping; making models; making handicrafts; sculpting; creating symbols.							

am skilled at	
	Additional Skill-Verbs Bank: Bringing order out of chaos, with masses of physical things; putting into working order.
	Additional Skill-Verbs Bank: Problem-solving; making decisions; eliminating; screening applicants; reducing the size of the database; separating the wheat from the chaff; reviewing large amounts of material and extracting its essence; writing a precis; making fiscal reductions; conserving; upgrading.
	Additional Skill-Verbs Bank: Having a photographic memory; having a memory for design; ability to visualize in three dimensions; conceiving symbolic and metaphoric pictures of reality; possessing color discrimination of a very high order; possessing instinctively excellent taste in design, arrangement and color; skilled at mechanical drawing; able to read blueprints; graphing and reading graphs.
	Additional Skill-Verbs Bank: Making practical applications of theoretical ideas; deriving applications from other people's ideas; able to see the commercial possibilities in a concept, idea or product.
	Additional Skill-Verbs Bank: Having conceptual ability of a high order; being an idea man or woman; having 'ideaphoria'; demonstrating originality; continually conceiving, generating and developing innovative and creative ideas; excellent at problem-solving; creative imagining; possessed of great imagination; improvising on the spur of the moment; developing; estimating; predicting; cooking new creative recipes; composing (music).
	Additional Skill-Verbs Bank: Devising; developing; generating; skilled at symbol formation.

Possible skills with Information *(CONCLUDED)*

27. PLANNING, DEVELOPING
*Determining the sequence of tasks, after reviewing pertinent data
or requirements, and often overseeing the carrying out of the plan.*
Reviewing pertinent data requirements; determining the need for
revisions of goals, policies and procedures; planning on the basis
of lessons from the past; determining the sequence of operations;
making arrangements for the functioning of a system; overseeing;
establishing; executing decisions reached; developing, building
markets for ideas or products; traveling.

28. EXPEDITING
*Speeding up the accomplishment of a task or series of tasks,
so as to reach an organizational objective on or ahead of time.*
Dispatching; adept at finding ways to speed up a job; establishing
effective priorities among competing requirements; skilled at
allocating scarce financial resources; setting up and maintaining
on-time work schedules; coordinating operations and details;
quickly sizing up situations; anticipating people's needs; acting on
new information immediately; seeks and seizes opportunities; deals
well with the unexpected or critical event; able to make hard
decisions; bringing projects in on time and within budget.

29. ACHIEVING
*Systematically accomplishing tasks in a manner that
causes objectives to be attained or surpassed.*
Completing; attaining objectives; winning; meeting goals;
producing results; delivering as promised; improving performance;
making good use of feedback; increasing productivity.

1 2 3 4 5 6 7

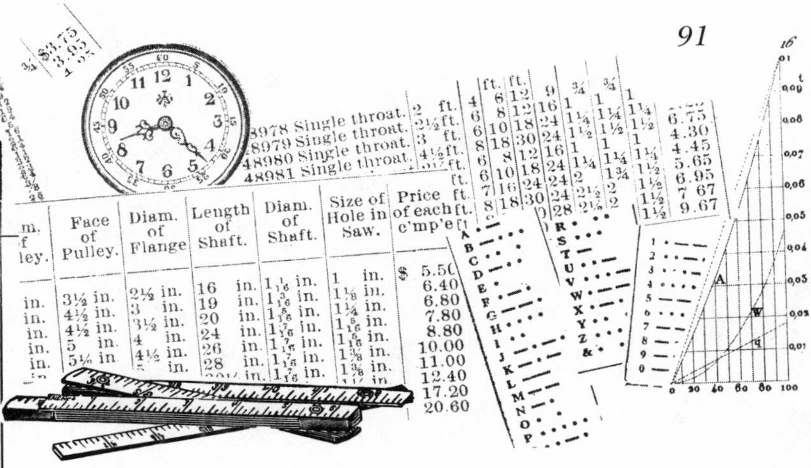

am skilled at

8978 Single throat.
8979 Single throat.
48980 Single throat.
48981 Single throat.

m. f ley.	Face of Pulley.	Diam. of Flange	Length of Shaft.	Diam. of Shaft.	Size of Hole in Saw.	Price of each ft. c'mp'e
in.	3½ in.	2½ in.	16 in.	1⅛ in.	1 in.	$ 5.50
in.	4½ in.	3 in.	19 in.	1⅛ in.	1⅛ in.	6.40
in.	4½ in.	3½ in.	20 in.	1⅜ in.	1¼ in.	6.80
in.	5 in.	4 in.	24 in.	1⅞ in.	1⅝ in.	7.80
in.	5¼ in.	4½ in.	26 in.	1⅞ in.	1⅝ in.	8.80
in.		in.	28 in.	1⅞ in.	1⅜ in.	10.00
				1⅞ in.	1⅜ in.	11.00
						12.40
						17.20
						20.60

Additional Skill-Verbs Bank: Organizes one's time expertly; able to handle a variety of tasks and responsibilities simultaneously and efficiently; continually searches for more responsibility; forecasting; instinctively gathering resources even before the need for them becomes clear; recognizing obsolescence of ideas or procedures before compelling data is yet at hand; anticipating problems or needs before they become problems; decisive in emergencies.

Skills you may have with
Things

Basically eleven skills

	1	2	3	4	5	6	7

30. HANDLING (OBJECTS)
Using one's hands or body to identify or move an object.
Feeling; fingering; washing; raising; lifting; carrying; balancing;
pushing; pulling; moving; taking; gathering; receiving; setting
(down); shipping; unloading; separating; sorting; distributing;
delivering; supplying.

31. BEING ATHLETIC
Using one's body as an instrument of accomplishment.
Displaying great physical agility; possessing great strength;
demonstrating outstanding endurance; maintaining uncommon
physical fitness; having excellent eye-hand-foot coordination;
possessing fine motor coordination.

32. WORKING WITH THE EARTH AND NATURE
Using earth's body as an instrument of accomplishment,
though under the limitations of the special laws that are written
into the behavior of the earth and growing things.
Clearing; digging; plowing; tilling; seeding; planting; helping
to grow; nurturing; weeding; harvesting.

33. FEEDING, EMPTYING (MACHINES)
Putting materials into or taking them out of machines,
often as they are running.
Placing; stacking; loading; feeding; emptying; dumping; removing;
disposing of.

34. MINDING (MACHINES)
Monitoring, adjusting, and servicing automatic machines,
usually as they are running.
Monitoring machines or valves; watching to make sure nothing
is wrong; tending; pushing buttons; starting; flipping switches;
adjusting controls; turning knobs; stopping; making adjustments
when machine threatens to malfunction, or does.

Your life stories/achievements ➔

1   2   3   4   5   6   7

am skilled at	
	Additional Skill-Verbs Bank: Having keen sense of touch; manual dexterity; good with one's hands; collecting.
	Additional Skill-Verbs Bank: Typing; printing; operating a computer; playing (a musical instrument); photographing; mastering machinery against its will.
	Additional Skill-Verbs Bank: Groundskeeping; landscaping; farming; logging; mining; drawing samples from the earth.

Possible skills with Things *(CONCLUDED)*

	1	2	3	4	5	6	7
35. USING (TOOLS) *Manipulating hand tools (electrically-powered or not)* *to accomplish that which the hands by themselves cannot.* The following skills are all accomplished with the aid of kitchen, garden or shop hand tools: using or utilizing (particular tools); manipulating (materials); working; eating; placing; guiding; moving; shaping; molding; filling; cutting; applying; pressing; binding; sewing (by hand); weaving; knitting; painting.							
36. OPERATING (EQUIPMENT OR MACHINES) *Performing some or all of the following operations upon a* *particular kind of (office, shop or other) machine or equipment.* You need to specify which equipment or machines you know how to perform these operations on (e.g., a computer or typewriter); and which operations: starting; operating; inputting; inserting; controlling; maintaining; monitoring; observing; checking; regulating; adjusting; changing; cleaning; refilling; producing (some kind of output, or product).							
37. OPERATING (VEHICLES) *Performing some or all of the following operations* *upon a particular kind of vehicle.* Driving; piloting; navigating; guiding; steering; regulating controls of; switching.							
38. PRECISION WORKING *Precise attainment of set limits, tolerances or standards.* Keypunching; drilling; sandblasting; grinding; forging; fitting; tuning; adjusting; having great finger dexterity; sketching; drawing; painting; sewing minute stitches; making miniatures; skilled at working in the micro-universe.							
39. SETTING UP (DISPLAYS, MACHINERY, EQUIPMENT) Preparing; clearing; laying; constructing; building; assembling; installing; displaying.							
40. REPAIRING *Putting something back into something like its original condition;* *or at least into good operating condition.* You will need to say what it is that you are good at repairing or restoring: fixing; repairing; doing preventative maintenance; trouble-shooting; restoring (as, art).							

I am skilled at

Additional Skill-Verbs Bank: Typing; printing; operating a computer; playing (a musical instrument); mastering machinery against its will.

Additional Skill-Verbs Bank: Giving continuous attention to the vehicle; offering a ready response to any emergency.

Additional Skill-Verbs Bank: Having great dexterity with small instruments (as, tweezers).

Now, You Need Priorities

Well, you did it. Seven stories all done. And analyzed for their skills. You've got a nice list called "I am skilled at ..." Good going!

Now what? Well, unfortunately, this new list of your skills *will do you absolutely no good if you do not then go on to say which skill you like best, which next best, etc.*

Why? Because, until you can say *that,* you can't even begin to define "Your Ideal Job or Career." *Almost every* job demands that you have skills with People, Information and Things—in one degree or another. It's that *degree* that determines *which* job or career we're talking about.

To define your next job or career you *must* prioritize your skills. Without this essential step, you will get bogged down for sure.

This prioritizing has two levels to it:

I. What you first need to know about yourself is: "Which kinds of skills do I most enjoy using? Those with People? Or those with Information? Or those with Things? Or, if all three, which is most important to me, which is next most important, and which is least important?" What career or job you choose next, will depend upon this discovery and this decision of yours, more than any other. Don't ever underestimate the importance of the distinction between PEOPLE, INFORMATION, and THINGS. It is the key to everything.

II. Then, within the three broad families of Skills (People, Information and Things), you MUST decide *which* "People Skills," and *which* "Information Skills," and *which* "Things Skills" are most important to you.

How Do You Prioritize? You begin by just trusting your intuition. Look over your colored-in pages: People, Information, and Things. Which skills do you like most to use, of the three? People? Information? or Things? Of the three, which is next? Which is your least favorite?

Next: look at the "People Skills" pages, all by themselves. Look at the skills you wrote down, in the "I am skilled at..." sections. On a separate piece of paper, copy these with your favorite at the top, your least favorite at the bottom. Cross out (or omit) any skills *you have* but don't enjoy using. You are only looking for *enjoy* here.

You may be able to do this prioritizing just by common sense. If not, use the "Prioritizing Grid" that you will find on page 116.

When you are done with your "People Skills," turn to the "Information Skills" pages, and follow the same procedure. Use a new piece of blank paper. Get all your "Information Skills" —in the "I am skilled at ..." sections— written down on this blank paper, in the order of their exact priority for you. Again, omit any skills you don't truly enjoy using.

When you are done with your "Information Skills," turn to the "Things Skills" pages, and again follow the same procedure, using a new piece of blank paper. Get your "Things Skills" too, into exact priority. And, once again, omit any skills you don't truly enjoy using.

NOW you have some truly useful information.

Incidentally, on page 118 you will find a place to *summarize* your findings. There is a picture of a Tree, there. And on the left-hand side of that tree, is a place for you to write your favorite *top three* or four "People Skills," AND your favorite *top three* or four "Information Skills," AND your favorite *top three* or four "Things Skills." Do save the papers, however, on which you have written out *all* your favorite People Skills, etc. For now, the *top three* of each, will do. But later, you may want to go back and look at the rest of the list.

"... and give me good abstract-reasoning ability, interpersonal skills, cultural perspective, linguistic comprehension, and a high sociodynamic potential."

WHAT USE IS ALL THIS INFORMATION?

Good question. And I'll tell you why. There are loads of job-counselors who think their task is to keep job-hunters busy. Period. As long as they keep you *busy* doing paper and pencil exercises, they believe they are doing their job. Unhappily, however, if you aren't clear as to where all this is leading, you will end up feeling like the hamster running on the treadmill. The first fifteen laps are sure fun, but after that . . . phooey. (Or fui.)

You need to know what use this information is. And it all boils down to this. Every time you decide to go about the job-hunt, you must be able to tell an employer convincingly what your strengths are; and, you must know them in their order of priority. "This is my greatest strength, this is my next greatest, etc."

Every time you decide not merely to do the job-hunt but also to make a career-change, you are essentially deciding to do two things: you are changing your field—your· field of knowledge, that is—AND you are rearranging the building blocks of your skills, in some new arrangement or constellation:

You are
aiming at
ultimately
being able
to fill in
this chart:

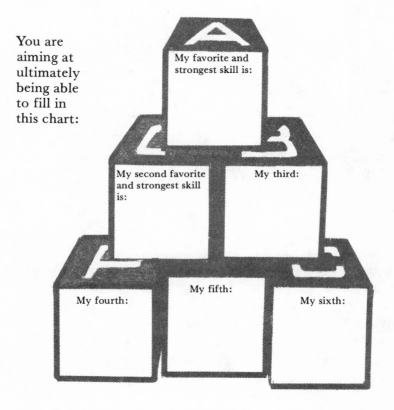

My favorite and strongest skill is:

My second favorite and strongest skill is:

My third:

My fourth:

My fifth:

My sixth:

So, even if you found—after doing the skill identification—that all the skills you identified were old familiar ones to you, with no surprises, it is still true that there will be NEWNESS in your new career—and that Newness is to be found in the new way in which those skills are arranged, with new ones in the top position. Hence, in the preceding exercises, the absolute importance of your taking the time to PUT YOUR SKILLS IN ORDER OF IMPORTANCE OR PRIORITY. If you skip over this step, you are committing job-hunting suicide.

SPECIAL PROBLEMS

In doing the foregoing exercise, it will not be surprising if you run into some problems. Let us look at the more common ones:

1. *"I don't see why I should look for skills I enjoy; it seems to me that employers will want to know what skills I do well, whether I enjoy using them or not."*

Well, yes. *Bad* employers will not care whether you enjoy a particular task—they will only want to know if you know how to do it. But *good* employers will care greatly. They know that unless a would-be employee has enthusiasm for his or her work, the lack of enthusiasm will be a killer.

It is important for you to find the skills you are enthusiastic about using, and you do this by looking for the skills that you enjoy. Enthusiasm and enjoyment are two different ways of stating the same thing. Years ago there was in our country a group of people who thought it sinful to enjoy oneself. They were called Puritans. They also railed against enthusiasm. They knew that enjoyment and enthusiasm were the same thing.

Enthusiasm, incidentally, comes from two Greek words, "en" and "theos," meaning God within us. In an earlier and healthier time, religious people understood that you could only be enthusiastic about something if you were divinely inspired, if God were within you, moving your heart to be attracted to that activity. In a later day, people became suspicious, came to distrust their heart, and to see sin in everything—even in enjoyment.

It would be nice, of course, if the Puritans had vanished from our culture by now; but, alas, the Puritan mentality is everywhere around us.

Puritans come in all sizes, shapes, genders, ages, and colors. Puritans allegedly believe in God; but, what a god! A Puritan believes that God didn't intend us to enjoy anything. And that if you enjoy it, it's probably wrong for you. Let us illustrate:

Two girls do babysitting. One hates it. One enjoys it thoroughly. Which is more virtuous in God's sight? According to the Puritan, the one who hates it is more virtuous.

Two Puritans met on the street. "Isn't this a beautiful day?"

said one. "Aye," said the other, "but we'll pay for it."

Puritans will talk about their failures, but hardly ever about their successes—and even then, always with a feeling that "God is going to get me, for such boasting." It's too enjoyable!

Given the Puritan's belief in God, what the Puritan fails to recognize is that enjoyment, in human life, isn't a fluke. It's part of God's plan. God wants us to eat; therefore God designs us so that eating is enjoyable. God wants us to sleep; therefore God designs us so that sleeping is enjoyable. God wants to have us procreate, love, and make love; therefore God designs us so that sex is enjoyable, and love even more so. *God gives us unique (or at least unusual) skills and talents; therefore God designs us so that, when we use them, they are enjoyable.*

That is, we gain a sense of achievement from them.

So, Puritans arise; if you believe in God, believe in One who believes in you. Downgrading yourself is out—for the duration.

"FRANKLY, IT'S NOT EASY BEING A PURITAN IN THIS 'HEDONISTIC SOCIETY!'"

2. *"I believe in doing this skill identification on myself; but I can't come up with enough good stories."*

If you are priming and priming the pump, but inspiration just isn't coming, there is another way. Instead of writing seven stories, you can try writing a diary of your life and your accomplishments, whether at work or at play.

The exercise is fully described in the companion book to this one, *Where Do I Go From Here With My Life?* by John Crystal and a friend of his.

For now, it may be sufficient to sketch the method. It has the following steps:

A. Write a diary of your entire life. An informal essay of where you've been, what you've done. Where you were working, what you did there (not in terms of job titles—forget them—but in terms of what you feel you achieved).

B. Boast a little. Boast a lot. Who's going to see this document, besides you, God, and any twenty people that you choose to show it to? Back up your elation and sense of pride with concrete examples, and figures.

C. Describe your spare time, in each place where you lived. What did you do? What did you most enjoy doing? Any hobbies? Avocations? Great. What skills did they use? Were there any activities in your work that paralleled the kinds of things you enjoyed doing in your leisure?

D. Concentrate both on the things you have done, and also on the particular characteristics of your surroundings that were important to you, and that you really enjoyed: green grass, the theater, golfing, warm climate, skiing, or whatever.

E. Keep your eye constantly on that "divine radar": *enjoyable*. It's by no means *always* a guide to what you should be doing, but it sure is more reliable than any other key that people have come up with. Sift later. For now, put down anything that helped you to enjoy a particular moment or period of your life.

F. Don't try to make this diary very structured. You can bounce back and forth in time, if that's more helpful; go back later, and use the questions above to check yourself out.

G. When your diary is all done, you may have a small book—it can run 30 to 200 pages. (My, you've done a lot of living, haven't you?) Now go back and find just one story in it

that you consider to be an achievement *for you.* Use that story as the first of your seven. After you are done analyzing it, go back to the autobiography and pick out a second story, in a different time period and a different arena of your life. Use that as your second story for skill identification. And so on.

This is more work than just trying to write stories, cold; but if the story approach isn't working for you, this is the only other way. Try it. As the commercials say: "You'll be so glad you did."

3. I've never had any experience in the world of work. I've been a homemaker all my life. I can think of stories or achievements within the home, but I'm not sure I could ever sell an employer on that."

You will want to write either to the National Center for Citizen Involvement's Readership Service, or to the Educational Testing Service, and ask for their I CAN lists. Their address is in section 9 of the Book Appendix, at the back of this book. The I CAN lists classify all the skills of the homemaker under various roles and job titles in business, such as: administrator/manager, financial manager, personnel manager, trainer, advocate/change agent, public relations/communicator, problem surveyor, researcher, fund-raiser, counselor, youth group leader, group leader for a serving organization, museum staff assistant, nutritionist, child caretaker, designer, clothing and textile specialist, and so forth. *Very* helpful.

4. "I have no difficulty finding stories to write up, from my life, that I consider to be achievements; but once these are written, I have great difficulty in seeing what the skills are, that I used in doing them—even with this skills list you have here."

You will want to consider getting two friends or two other members of your family to sit down with you, and do some warm-up on skill identification through the practice of "Trioing." This practice is described at some length in *Where Do I Go From Here With My Life?*, listed at the beginning of the Book Appendix in the back.

5. "How do I know if I've done this all correctly? What if I just think I understood what I was supposed to do, but I really didn't?"

Well, that's a reasonable anxiety, it seems to me.

So, here are a few questions, to help you check out how you did:

1. Since all transferable skills are used either with Data, or People, or Things, do you now know which you most prefer working with? Is it some kind of Data, or some kind of People, or some kind of Things? What kind?

2. What's your second preference? Your third?

3. Have you got the skills to be more than one word? One word won't do. "I'm good at organizing" don't tell us *nothing*. Organizing what? People, as at a party? Nuts and bolts, as on a workbench? Or lots of information, lying in a computer? Those are three *entirely different skills*. The one word "organizing" doesn't tell us which one, at all. Sooooo, have you gone back over the skills you pulled out of the skills grid, and made sure that each one-word definition gets *fleshed out* with an *object*—some kind of Data/Information, or some kind of People, or some kind of Thing—and maybe also an adverb or adjective? "I'm good at analyzing people *painstakingly*," and "I'm good at analyzing people *in a flash, by intuition*," are two *entirely different skills*. The difference between them is found in the adjectival or adverbial phrase there at the end. So, have you expanded each definition as much as you can, by an object at least, and maybe an adverb or adjective? If so, great. If not, *go do it*.

4. Have you got all your skills arranged *in order of importance, or priority, for you? Anytime* you have a bunch of

information about yourself, it is relatively useless to you, *until you have put it in order of priority.* "Here's what I most enjoy doing, this is next, this is next, and so on." This is *especially* true of your skills. Looking ahead to your next job or career, which skill do you *most* hope you will get to use "on the job," which next, which next? and so on.

5. Have you avoided stating your skills in the jargon or language of your past career? This is a point on which clergy, in particular, often stumble and fall. "I am good at preaching" is not a very useful skill identification. It is still cloaked in the jargon and language of *one career and one career only.* What is its *larger* form? "Teaching?" Perhaps. "Motivating people?" Perhaps. "Moving people to their depths?" Perhaps. Only you can say. But get your skills out of any jargon from your past.

6. Have you thus far steered clear of putting a job title on what you're aiming toward? Skills can point to many different jobs, which have a multitude of titles. Don't lock yourself into a box prematurely. "I'm looking for a job where I can use the following skills," is fine. But, "I'm looking for a job where I can *be* a (job title)" is a no-no, until you've done more homework and more research.

7. Are you hanging loose, willing to look at a number of alternatives, as you move through the homework and research? Or is your desire for finishing this off *fast* leading you to push prematurely for just one way to go? Stay loose. Preserve *all* your options.

8. As you have been working on the question of your future career or future job, have you begun to get some insights into your whole life and being? Keep yourself sensitive to these things, as they pop up. Properly speaking, what you're engaged in is not merely career planning, but *life* planning or life *designing,* if you prefer. You will become, in all likelihood, increasingly conscious of your *values* as you go along. As David Maister says, "Play to your evil secrets." They're not really so evil; you just *think* they are. But, speaking candidly and to yourself alone, what *are* your values? Truth, beauty, righteousness, ambition, compassion, security, service, popularity, status, power, friends, achievement, love, authority, freedom, glamor, giving, integrity, honesty, loyalty, sensitivity, caring—which holds the *most* meaning and importance for

you? These things will almost certainly come clearer for you, as you move on through your job-hunting or career-planning homework. Stay alert and sensitive to these. You will get much clearer about who you are willing to work with and for, and who you are not. Those who *share* your values will be on your hit parade; those who don't, won't.

ARE THERE ANY SHORTCUTS I COULD TAKE, INSTEAD OF IDENTIFYING MY SKILLS SO PAINSTAKINGLY?

You've probably gotten to this point in the chapter, without having yet done the actual skill identification exercise. You like to read ahead and get the overall picture first. Right? But now that you are here, you're debating, whether to go do it or not.

Well, what can I tell you? You could be forgiven for not wanting to do all this work. And for wanting to know if there are any "Alternatives for the Lazy." Well, sure. I'll tell you at least a couple of ways that some job-hunters have gone about Avoiding Skill Identification:

1. What do you want to be? My friend John Holland first proposed this one. In his earliest book, now out of print, he wrote: "Despite several decades of research, the most efficient way to predict vocational choice is simply to ask the person what he wants to be; our best devices do not exceed the predictive value of that method."

So, if you don't want to think out your future in terms of skills, try thinking it out just in terms of this question: "What do you want to be?" Sit in a quiet place, pen in hand, and write it out.

2. Whose job do you most admire? One woman I know declined to do any of the skill identification exercises in this chapter. *But* she decided to pose for herself this question: Among all the people that I know or have seen or read about, whose job would I most like to have? She decided that the person she most admired, whose job she most coveted, was a woman who appeared as hostess on a television program for children. Accordingly, she went to a local TV station with a carefully written, well-thought-out proposal for a similar children's television program. They not only eventually bought the idea, they asked her to be the hostess of it. Thus did she find her ideal job. "Without," she added triumphantly, "doing a single exercise in your book."

THE PERIL OF SHORTCUTS

Nice, eh. It's always nice to think that there are shortcuts. Only just remember the principle enunciated earlier: the job-hunt in this country is essentially a matter of sheer luck. The more time you are willing to spend on some proven job-hunting or career-changing techniques, the more you cut down on how much of your job-hunt depends on luck.

Conversely—and this is the point you especially want to remember here—the less time you are willing to spend on your own homework, the more you are returning to a dependence on sheer luck. So, try any shortcuts you want to. If you succeed in finding a fabulous job, then luck was obviously on your side.

But, *on the other hand* if you try these shortcuts and you *don't* find a job, then YOU KNOW WHAT YOU MUST DO: go back, and do the skills grid IN DETAIL.

Practical Exercise (Cooling Down?)

If two weeks after putting down this chapter, you pick it up again, and realize you still haven't even begun identifying your skills through *any* of these exercises, then let's face it: you're going to *have to* pay someone to aid you. Too bad, because chances are that if you'd just try this on your own, you could do as well or better by yourself. But better this than nothing: turn to Appendix B, choose three possible counselors or places, and go ask them questions. Choose one. Pay them, and *get at this.*

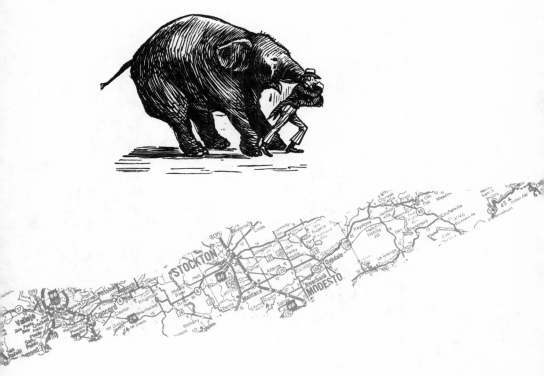

Students spend four or more years
learning how to dig data out of the library
and other sources, but it rarely occurs
to them that they should also apply some of
that same new-found research skill to their
own benefit—to looking up information
on companies, types of professions, sections
of the country that might interest them.

Professor Albert Shapero
The William H. Davis Professor
of The American Free Enterprise System
at Ohio State University

CHAPTER FIVE

The Systematic Approach To The Job-Hunt and Career-Change:

PART II

Where

Do You Want To Use Your Skills?

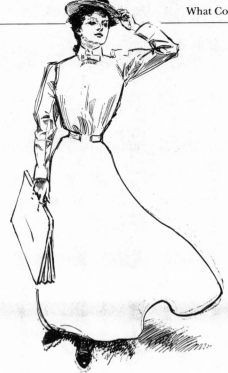

Okay, once you've figured out the "WHAT?", you turn to the "WHERE?" Once you've figured out what are your favorite and strongest skills, you turn to the question:

Where do I want to use these skills? What occupation or occupations will use as many of my strongest skills, and on as high a level as possible—so that I will be doing my most effective work, and also my most enjoyable work?

The "WHERE?" is important. Suppose your strongest and most favorite skills involve welding. The "WHERE?" question is: Do you want to weld together a wheel, or do you want to weld the casing of a nuclear bomb? You can see, the "WHERE?" is *terribly* important. Again, suppose your strongest and most favorite skills are secretarial ones. The "WHERE?" question is: Do you want to be working in a legal office, or in an office of a gardening store? Again, the "WHERE?" can make all the difference in the world.

It is not sufficient, therefore, merely to know WHAT are your favorite skills. You must press on, to this next step in your systematic approach to job-hunting and career-change: WHERE do you want to use them?

HOW MUCH CAN I DREAM?

You are starting here at exactly the opposite place from where most job-hunters begin. They begin with Vacancies. They comb the newspapers, professional journals, agencies and other places to try to find out where there are Vacancies. You aren't beginning there. You're starting with the issue of *where you would LIKE to work.* LATER, you can inquire whether or not those places have vacancies.

So-called Realists scorn this step, of course. "Dreamers," they snort, to all who would take this step. Maybe. And maybe not.

Most of us have visions and dream dreams. It's only when we come to our job that we think our visions and dreams should be shelved. In career planning there used to be certain professionals who loved to play the game of getting you to say what you really wanted to do with the rest of your life, and then "bringing you down to earth" by saying, "All right; now, let's get realistic." What they should have asked was, "Are you *sure* this is what you really want? because if it is, chances are you will find some way to do it."

Never mind "being realistic." For every person who "over-dreams"—of doing more than their merits would justify—there are four people who "under-dream," and sell themselves short. Remember, according to the experts, 80% of the workers in this country are "under-employed." You may end up in the same fix, if you try to keep one eye fixed on your dreams, and one eye fixed on what you *think* you know about the job market, e.g., "I'd like to be able to do this and that at my job, but I *know* there is no job in the world like that." You don't know any such thing.

Granted, you may not be able to find a job that has *all* that you want. But why not aim for it, and then settle for less if and when you find out that you simply have to? Don't foreclose your future prematurely. You'd be surprised at what you may be able to turn up.

To be sure, dreams sometimes have to be taken in stages. If you want to be president of a particular enterprise, for example, you may have to work your way toward it through two or three steps. But it is quite likely you will eventually succeed—*if your whole heart is in your dream.*

Now, let us do a warm-up exercise to surface some of our ancient dreams:

ON THE LAST DAY OF MY LIFE

Spend as much time as necessary writing an article entitled "Before I die, I want to . . ." (Things you would like to do, before you die.) Confess them to yourself now, and maybe you can begin to make them happen.

You may prefer to write an article on a similar topic: "On the last day of my life, what must I have done or been so that my life will have been satisfying to me?" Spend an hour or two on this. When finished, go back over it and make three lists: Things Already Accomplished, and: Things Yet To Be Accomplished, and: a third column, beside the second, listing the particular *steps* that you will have to take, in order to accomplish these things:

1 Things already accomplished.	2 Things yet to be accomplished. *(Then number them in the order in which you would like to accomplish them.)*	3 Steps needed in order to accomplish the things in column 2

As you get involved with this exercise, you may notice that it is impossible to keep your focus only on your career. You will find some dreams creeping in concerning your leisure or your life-long learning—of places you want to visit, and experiences you want to have—that are not on-the-job. *Don't omit these.* Be just as specific as possible.

Now, to get down to the nitty-gritty of figuring out WHERE you would like to use your strongest and most enjoyable skills. This activity *sounds* like Dreaming, and in some ways I suppose it is. But it is actually an immensely practical activity, with an immensely practical purpose: to narrow down the territory that you will have to go explore.

YOU START WITH
THE WHOLE JOB-MARKET
IN THIS COUNTRY—

1 You narrow this down by deciding just what area, city or county you want to work in. This leaves you with however many thousands of job markets there are in that area or city. **2** You narrow this down by identifying your Strongest Skills, on their highest level that you can legitimately claim, and then thru research deciding what field you *want* to work in, above all. This leaves you with all the hundreds of businesses/community organizations/ agencies/schools/hospitals/projects/associations/ foundations/institutions/firms or government agencies there are in that area and in the field you have chosen. **3** You narrow this down by getting acquainted with the economy in the area thru personal interviews with various contacts; and supplementing this with study of journals in your field, in order that you can pinpoint the places that interest you the most. This leaves a manageable number of markets for you to do some study on. **4** You now narrow this down by asking yourself: *Can I be happy in this place, and do they have the kind of problems which my strongest skills can help solve for them?* **5** This leaves you with the companies or organizations which you will now carefully plan how to approach for a job, in your case, *the* job.

14,000,000 JOB MARKETS

Job-hunters begin by thinking there are too few job markets (and therefore, too few jobs) "out there." We argue just the opposite. There are too many. If you try to hit them all (shotgun style) you will only diffuse your energies and your effectiveness.

It is, of course, nice to 'stay loose' and be willing to use your skills any place that there is a vacancy. Unfortunately, experts say that 80% of all the vacancies which occur in this country, above entry level, are never advertised through any of the channels or avenues that job-hunters traditionally turn to.

So, you're going to have to approach any place and every place that looks attractive to you.

Thus, you can't rule out any place that looks interesting to you, because it's just possible they have a vacancy that you don't know about. Or will develop one *while you're there.* Or will decide (since they may be expanding) to create a job just for you.

Since you can't go visit EVERY place that looks interesting, you've GOT to "cut the territory down" to some manageable size, by using: Some Principles of Exclusion for Narrowing Down the Area You Need to Focus On.

Some Principles of Exclusion For Narrowing Down The Area You Need To Focus On

1 Special Knowledges. The First Principle for Narrowing Down the Organizations You Will Need to Take A Look At: WHAT SPECIAL KNOWLEDGES DO YOU WANT TO BE ABLE TO USE ON THE JOB?

● **Set Up A Form.** Here you will need another blank sheet of paper. Divide it into four columns, and put the following headings on those columns:
1. Special Knowledges I Picked Up In School or College.
2. Special Knowledges I Picked Up On The Job, Or Just By Doing (At Home or Work).
3. Special Knowledges I Picked Up From Seminars or Workshops, Etc.
4. Special Knowledges I Picked Up Just By Reading Avidly Or Talking With People.

Down the left-hand side, you can put the Years, working back from the present, in five-year increments: e.g., 1986-1982, 1981-1977, 1976-1972, etc.

List the Knowledges You Have. Now you are ready to start filling it in. Using your memory, or borrowing that of a longstanding friend, list EVERY knowledge you have ever picked up anywhere. See examples on the next page.

Special Knowledges I Picked Up In School or College	Special Knowledges I Picked Up On The Job, Or Just By Doing (At Home or Work)	Special Knowledges I Picked Up From Seminars, or Workshops, Etc.	Special Knowledges I Picked Up Just By Reading Avidly Or Talking With People
Spanish; Psychology; Biology; Geometry; Accounting; Music appreciation; Sociology.	How to Operate a computer; How a volunteer organization works; Principles of financial planning and management.	The way the brain works; Principles of art; Speed reading; Drawing on the right side of the brain.	How computers work; Principles of comparison shopping; Principles of outdoor survival; Knowledge of antiques.

Circle the Ones You Love. When you are all done with *your* list (not mine), go back and *circle* all the knowledges you would *love* to be able to use in your next job or career.

Put Them in Priority. Then, choose your top ten, and get them into *exact order*—from most favorite, to least favorite. Use this "Prioritizing Grid," in order to help you do this.

Prioritizing Grid

For Ten Items. Here is a method for taking (say) 10 items, and figuring out which one is most important to you, which is next most important, etc.:

List, Compare. Make a list of the items and number them. *In the case of Specific Knowledges, make a list of the ten subjects you know the most about, then number them 1 thru 10.* Now, look at the top line of this grid. You see a 1 and 2 there. So, compare items one and two on your list. Which one is more important to you? *State the question any way you want to: in the case of Specific Knowledges, you might ask yourself: if I was being offered two jobs, one which used knowledge #1, and one which used #2, other things being equal, which would I prefer?* Circle it. Then go on to the next pair, etc.

```
1  2
1  3   2  3
1  4   2  4   3  4
1  5   2  5   3  5   4  5
1  6   2  6   3  6   4  6   5  6
1  7   2  7   3  7   4  7   5  7   6  7
1  8   2  8   3  8   4  8   5  8   6  8   7  8
1  9   2  9   3  9   4  9   5  9   6  9   7  9   8  9
1 10   2 10   3 10   4 10   5 10   6 10   7 10   8 10   9 10
```

Circle, Count. Total Times Each Number Got Circled:

1 ___ 2 ___ 3 ___ 4 ___ 5 ___ 6 ___ 7 ___ 8 ___ 9 ___ 10 ___

When you are all done, count up the number of times each number got circled, all told. Enter these totals in the spaces at the bottom of page 116.

Recopy. Finally, recopy your list, beginning with the item that got the most circles. This is your *new #1*. Then the item that got the next most circles. This is your *new #2*.

In case of a tie (two numbers got the same number of circles), look back on the grid to see when you were comparing those two numbers there, which one got circled. That means you prefer That One over the other; thus you break the tie.

P.S. If you need to compare any list that has more than 10 items to it, just keep adding new rows to the bottom of the grid. Thus: 1 *11*　　2 *11,*　　etc. Until you have all the numbers compared.

Copy This Prioritized List. When you are done, copy the 10 in their exact order of priority now on that (formerly) blank sheet of paper—one side or the other—that you have been working on.

Summarize It on the Tree Diagram. Turn to page 118, if you will, and in the place provided there on the left-hand side of the Tree, put your top four or five Special Knowledges.

If You Want to Do Several Different Part-Time Jobs. If you want to have a Composite Career—combining two or three different jobs into one Career—copy the picture of the Tree onto more than one larger pieces of paper. Have a separate Tree for each separate career or job, and put different skills and different Special Knowledges (from your prioritized list) on separate Tree diagrams. Do remember, however, to save the paper that you have been copying from. It may be you will want to consult it later, to see where you might use the rest of your favorite special knowledges—in your leisure, for example.

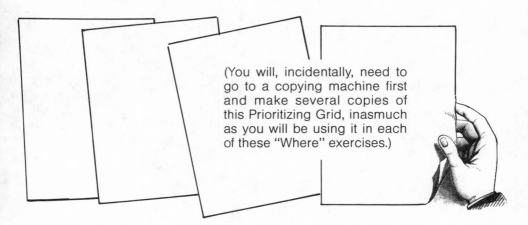

(You will, incidentally, need to go to a copying machine first and make several copies of this Prioritizing Grid, inasmuch as you will be using it in each of these "Where" exercises.)

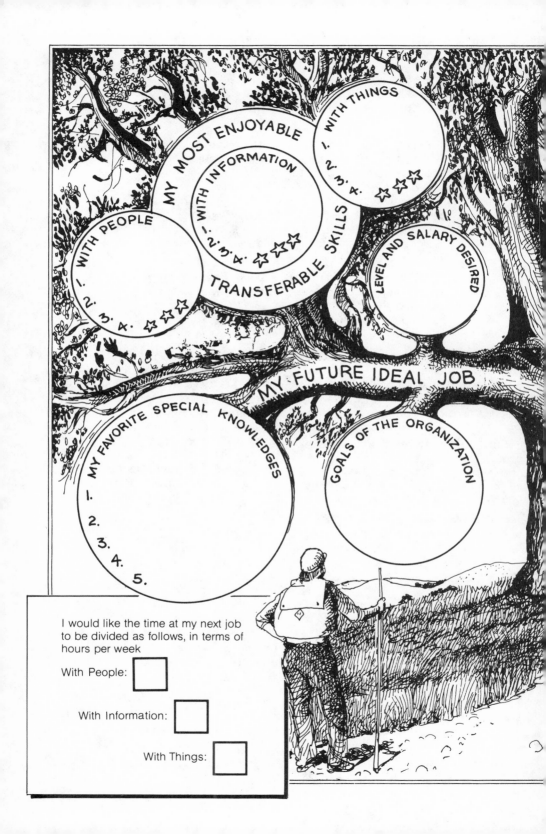

WORKING CONDITIONS

TYPES OF PEOPLE WORKED WITH

HOW I WILL CHOOSE BETWEEN ORGANIZATIONS

PREFERRED GEOGRAPHY

FACTORS

MY IDEAL JOB

Color in the stars in the Skills section as follows: color all three stars for your favorite skills arena—People, or Information, or Things. Color two of the stars in your next favorite skills arena. And, of course, color only one of the stars in your third favorite arena.

Copy this on a larger sheet of paper (perhaps two sheets taped together) and fill it in.

**The Second Principle
For Narrowing Down The
Organizations You Will
Want To Take A Look At:**

2 WHAT DO YOU WANT THE GOALS OF THE ORGANIZATION TO BE, WHERE YOU WILL BE WORKING?

A Product, A Service, or Information? That's the first question. Do you dodge this question by saying simply, "I want to work for a place that makes money." The response is: "Makes money doing WHAT?" We are back to the question above: Do you want to work in a place (of your own choosing or your own devising) whose goal is to produce a product? Or, would you prefer to work in a place whose goal is to render some kind of service to people? Or, would you prefer to work in a place whose business it is to get information out to people?

You have to make a decision about the goals of the organization NOW or later. You can postpone it. But you cannot evade it.

If You Choose a Product, What *Kind* of Product? What kind of product do you want the place to be *producing,* OR what kind of product do you want to be able to *work with, or use,* at this place? Either answer will help you narrow down the kinds of places. If, for example, you say, "I want to work at a place where I could use a drill press," that will help narrow down the places you need to take a look at, in your given city or area.

So, read over this list, and circle any products/things/whatever that interest you and that you would like to work with, *or* help produce. (Do say which, please.)

Machines
Tools
Toys
Equipment
Products
Desk-top
   supplies
Crops, plants,
   trees
Dollies,
   handtrucks
Boxes
Automatic
   machines
Paper
Laundry
Dishes, pots
   and pans
Controls,
   gauges
Copying
   machines
PBX switch-
   boards
Valves, switches,
   buttons
Computer
Tables
Portable power
   tools
Kitchen and
   garden tools
Meats
Typewriters
Mimeograph
   machines
TV camera
Vehicles
Transparencies
Therapy center
Cranks, wheels,
   gears, levers
Hoists, cranes
Matches
Candles
Lanterns,
   oil lamps
Light bulbs
Fluorescent
   lights
Laser beams
Windmills
Waterwheels
Water turbines

Gas turbines
Steam turbines
Steam engines
Fuel cells
Batteries
Transformers,
   electric motors,
   dynamos
Engines, gas,
   diesel
Dynamite
Nuclear reactors
Other things
   belonging to
   the field of
   Energy:
Electronic
   devices
Electronic
   games
Calculators
Lie detectors
Radar
   equipment
Clocks
Telescopes
Microscopes
X-ray machines
Pens, ink, felt-tip,
   ballpoint
Pencils, black,
   red or other
Printing presses,
   type, ink
Woodcuts,
   engravings,
   lithographs
Paintings,
   drawings,
   silk-screens
Books
Braille
Newspapers
Magazines
Teleprinters
Telephones
Telegraphs
Radios
Records
Phonographs
Stereos
Tape recorders
Cameras
Movies

Television sets
Video recorders
Games
Amusements
Cards
Board games,
   checkers,
   chess, etc.
Kites
Gambling
   devices or
   machines
Musical
   instruments
Money
Cash registers
Financial
   records
Roads
Bicycles
Motorcycles
Mopeds
Cars
Parking meters
Traffic lights
Railways
Subways
Canals
Boats
Steamships
Gliders
Airplanes
Parachutes
Balloons
Foods
Food
   preservatives
Artificial foods
Health foods
Vitamins
Can openers
Refrigerators
Microwave ovens
Wells
Cisterns
Bathtubs
Soaps
Umbrellas
Clothing
Spinning wheels,
   looms

Patterns, safety
   pins, buttons,
   zippers
Dyes
Cloths
Sewing
   machines
Shoes
Beds
Furniture
Sheets, blankets,
   electric blankets
Towels
Washing
   machines,
   dryers
Wash-day
   products,
   bleach
Cosmetics
Toiletries
Drugs
Cigarettes
Tents
Plywood
Bricks
Cement
Concrete
Cinder-block
Carpenters' tools
Chimneys
Columns
Domes
Paint
Wallpaper
Heating
   elements,
   furnaces
Carpeting
Fire
   extinguishers
Fire alarms
Burglar alarms
Crafts-materials
Paper-mache
Hides
Pottery
Pewter
Paraffin, pitch
Bronze, brass
Cast iron,
   ironworks

Steel, aluminum
Rubber
Plastics
Textiles
Felt
Synthetics
Elastic
Gym equipment
Medicines
Vaccines
Anesthetics
Thermometers
Hearing aids
Dental drills
False parts
   of human body
Spectacles,
   glasses,
   contacts
Fishing rods,
   fishhooks, bait
Traps, guns
Beehives
Ploughs
Fertilizers
Pesticides
Weed killers
Threshing
   machines,
   reapers,
   harvesters
Shovels
Picks
Lawnmowers
Dairy equipment
Wine-making
   equipment
Bottles
Cans

What Kinds of People Would You Most Like to Work With?

Underline or circle any descriptions below that are a part of your answer to this question.

Individuals	People in their thirties
Groups of eight or less	The middle-aged
Groups larger than eight	The elderly
Babies	All people of all ages
School-age children	Men
Adolescents or	Women
young people	Heterosexuals
College students	Homosexuals
Young adults	All people regardless
	of sex

People of a particular cultural background

(Namely, _____)

People of a particular economic background

(Namely, _____)

People of a particular social background

(Namely, _____)

People of a particular educational background

(Namely, _____)

People of a particular philosophy or religious belief

(Namely, _____)

Certain kinds of workers (blue-collar, white-collar, executives, or whatever)

(Namely, _____)

People who are powerless

(Namely, _____)

People who wield power (e.g., opinion-makers, etc.)

(Namely, _____)

People who are easy to work with
People who are difficult to work with
  ("a challenge," as we say: i.e., prima donnas)
People in a particular place (the Armed
  Services, prison, etc.)

(Namely, _____).

When you're done with the list, PLEASE prioritize it. Put the services in order, from your most favorite to your least favorite. Also, the kind of people you would like to serve. Again, don't hesitate to copy and use the "Prioritizing Grid."

If You Choose To Work For An Organization That Collects or Dispenses Information, What *Kind* of Information or Data?

You may already know. Instantly. No need to work through the list below at all. On the other hand, maybe you know that you like to work with information—but you're not clear about what kind of information. If so, go over the list below, and circle the sorts of things you *love* to work with—or *would* love to work with:

Data in General

Knowledge	Words
Conceptions or	Symbols
ideas or theories	Facts
Numbers or	Information
statistics	History

Data Primarily Dealing With Things

Parameters	Designs
Boundary conditions	Blueprints
Frameworks	Wall-charts
Specifications	Time-charts
Precision requirements	Schema
Principles	Schematic analyses
Principles' applications	Techniques
Standards	Methods
Repeating requirements	Procedures
Variables	Specialized procedures

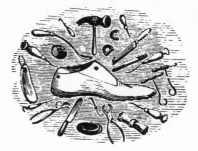

When you're done with the list, PLEASE prioritize it. Put the products in order, from your most favorite to your least favorite. Use the "Prioritizing Grid."

If You Choose A Service, What *Kind* of Service? Do you want to service or repair some kind of product? If so, review the list above, please—with that in mind. Copy down what sort of product you would like to service.

Is the kind of service you want to offer related to helping people with some kind of personal problem? If so, what kind of people, and what kind of problem? Here is a list, to get your imagination going. Circle any that enchant you.

People needing help with the following special problems:
Life adjustment or life/work planning
Unemployment or job-hunting
Being fired or laid-off
Stress
Relationships
  Shyness
  Meeting people, starting friendships
  Complaints, grievances
  Anger   Rape
  Love   Abuse
  Marriage   Parenting
  Sex   Divorce
Possessions
  Personal economics
  Budgeting
  Debt, bankruptcy
  Financial planning
Problems Generally Regarded As Related Primarily to the Mind
  Mental retardation
  Personal insight, therapy
  Communications, thoughts-feelings
  Illiteracy, educational needs
  Industry's in-house training
Problems Generally Regarded As Related Primarily to the 'Heart' (Beauty, Feelings, etc.)
  Expressed feelings
  Learning how to love
  Self-acceptance and acceptance of others
  Boredom
  Loneliness
  Anxiety
  Fear
  Anger
  Depression
  Mental illness
  Psychiatric hospitalization
  Death and grief

Problems Generally Regarded As Related Primarily to the 'Will" (Perfection, Ethics, Actions, Doing)
  Prescribed actions
  Competing needs
  Performance problems, appraisal
  Discipline problems, self-discipline
  Personal powerlessness
  Work satisfaction
  Values
  Ethics
  Philosophy or religion
Problems Generally Regarded As Related Primarily to the Body
  Physical handicaps
  Physical fitness
  Sexual dysfunction
  Pregnancy and childbirth
  Overweight
  Nutritional problems
  Low energy
  Allergies
  Sleep disorders
  Hypertension
  Pain
  Disease in general
  Terminal illness
  Self-healing, psychic healing
  Treatment or drug addiction
  Alcoholism
  Smoking

[*As the line between psyche and soma is very thin, many will prefer all or some of the listings immediately above to be listed under "the mind," rather than under "the body."*]

Problems Generally Regarded As Related Primarily to the 'Spirit'
  Religion
  Stewardship
  Worship
  Psychic phenomena
  Life after death
Problems Regarded by Some as Holistic— Embracing Body, Spirit, Mind, Heart and Will
  Any of the above may be so-regarded
  Holistic health
  Holistic medicine or healing

Data Primarily Dealing With People

Many of the above may be so-regarded or used. Also:

Intangibles	Objectives
Intuitions	Goals
Sequences	Project goals
Solutions	Tactical needs
New approaches	Needs
Public moods	Organizational contexts
Opinion-collection	Operations
Points of view	Systems
Sources	Work assignments
Programs	Reporting systems
Projects	Controls systems
Surveys	Performance character-
Investigations	istics
Research projects	Proficiencies
Research and develop-	Deficiencies
ment projects	Records management
Inputs	Catalogs
Outputs	Handbooks
Reports	Trade or professional
Conclusions	literature
Findings	Data analysis studies
Recommendations	Statistical analyses
Policy recommendations	Financial needs
Policy formulations	Costs
Plans	Accountings

When you're done with the list, PLEASE prioritize it. Put the types of information in order, from your most favorite to your least favorite. Again, don't hesitate to copy and use the "Prioritizing Grid."

Summarize It All, on Your Tree Diagram. Turn to page 118 again, if you will, and in the place provided there on the left-hand side of the Tree, put your summary of 'GOALS OF THE ORGANIZATION.' It should state whether Product, Service, Information or any fourth alternative that you made up. And *which* kind, in specifics.

Combine Wherever Possible. It doesn't have to be Product OR Service OR Information. It can be any two of the above. Or any three. For example, you might decide that the kind of Information you would most like to get out to people would be a catalog. Fine, but then if that's the only thing you can say

about yourself, you're going to have to cover every place in your entire 'target' geographical area, that produces a catalog of some sort. If however, you discovered that on the Product list, you liked the idea of Gym Equipment, that should be added to "catalog." It now reads "Producing catalogs of gym equipment." *That* narrows down the field in a much more satisfactory manner. You now have a *manageable* number of places to locate, investigate, and visit.

The Third Principle For Narrowing Down The Organizations You Will Want To Take A Look At:

3 AT WHAT LEVEL WITHIN THE ORGANIZATION DO YOU WANT TO BE FUNCTIONING, AND AT APPROXIMATELY WHAT SALARY?

You've GOT to make some decisions about this, at some point. For, your answer to this question will determine at what level you do your investigating, in the "HOW" section of chapter 6.

Here are some of the possible levels you may choose from: Volunteer • Intern • Entry-level worker • One who supervises others • One who works essentially alone •

One who works with one other, in tandem • One who works as a member of a team • The head of the organization • The founder of the organization.

Level on the job is generally intimately related to how high a level your skills are on. And how rare they are—not separately, but in the way you have combined all your skills, and caused them to be interrelated to one another.

Level on the job determines what your salary will be. So now is as good a time as any for you to sit down and

figure out what salary you need. We suggest for this purpose that you make up two budgets.

First: the 'rock-bottom need' budget —what you *need* to just survive, if you found yourself and your loved ones between a rock and a hard place. Second: the 'I hope' budget—what you *hope* you will have to live. The categories, for both budgets include, of course:

Food—at home; Food—out
Housing—rent/mortgage, tax, insurance
Housing—furnishings
Housing—utilities and household supplies
Transportation—car payments, insurance, parking, gas, other maintenance; public transportation
Clothing—purchases, maintenance
Hairdos, toiletries
Medical—insurance, physicians' visits, other, including dental
Education—tuition, books, loan repayment
Recreation
Gifts, contributions
Life insurance
Union dues
Savings
Payments on debts
Pension contribution
Social Security; federal/state income taxes
and—

Plus 15% . . .
To each budget add 15% more, because we all habitually underestimate our needs, and by about that much.

What you have now is your range: the amounts *between which* you can bargain, at the conclusion of a promising job interview, and the level at which you want to do your exploring, now.

Summarize It All, on Your Tree Diagram. Turn to page 118 again, if you will, and in the place provided there on the left-hand side of the Tree, put your summary of "LEVEL AND SALARY DESIRED."

Good.

You now have all the basic raw materials for finding out what your ideal future job might be.

But What about the *Right* Side of the Tree Diagram? Ah, yes. There *are* three more "principles of exclusion." *However,* these will *probably* only be useful to you *after* you have narrowed your search down to three or four places that truly interest you; and you are then trying to make up your mind between them.

At that point you will need some further principles of exclusion, to narrow down the territory. At that point, "working conditions," and "types of people you will be working with," and "preferred geography factors" will help you decide. But let's do the homework on these principles of exclusion now, so as to get them all nailed down:

The Fourth Principle For Narrowing Down The Organizations,—Usually *After* You've Taken A Look At Them:

4 WHAT KINDS OF WORKING CONDITIONS DO YOU WANT?

Figure Out What's Important To You. *When* you are looking at, and weighing, two or more organizations, you will be able to give preference to one above the others *if you know under what conditions you do your best work.* This can include *anything!* Such as:

- Do you prefer work outdoors, or indoors?
- Do you want to work for an organization with 20 or less employees?

100 or more? 500 or more? 1000 or more?

- Do you want to work in a place where you know everyone, or not?
- Do you want to work in a room with windows, or don't you care?
- Do you want to be working in close physical proximity to others, or not?
- What distasteful working conditions from your past do you want to be SURE not to repeat?
- What kind of dress code, supervision, use of authority, openness to change, do you want to have—in order to do your most effective work?

Write these answers out on a separate piece of blank paper.

Prioritize The List. Then (you know by now): PRIORITIZE the list, using another copy of the "Prioritizing Grid."

Summarize It on the Tree Diagram. Turn to page 119, and enter your top five answers in the appropriate place on the right-hand side of the Tree diagram. As you stare at it, it will *of course* occur to you that *some* of the list here *may be useful to you before* you begin your search. For example, if you decide you want to work for an organization with 20 or less employees, *that* will be an important principle to have in hand *before* you begin your search—as it will determine *which* organizations you focus your attention on.

Generally speaking, however, as we said earlier, these "preferred working conditions" will be more useful to you after you have three or four particular organizations in mind.

The Fifth Principle For Narrowing Down The Organizations,—Usually *After* **You've Taken A Look**

5 WHAT KINDS OF PEOPLE WOULD YOU LIKE TO BE WORKING WITH?

WHAT "Kinds of People" usually means two things. *What kinds of people do you want to be dealing with as clients, customers, consumers, students, or whatever?* AND: *What kinds of people do you want to have working beside you within your organization? beside you, with you, under you, and over you?*

Who Do You Want To Serve? The answer to the first part lies in the list we saw, back when we were dealing with WHAT KINDS OF SERVICES DO YOU WANT TO OFFER, AND TO WHOM? If you need help here, now, go back and look at that list. It should give you some helpful starts toward this subject.

Who Do You Want Beside You? As for "the kinds of people you would like to have working beside you, within your organization"—all you have to do is take a blank piece of paper and make a list of all the kinds of people you have already worked with (at home or at work), and hope you will never have to work with again.

Negatives Into Positives. Then turn those "negative" factors into "positive factors"—which will often, but not always, be their opposites.

Prioritize the list (of course) and you will have a splendid list of what to look for. When at a later point in your job-hunt you have three or four places under consideration, and they look rather equally attractive to you, *this* list will separate the men from the boys, and the women from the girls. Also the sheep from the goats.

Here Come Your Values. *Most often* you will discover that "Types of People" is utterly dependent upon your "value system." You would call them your "traits." In the jargon of vocational experts, they are called "Self Management Skills." Whatever the language, we are obviously referring to all those traits (or skills) that you were missing seeing in the WHAT part of this process. Traits/skills such as these:

Some Typical Self-Management Skills/Traits

A
Adept(ness)
Adventuresome(ness)
Alert(ness)
Assertive(ness)
Astute(ness)
Attention to details
Authentic(ity)
Authority, handles well
Aware(ness)
B
C
Calm(ness)
Candid(ness)
Challenges, thrives on
Character, has fine
Clothes, dresses well
Committed, commitment to growth
Competent (competence)
Concentration
Concerned
Conscientious(ness)
Cooperative (cooperation)
Courage(ous)
Creative, manifests creativity
Curious (curiosity)
D
Dependable (dependability)
Diplomatic (diplomacy)
Discreet
Driving (as, in ambition), drive
Dynamic(ness)
E
Easygoing(ness)
Emotional stability
Empathy (empathetic)
Enthusiastic (enthusiasm)
Exceptional
Experienced
Expert
Expressive(ness)
F
Firm(ness)
Flexible (flexibility)
G
Generous (generosity)
Gets along well with others
H
High energy level
Honest(y)
Humanly-oriented (warm)
I
Imaginative
Impulses, controls well
Initiating (initiative)
Innovative (innovation)
Insight(ful)
Integrity, displays constant
J
Judgment, has good
K
L

Loyal(ty)
M
Material world, deals well with the
N
Natural(ness)
O
Objective
Openminded(ness)
Optimistic (optimism)
Orderly (orderliness)
Outgoing(ness)
Outstanding
P
Patient (patience)
Penetrating
Perceptive(ness)
Persevering (perseverance)
Persisting (persistence)
Pioneering
Playful(ness)
Poise
Polite(ness)
Precise attainment of set goals,
    limits or standards
Punctual(ity)
Q
R
Reliable (reliability)
Resourceful(ness)
Responsible (responsibility)
Responsive(ness)
Risk-taking
S
Self-confident (confidence)
Self-control, good
Self-reliant (reliance)
Self-respect
Sense of humor, great
Sensitive (sensitivity)
Sincere (sincerity)
Sophisticated
Spontaneous (spontaneity)
Strikes balance, happy medium
Strong (as, under stress)
Successful
Sympathetic (sympathy), warm
T
Tactful(ness)
Takes nothing for granted
Thinks on his/her feet
Thorough(ness)
Tidy (tidiness)
Time, deals with well
    punctual (punctuality)
Tolerant (tolerance)
U
Uncommon
Unique
V
Versatile (versatility)
Vigor(ous)
W X Y Z

Use This List Twice: Underline. There are two ways to approach this list. First think of it as a list of *your own* possible Traits. *Underline* the ones which you think distinguish *You.*

And Then Circle. *Then* go back to the beginning, and this time approach the list as a list of People you would like to be surrounded by, at work. *Circle* the Traits that are most important to you, in the people you work with. If you desire different traits in your boss, from the traits you desire in your co-workers, or in those under you, make up three lists.

Compare. When you are done circling, do two things. First of all, compare *your* Traits with those you want to find in those around you at work. Are they the same? Don't be surprised if they are. Honest people usually like to be surrounded by honest people, and not by a bunch of liars. Etc. Etc.

And Prioritize. Secondly, of course, prioritize the list of stuff you want to have in those who surround you at work —unless you are going to be working alone, in which case, this is irrelevant. It may however have something to do with your clients or customers, so don't leap over this *too* quickly! Enter the results as usual on page 119.

The Sixth Principle For Narrowing Down The Organizations,—Usually *After* You've Taken A Look At Them:

6 WHERE DO YOU WANT TO BE, GEOGRAPHICALLY SPEAKING?

It may be that you have no choice. Your mother lives nearby, at present, and she is on in years, and needs you to be near. And, you want to be near. So, geography may not look like a very important issue for you.

Mini-Geography. But, suppose you find as you go on, that there are two places which interest you. One is a 75-minute commute, and the other is a 10-minute commute. If you care about the length of your daily commute, then as you see, geography becomes a useful tool for deciding which one to go after. Mini-geography is operative here (one area or another, within your county or state). Maxi-geography might be operative at some other time of your life (whether to move from New York to California, or not).

Maxi-Geography. Indeed, it may be operative now, for you. To such an extent that you intend to go to the State of your choice, and there conduct your job-hunt, from the beginning. Or, to a lesser extent—such that, if two places come to your attention, and one is in your favorite City in the whole country (or world), while the other is not, the balance would be tipped for you in favor of the one which is in the City of your dreams.

Learn the Geography Lessons from Your Past. So, you need to think this out. If you want to move, need to move, but haven't the foggiest notion *Where,* try making a list of all the distasteful factors you have endured—geographically—since you were a small lad or lass. Conditions you hope you will never have to deal with again, as long as you live. Then turn those "negative" factors into "positives" again, prioritize them, and see what city or area it *sounds* like. Show the list to a number of your family or friends, if you have no clue.

Summarize It on the Tree Diagram. Whatever you come up with, mini-geography or maxi-, summarize it on the appropriate place, in the right side of the Tree diagram on page 119 —well, you surely know it by now.

Passive vs. Active Geography. Needless to say, you may be saving this Geography consideration just to help you weigh various attractive organizations, as you get down to the wire later on. On the other hand, Geography may be what's *driving* you, right now. If so, write the name of your "target" city or area, over near the "Goals of the Organization."

Well, there you have it. The six factors which will help you decide "WHERE?" you want to use your skills. You've finished with the homework on *yourself.* Time now to take this information, and with it in hand, go out and do some research about *what's available, out there* that matches the stuff you've just uncovered.

ON TO THE RESEARCH PART OF THIS JOB-HUNT OR CAREER-CHANGE

Yes, research. Don't let your stomach turn weak, or your knees to jelly. It's not difficult at all. It never is *when you're researching something you LOVE.* And that was the whole point of the Six Principles of Exclusion, wasn't it: to nail down what it is you LOVE, in each of those six arenas?

Courage, then. This research shouldn't be difficult at all, IF you keep in mind the questions you are trying to find answers to. There are FOUR such questions that you need to work your way through, step-by-step. And they are:

1 What are the names of jobs that would use my strongest and most enjoyable skills and fields of knowledge?

2 What kinds of organizations have such jobs?

3 What are the names of the organizations that I particularly like, among those uncovered in Question #2?

4 What needs do they have that my skills could help with?

Can you find out all this stuff? Sure; this is an information society with no limits on what you can find out, if you're just persistent and imaginative enough.

DON'T PAY SOMEONE TO DO THIS RESEARCH FOR YOU, WHATEVER YOU DO

There are a number of reasons why *no one else* can do all of this job-hunting research for you; not a job-counselor, not a friend, not anyone.

1. Only *you* really know what things you are looking for, and what things you want to avoid if possible.

2. You need the self-confidence that comes to you as you practice this researching. You need it *before* you go after the organizations that interest you.

3. The skills you use to *find* a job are close to the skills you use to *do* the job, after you get it. Therefore, by doing all this research you are increasing your qualifications for the job itself. Thus, this conclusion: the more research you do, the more qualifications you will have.

Can you do this research yourself, then?

Of course you can.

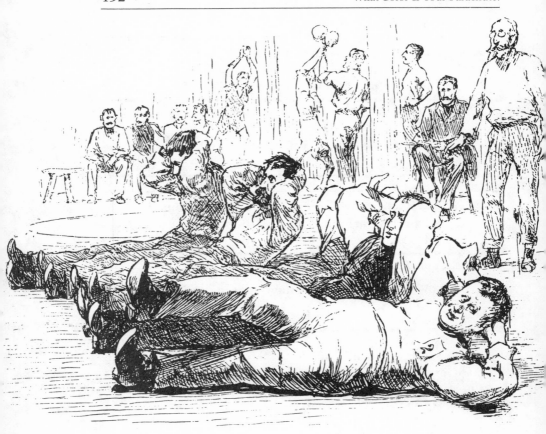

THE PRACTICE

If you want to do some Practice, first, there is an exercise which John Crystal invented; it's called "The Practice Field Survey." You pick a hobby or a curiosity or an issue or some enthusiasm of yours—say, the movies. The important thing is, it must have *absolutely* no possibility in your mind as a future job for you. You might have always been curious to know how they predict the weather, or how a bookstore gets started, or how a projectionist shows a movie. You might have an interest in affirmative action, or ecology, or lower taxes, or whatever. You use the yellow pages to find someone who could enlighten you about your curiosity, or your issue. Or to find someone who might share your enthusiasm, whatever it is. You then go to talk with them. You ask them whatever questions you have on your mind; but if none occur to you, try these:

1. How did you get involved with all this?
2. What do you like best about it?
3. What do you like the least about it?
4. Who else would you suggest I go talk to? May I tell them you recommended that I talk with them? Can I use your name? Would you be willing to call ahead, so that they will know who I am when I go over there?

Then go see whoever they lead you to. Thus will you get practice in talking with people, and thus will you learn how easy it is when it is a mutual enthusiasm that you both are discussing.

You say YOU ARE TOO SHY TO DO ALL THIS STUFF? Well, me too. BUT you've *got* to go face-to-face with people if you're going to get a job. So, might as well get started. And, shyness will yield, IF it's a true enthusiasm that you're talking to someone about. If you *love* computers, then you probably forget all about your shyness *when* you're talking to someone else about computers. So, just remember, during this research of your ideal job, when it is time for Shy You to go talk with people, it's your ENTHUSIASM you're exploring —the thing in this world you're dying to know more about, than any other subject.

Also, during this first stage of your research, it is *perfectly permissible to take somebody with you*—anyone, though I don't particularly recommend that it be your mother, or your dog Ralph.

Your shyness is *your* servant. You are not its servant. Make it serve you. Put on your best clothes, stand tall and straight, shoulders back, and get out there. Conduct yourself *as quietly confident that you would be an asset to any organization that you ultimately decide to serve.* You will be, indeed. The thoroughness with which you're doing this research, shows *that.*

Okay, let's see how you go about tackling each of these
FOUR questions in turn:

The First Step in Your Research:
WHAT ARE THE NAMES OF JOBS
THAT USE MY SKILLS?

In effect, what you are doing here is trying on jobs to see
if they fit; and you do this by going out and talking to people
who are actually doing work that you think you might like
to do.

How do you decide who to go see? That's easy. Go back to
the diagram of the TREE that you so laboriously filled in
(you did, didn't you?) earlier in this chapter. Of all the factors
on the left-hand side of that tree, which one is most important
to you, in your next job or career? I'll give you a clue. It will
usually turn out to be your favorite Transferable Skill (whether
with People, Information, or Things) AND/OR your favorite
FIELD of (Special) Knowledge.

Put this KEY FACTOR down as number 1 on the following
chart, in all four places where number 1 appears.

Okay, now, what's the next most important factor to you,
in your next job or career? (Look at the left-hand side of
the TREE diagram, again.) Put it down as number 2, in the
three places where the number 2 appears.

Continue in this fashion, until you have the chart filled in.
As you will note at the bottom of that chart, you can copy it
on to another piece of paper and extend it so as to
include as many factors as you wish.

RESEARCHING YOUR IDEAL JOB

As my first person to interview, I'm going to identify someone whose job uses/is characterized by

1. _____

As my second person to interview, I'm going to identify someone whose job uses/is characterized by

1. _____ *AND*

2. _____

As my third person to interview, I'm going to identify someone whose job uses/is characterized by

1. _____ *AND*

2. _____ *AND*

3. _____

As my fourth person to interview, I'm going to identify someone whose job uses/is characterized by

1. _____ *AND*

2. _____ *AND*

3. _____ *AND*

4. _____

As my fifth person to interview, I'm going to . . .
(You can surely finish this diagram for yourself, on a separate sheet of blank paper.)

Having finished filling in this chart, you are ready to go out and talk to someone whose job uses the first factor on the chart. Never mind if nothing else matches about their job and your Tree. They can still give you valuable information, and they can still lead you to the second person you want to talk to.

If you don't know even how to find the first person, ask your family and friends for help and suggestions.

Incidentally, if you don't want to be so logical and orderly as this chart implies, then just show a list of your favorite

Transferable Skills and your favorite Special Knowledges to all your family and friends, and ask them what jobs come to mind, that they think would use such Skills and such Knowledges. You can then ask them where they think you would find such people.

Do remember, that at this stage of your research you are *not* interested in talking to employers, or people who have the power to hire. Rather, you are interested in talking to *people who are actually doing the work* that you think you might enjoy doing.

Each time that you find such a person, these are the questions you will find most useful to ask:

1. How did you get into this work?
2. What do you like the most about it?
3. What do you like the least about it?
4. And, where else could I find people who do this kind of work OR this kind of work PLUS? (And here you trot out the next factor on your list.)

Then you go visit the people they suggest.

*"I used to ask myself,
'What can I do to help my fellow man?' but
I couldn't think of anything that wouldn't have put me
to considerable inconvenience."*

You should always ask them for more than one name, so that if you run into a dead end at any point, you go back and visit the other people they suggested.

Remember, what you are doing here is Trying On Jobs without actually taking them—just as you might go to a clothing store and Try On some clothes. Your basic object is to see if they fit you. So here.

Now think how immensely intelligent this process is. In a survey done in the San Francisco Bay Area it was found that of those people placed in jobs by the U.S. Employment Service, 57% of them were not in that job just thirty days later. Granted that some of them probably only wanted work for a few days, it is still true that many tried out the job and found out that they didn't like it, because it didn't fit them. But, in order to find this out, they had to go through all the hassle of searching for that job, convincing the boss that they were right for that job, taking that job, starting work, telling all their friends that they had found a job, and then—finding to their dismay that it didn't fit them—having to either quit, or be fired. How much more intelligent it is to go talk to people about their jobs BEFORE you try to get hired in that line of work. How much more intelligent to find out ahead of time that the job doesn't fit you. Or, that it does. That is what you are doing, here.

As you go about this phase of your research, you will discover that the separate and distinct things that you wrote out on the left-hand side of your TREE diagram begin to fit together. You will become better and better at figuring out *who* can give you the information you need. For example, suppose that you have discovered you are skilled in: counseling people, particularly in one-to-one situations; that you are well-versed in psychiatry; and that you love carpentry and plants.

How do you put all this together into one unified career? Well, begin by translating each of the skills, knowledges or interests you have, into a corresponding PERSON. Counseling = counselor, psychiatry = psychiatrist, carpentry = carpenter, plants = gardener.

Next, ask yourself which of these persons is most likely *to have the largest overview?* This is often, but not always, the same as asking: who took the longest to get their training? The particular answer here: the psychiatrist.

In the place where you presently are, then, plan to go see a psychiatrist (pay them for fifteen minutes of their time—if there is no other way) or go see the head of the psychiatry department at the nearest college or university, and ask them: Do you have any idea how to put all the above together in a job? And if *you* don't, *who* might?

If you carry out this plan, in this particular case, you will eventually be told: Yes, it can all be put together. There is a branch of psychiatry that uses plants to help heal people. You can use all your skills and interests. You can even use your carpentry to build planters for those plants.

Once you have begun to get a pretty good idea of what jobs interest you the most, because they use your favorite Skills and your favorite Special Knowledges, you are ready for

The Second Step in Your Research:
WHAT KINDS OF ORGANIZATIONS
HAVE SUCH JOBS?

You will of course have already stumbled on some of this information, while you were going about interviewing people whose jobs you thought you might like to do. But now it is time to focus your research solely on this issue. You want to find out *all* the different places you might consider, in looking for the kinds of jobs you've decided you would like to do.

Now, to give you an example of what I mean, let us consider the job of teacher. Let us suppose that you want to teach. But what kinds of organizations have such jobs? Not just schools, as you might at first suppose. There are countless kinds of organizations and agencies out there which have a teaching arm, and therefore employ teachers. You want to find out all such places, so that—as Confucius says—you are choosing a card from a full deck.

Here are *the kinds of questions* that you are (hopefully) trying to find the answers to, as you do this part of your research:

☐ 1. Do I want to work for a profit-making company, a non-profit firm, agency, college, association, foundation, small business, the government, or what?

☐ 2. Do I want to work for an older and larger organization, or get in on the ground floor of a new and smaller one, with growth possibilities? If you're in an area where hiring is "tight," look *long and hard* at the new and smaller organizations. It's true that their failure rate is high; *but* it's also true that that's where two-thirds of all new jobs get created—in businesses with twenty or less employers.

☐ 3. Do I want to advance rapidly? If so you need an organization with solid plans for expansion—overseas or at home.

☐ 4. Do I want to work for a "going concern" or for "a problem child" type of operation? As the experts say, a company in trouble is a company in search of leadership. The same goes for foundations, agencies, etc. If that is your cup of tea (well, is it?), you can probably find such places without too much investigation. Some experts say if you go for such a challenge, give yourself a time limit, say three to five years, and then if you can't solve it, get out. The average job in this country only lasts 3.6 years, anyway.

☐ 5. Other questions: what do I want to accomplish with my skills? what working circumstances do I want? what opportunities? what responsibilities? what kinds of job pressures am I willing to exist under, and do I feel capable of handling? what kinds of people do I want to work with? starting salary? salary five years from now? promotion opportunities?

WRITTEN STUFF AND PEOPLE

In doing this phase of your research, you will be dealing *alternately* with written materials—such as books, journals, magazines, or other materials which librarians can direct you to—AND with people, who can tell you what you need to know. In general, the pattern is: you Read, until you need some information that no book seems to have. Then you go Talk to people until you have found out what you needed to know. Back then to do some more reading.

I caution you to do as much reading as you possibly can *before* you go and visit people. In the very nature of the case, people who have jobs are busy people and usually they do not appreciate *answering questions that you could just as easily have looked up in some directory or book*. They *do* appreciate answering questions that only they know the answer to.

You will normally be accorded a cordial welcome by *most* people you go to see:

a. *provided* that you know what questions you are trying to find answers to, and the answers can't easily be found in printed materials, microfiche, or on disks.

b. *provided* that you approach no organization until you've first gotten your hands on everything they've got in print, about who they are and what they do—and provided that *you've thoroughly digested this stuff* before you go in to see them.

c. *provided* that when it is time for you to approach people, you approach first of all those people whose business it is to give out information to the public, and find out every-thing they know about the questions or curiosities that are plaguing you. I am thinking of such people as the front desk in personnel offices, receptionists, public relations officers, librarians, and the like.

d. *provided* that when you approach an organization, you talk to those in lesser authority first, to find out everything that they know, before you approach someone higher up in the same organization. The principle here is that you only approach people for *the information that they alone know*.

e. and, *provided* that before you approach someone higher up, you ask that organization for everything they have in print about that person. This information will normally be in the hands of the receptionist if the place is small, or the personnel department if the place is large. If the person who alone has the information you want is a senior person in that organization, your local library or business library may have clippings, etc. about him or her. Incidentally, visiting a senior person in that organization unannounced ("I just happened to be in the neighborhood") is universally perceived as the conduct of an amateur. If you would like to be seen as a professional, make an appointment; and state at that time what information it is that you are trying to find out. It may be someone else has that information, and you will save yourself from a fruitless errand.

WHAT KINDS OF BOOKS WILL LIKELY BE USEFUL?

The kinds of books that you will likely find useful to you at this stage of your research, as well as subsequently, are the following. Most of them are to be found down at your local library.

American Men and Women of Science.

American Society of Training and Development Directory.
Who's Who in Training and Development, Ste. 305, 600 Maryland Ave. SW, Washington, DC 20024.

Better Business Bureau report on the organization (call the BBB in the city where the organization is located).

Business Information Sources, by Lorna M. Daniels.
University of California Press, Berkeley, CA 94720.
Annotated guide to business books and reference sources.

Career Guide to Professional Associations. Garrett Park Press, Garrett Park, MD 20766.

Chamber of Commerce data on the organization (visit the Chamber there).

College library (especially *business school* library), if there is one in your chosen area.

Company/college/association/agency/foundation *Annual Reports.* Get these directly from the personnel department or publicity person at the company, etc., or from the Chamber or your local library.

Consultants and Consulting Organizations Directory, 6th ed.
Gale Research Co., Book Tower, Detroit, MI 48226.
Editors: Paul Wasserman and Janice McLean. 1984.

Contacts Influential: Commerce and Industry Directory.
Business in particular market area listed by name, type of business, key personnel, etc. Contacts Influential, Market Research and Development Services, 321 Bush St.,

Ste. 203, San Francisco, CA 94104, if your library doesn't
have it.

The Dictionary of Holland Occupational Codes.

The Dictionary of Occupational Titles.

Directory of Corporate Affiliations. National Register
Publishing Co., Inc.

Directory of Information Resources in the United States.
(Physical Sciences, Engineering, Biological Sciences)
Washington, DC. Library of Congress.

YOU'LL LIKE THIS JOB, EXCEPT EVERY NOW
AND THEN, WHEN THEY DUMP A LOT OF
PAPER WORK ON YOU.

Dun & Bradstreet's Million Dollar Directory. Very helpful.

Dun & Bradstreet's Middle Market Directory. Very helpful.

Dun & Bradstreet's Reference Book of Corporate Managements.

Encyclopedia of Associations, Vol. I, National Organizations.
Gale Research Co. Lists organizations that are in the
business of giving out information.

Encyclopedia of Business Information Sources, 4th ed.
(2 volumes). Gale Research Co.

Fitch Corporation Manuals.

F & S Indexes (recent articles on firms).

F & S Index of Corporations and Industries.
Lists "published articles" by industry and by company
name. Updated weekly.

Fortune Magazine's 500.

Fortune's Plant and Product Directory.

The Foundation Directory.

How to Reach Anyone Who's Anyone, by Michael Levine. Price/Stern/Sloan Publishers, Inc. 410 N. La Cienega Blvd., Los Angeles, CA 90048.

Industrial Research Laboratories of the United States. R.R. Bowker Co., 205 E. 42nd St., New York, NY 10017.

Investor, Banker, Broker Almanac.

MacRae's Blue Book.

Moody's Industrial Manual (and other Moody manuals).

National Directory of Addresses and Telephone Numbers. Concord Reference Books, 240 Fenel Lane, Hillside, IL 60162.

National Recreational Sporting and Hobby Organizations of the U.S. Columbia Books, Inc., 777 14th St. NW, Washington, DC 20005.

National Trade and Professional Associations of the United States and Canada and Labor Unions. Garrett Park Press, Garrett Park, MD 20766.

Occupational Outlook Handbook.

Occupational Outlook Handbook for College Graduates.

Plan Purchasing Directory.

Register of manufacturers for your state or area (e.g., *California Manufacturers Register*).

Research Centers Directory, 6th ed. Gale Research Co. Also: *New Research Centers,* updating the original 1979 volume.

Standard and Poor's Corporation Records.

Standard and Poor's Industrial Index.

Standard and Poor's Listed Stock Reports (at some
brokers' offices).

*Standard and Poor's Register of Corporations, Directors and
Executives.* Key executives in 32,000 leading companies,
plus 75,000 directors.

Telephone Contacts for Data Users. Customer Services Branch,
Bureau of the Census, 301-449-1600 for statistical
information on any subject.

Thomas' Register of American Manufacturers.
Thomas Publishing Co.

Trade association periodicals.

Trade journals.

Training and Development Organizations Directory, 3rd ed.
Gale Research Co., Book Tower, Detroit, MI 48226.
Editor: Paul Wasserman. 1983.

United States Government Manual. Or call the Federal
Information Center of the General Services Administration
at 202-755-8660 to find the names of experts in any field.
For help on a question no one seems to know the answer
to, try the National Referral Center at the Library of
Congress, 202-287-5670.

Value Line Investment Survey, from Arnold Bernhard and Co.,
5 E. 44th St., New York, NY 10017. (Most libraries have
a set.)

Walker's Manual of Far Western Corporations and Securities.

Who's Who in Finance and Industry, and all the other Who's
Who books. Useful once you have the name of someone-
who-has-the-power-to-hire, and you want to know more
about them.

If all of the above seems like an embarrassment of riches, and you don't know where to begin, there's even a guide to all these directories. If you don't know which directory to consult, see—

- Klein's *Guide to American Directories*
  or
- Gale Research Company's *Directory of Directories*
  or
  when you are about to throw up your hands in despair,
- remember there is a person who knows how to use *all* these books: your friendly neighborhood librarian.

Besides these directories, some periodicals may be worth perusing: *Business Week, Dun's Review, Forbes, Fortune,* and the *Wall Street Journal.*

One way or another, through people or books, you should be able to identify the kinds of organizations which have the kinds of jobs you are interested in. This then brings you to

The Third Step in Your Research:
WHAT ARE THE NAMES OF SUCH ORGANIZATIONS THAT I PARTICULARLY LIKE?

Your problem here is cutting down the territory. You can't, after all, go visit 2,000 organizations. You must focus down. Two of the exercises you did earlier will be of particular relevance and helpfulness, at this point: Geography, and Working Conditions. Geography, for one, will save you from trying to stay too broad. Instead of your saying, "I'm looking for the names of organizations which hire welders," for example, you will be forced by your Geography statements to a more focused and manageable goal, such as: "I'm looking for the names of organizations in the San Jose area which hire welders." Your preferred Working Conditions will further aid you in cutting down the territory. If you stated that you preferred to work for an organization with fifty or less employees, then your targets become: "I'm looking for the names of organizations having fifty or less employees which hire welders, in the San Jose area." If, on top of this, you throw in other statements from your Tree diagram or your earlier research, your task will get easier still. Suppose you decided you wanted to work for an organization which produced wheels. Then your targets become: "I'm looking for the names of organizations in the San Jose area, which produce wheels, hire welders, and have fifty or less employees."

As you can see, *the more detailed you are, the easier it will be for you to find the names of such organizations.* And conversely, the less specific you are willing to be, the harder it will be for you to find the names of specific organizations which might hire you.

Once you're able to say just exactly and most specifically what kinds of organizations you want to find the names of, then what?

Well, you know: books, and people, books and people.

Into this quest, you press every contact that you have. That

means members of your family. Every friend. Your relatives. Your doctor, dentist, gas station attendant (a vanishing race), and the check-out clerk at your supermarket. Everyone you meet, anywhere, during the week.

Whenever a job-hunter writes me and tells me they've run into a brick wall, as far as finding out the names or organizations is concerned, I know what the problem will usually turn out to be. They aren't making sufficient use of their contacts.

The more people you know, the more people you meet, the more people you talk to, the more people you enlist as part of your own personal job-hunting network, the better your job-finding success is likely to be. Keep their names on 3 x 5 file cards with addresses, phone numbers, and anything about where they work or who they know that may be of use at a later date.

To do your job-hunt well, you need to be in twenty places at once, with your eyes and ears wide open. You can't be,

really. But your contacts *can* be. IF they know what you are looking for, and IF you have enlisted them to keep their eyes and ears open on your very specific behalf.

Some job-hunters cultivate new contacts whenever they can. If they go to hear a speaker on some subject *that interests them,* they make it a point to join the crowd that gathers 'round the speaker at the end of the talk, and—with notebook poised—ask such questions as: "Is there anything special that people with my technical expertise can do?" And then you mention your specialty: computer scientist, health professional, chemist, writer, or whatever. Very useful information may thus be turned up. You can also ask if you can contact the speaker for further information—"and at what address?" Conventions, likewise, afford rich opportunities to make contacts. Says one college graduate: "I snuck into the Cable Advertisers Convention at the Waldorf in N.Y.C. That's how I got my job."

If you decide that your target is in some entirely different geographical area from where you presently reside, you can still find out the names of organizations there. Complete detailed instructions as to how to do this are to be found in Appendix C.

We come now to

The Fourth and Last Step in Your Research:
WHAT NEEDS DO THEY HAVE THAT
MY SKILLS COULD HELP WITH?

"Needs" is a polite word. You know what we're *really* talking about here. We're talking about

AN ORGANIZATION'S PROBLEMS

All organizations have money—to one degree or another. What you are looking for are *problems*—specifically, *problems that your skills can help solve. What problems are bugging this organization? Ask; look. (If you know some people within a company or organization that looks interesting to you, ask them ever so gently:* What is the biggest challenge you are facing there?)

The problem does not have to be one that is bothering only *that* organization. You may want to ask what problem is common to the whole industry or field—low profit, obsolescence, inadequate planning, etc.? Or if there is a problem that is common to the geographic region: labor problems, minority employment, etc. All you really need is one major problem that you would truly delight to help solve.

If this idea is new and puzzling, still, to you: that your getting a job depends upon *your seeing and selling yourself as a solution to some problem,* then consider the following. You yourself know already how *problems* affect an organization's profits. Think of five stores you have been in, where you debated whether you would ever go back. Why was that? Well, of course, because of some problem they had. What kind of problem? You weren't waited on, when it was your proper turn? You weren't told all the information you needed to know, in order to make an intelligent purchase? The person with whom you were dealing insisted on going by the rule book, no matter what common sense and compassion would otherwise dictate? The person with whom you were dealing had some small amount of power but was misusing that power

for all it was worth? The organization had installed a computer where a person used to be, and the person between you and the computer seemed to be taking orders from it, rather than vice versa? The organization had, in a word, lost the human touch? Or what? You will quickly realize, you are more aware of an organization's problems than you thought you were.

All you have to do now is polish this awareness of yours. Assuming you did the work outlined in the previous section, you've got a (manageable) list of places that interest you. What you now need BEFORE YOU GO THERE (or BACK THERE) is to identify—within the area, department or tasks that interest you—what kinds of problems you could help solve, if they hired you.

Some of this you can figure out, just by thinking, and logical analysis. You may, for example, want to think how an unsatisfactory employee would behave in the job you are going to go after, and what problems such behavior would create. You of course intend to be a very competent, and enthusiastic employee, if you get that job. Therefore, you already can think of some problems you would eliminate, just by your extreme competency and enthusiasm for the work.

Beyond this, however, you want to learn as much as you can about the workings of the companies or organizations that interest you: what they are trying to accomplish, how they go about it, and—like that. There is only one name for this kind of investigation on the part of a job-hunter (You)— and that is: "intensive research."

As you go through all this intensive research concerning the places where you might like to work, two things will happen:

1. Your list will get smaller, as you discover some of the places that interested you *did not have the kind of problems or difficulties that your strongest skills could* a) solve; and b)let you enjoy doing so, during the process. Eliminate these places from your list. You would be unhappy there, even if they hired you. Know that now, and cross them off.

2. You will get to know *a great deal* about the remaining organizations which still interest you, including—most specifically—*their problems, and what you could do to help solve them.*

RULES FOR FINDING OUT IN DETAIL THE NEEDS
OR PROBLEMS OF AN ORGANIZATION

- **Rule No. 1:** **If it's a large organization that interests you, you don't need to discover the problems of the whole organization. You only need to discover the problems that are bugging the-person-who-has-the-ultimate-responsibility (or power) -to-hire-you.** The conscientious job-hunters always bite off more than they can chew. If they're going to try for a job at the Telephone Company, or IBM or the Federal Government or General Motors or—like that—they assume they've got to find out the problems facing that whole organization. *Forget it!* Your task, fortunately, is much more manageable. Find out what problems are bugging, bothering, concerning, perplexing, gnawing at, the-person-who-has-the-power-to-hire-you. This assumes, of course, that you have first *identified* who that person is. Once you have identified her, or him, *find out everything you can about them.* The directories will help. So will the clippings, at your local library. So will any speeches they have given (ask their organization for copies, of same).

  If it's a committee of sorts that actually has the responsibility (and therefore Power) to hire you, you will need to figure out who that one individual is (or two) who sways the others. You know, the one whose judgment the others respect. How do you find that out? By using your contacts, of course. Someone will know someone who knows that whole committee, and can tell you who their *real* leader is. It's not necessarily the one who got elected as Chairperson.

● <u>Rule No. 2</u>: **Don't assume the problems have to be huge, complex and hidden. The problems bothering the-person-who-has-the-power-to-hire-you may be small, simple, and obvious.** If the job you are aiming at was previously filled by someone (i.e., the one who, if you get hired, will be referred to as "your predecessor"), the problems that are bothering the-person-who-has-the-power-to-hire-you may be uncovered simply by finding out through your contacts what bugged your prospective boss about your predecessor. Samples:

"They were never to work on time, took long lunch breaks, and were out sick too often"; OR

"They were good at typing, but had lousy skills over the telephone"; OR

"They handled older people well, but just couldn't relate to the young"; OR

"I never could get them to keep me informed about what they were doing"; etc.

Sometimes, it's as simple as that. Don't assume the problems *have to be* huge and complex. In your research you may be thinking to yourself, "Gosh, this firm has a huge public relations problem; I'll have to show them that I could put together a whole crash P.R. program." That's the huge, complex and hidden problem that you think the-person-who-has-the-power-to-hire-you *ought to be concerned about*. But, in actual fact, what they *are* concerned about is whether (unlike your predecessor) you're going to get to work on time, take assigned lunch breaks, and not be out sick too often. Don't overlook the Small, Simple and Obvious Problems which bug almost every employer.

● <u>Rule No. 3</u>: **In most cases, your task is not that of educating your prospective employer, but of trying to read their mind.** Now, to be sure, you may have uncovered—during your research—some problem that the-person-who-has-the-power-to-hire-you is absolutely unaware of. And you may be convinced that this problem is *so crucial* that for you even to mention it will instantly win you their undying gratitude. Maybe. But don't bet on it. Our files are filled with sad testimonies like the following:

"I met with the VP, Marketing in a major local bank on the recommendation of an officer, and discussed with him a program I devised to reach the female segment of his market, which would not require any new services, except education, enlightenment and encouragement. His comment at the end of the discussion was that the bank president had been after him for three years to develop a program for women, and he

wasn't about to do it because the only reason, in his mind, for the president's request was reputation enhancement on the president's part. . . ."

Inter-office politics, as in this case, or other considerations may prevent your prospective employer from being at all receptive to Your Bright Idea. In any event, you're not trying to find out what *might* motivate them to hire you. Your research has got to be devoted rather to finding out what *already does* motivate them *when they decide to hire someone for the position you are interested in.* In other words, you are trying to find out What's Already Going On In Their Mind. In this sense, your task is more akin to a kind of mind-reading than it is to education. (Though *some* people-who-have-the-power-to-hire are *very* open to being educated. You have to decide whether you want to risk testing this.)

• **Rule No. 4:** There are various ways of finding out what's going on in their mind; don't try just one way. We will give a kind of outline, here, of the various ways. (You can use this as a checklist.)

A   *Analyzing the Organization at a Distance and Making Some Educated Guesses.*

1. If the organization is expanding, then they need:
   a. More of what they already have; OR
   b. More of what they already have, but with different style, added skills, or other pluses *that are needed;* OR
   c. Something they don't presently have: a new kind of person, with new skills doing a new function or service.

2. If the organization is continuing as is, then they need:

   a. To replace people who were fired (find out why; what was lacking?); OR

   b. To replace people who quit (find out what was prized about them); OR

   c. To create a new position. Yes, this happens even in organizations that are not expanding, due to—

      1) Old needs which weren't provided for, earlier, but now must be, even if they have to cut out some other function or position.

      2) Revamping assignments within their present staff.

3. If the organization is reducing its size, staff, or product or service, then they—

   a. Have not yet decided which staff to terminate, i.e., which functions to give low priority to (in which case *that* is their problem, and you may be able to help them identify which functions are "core-functions"); OR

   b. *Have* decided which functions or staff to terminate (in which case they may need multi-talented people or generalists able to do several jobs, i.e., functions, instead of just one, as formerly).

B *Analyzing the problems of the-person-who-has-the-power-to-hire-you by talking to them directly.*

It may be that your paths have accidentally crossed (it happens). Perhaps you attend the same church or synagogue. Perhaps you eat at the same restaurant. In any event, if you *do* ever have a chance to talk to her or him, listen carefully to whatever they may say about the place where they work. The greatest problem every employer faces is finding people who will listen and take them seriously. If you listen, you may find this employer discusses their problems—giving you firmer grounds to which you can relate your skills.

C *Analyzing the problems of the person-who-has-the-power-to-hire-you by talking to their "opposite number" in another organization which is similar (not to say, almost identical) to the one that interests you.*

If, for some reason, you cannot approach—at this time—the organization that interests you (it's too far away, or you don't want to tip your hand yet, or whatever), what you can do is pick a similar organization (or individual) where you are—and go find out what kind of problems are on their mind. (If you are interested in working for, say, a senator in another state, you can talk to a senator's staff here where you are, first; the problems are likely to be similar.)

D   *Analyzing the problems of a prospective employer*
by talking to the person who held the job before you—
OR by talking to their "opposite number" in another
similar/identical organization.

Nobody, absolutely nobody, knows the problems bugging a boss so much as someone who works, or used to work, for them. If they still work for them, they may have a huge investment in being discreet (i.e., not as candid as you need). Ex-employees are not necessarily any longer under that sort of pressure. Needless to say, if you're trying to get the organization to create a new position, there is no "previous employee." But in some identical or similar organization *which already has this sort of position,* you can still find someone to interview.

E *Using your contacts/friends/everyone you meet,*
   in order to find someone who:

1. Knows the organization that interests you, or knows
   someone who knows;
2. Knows the-person-who-has-the-power-to-hire-you, or
   knows someone who knows;
3. Knows who their opposite number is in a similar/identical
   organization;
4. Knows your predecessor, or knows someone who knows;
5. Knows your "opposite number" in another organization,
   or knows someone who knows.

F *Supplementary Method: Research in the library,* on the
   organization, or an organization similar to it; research
on the-individual-who-has-the-power-to-hire-you, or on their
opposite number in another organization, etc. (Ask your
friendly librarian or research librarian for help—tell them
what you're trying to find out.)

See also the books listed in Appendix A on
page 229: Executives and the Business World.

ANALYZING AN ORGANIZATION'S PROBLEMS

[ ] If it's a decent-sized company, send for (or go pick up) their annual report to stockholders; granted it's a public relations piece, it still may help quite a bit. If the organization is too small to have an annual report, get whatever pamphlets they have, describing their work. Also, use your contacts to try to find people who know a lot about them. Then, after studying what you find out, you will want to weigh the following questions:

IF IT IS A LARGE COMPANY:

[ ] How does this organization rank within its field, or industry? Is this organization family owned? If so, what effect has that on promotions? Where are its plants, offices or branches? What are all its projects or services? In what ways have they grown in recent years? New lines, new products, new processes, new facilities, etc.? Existing political situations: imminent proxy fights, upcoming mergers, etc.? What is the general image of the organization in people's minds? If the organization sells stock, what has been happening to it (see an investment broker and ask).

QUESTIONS TO BE ASKING YOURSELF
REGARDLESS OF THE COMPANY'S SIZE:

[ ] What kind of *turnover of staff* have they had? What is the attitude of employees toward the organization? If you've been there, are their faces happy, strained, or what? Is promotion generally from within, or from outside? How long has the chief executive been with the organization?

[ ] Do they encourage their employees to further their educational training? Do they help them pay for it?

[ ] How do *communications* work within the organization? How is information collected, and by what paths does it flow? What methods are used to see that information gets results — to what authority do people respond there? Who reports to whom?

[ ] Is there a "time-bomb" — a problem that will kill the organization, or drastically reduce its effectiveness and efficiency if they don't solve it real fast?

● <u>Rule No. 5</u>: Ultimately, this is a language-translation problem. You're trying to take your language (i.e., a description
of your skills), and translate it into their language (i.e., thcir
priorities, their values, their jargon, as these surface within
their concerns, problems, etc.). You should be aware to
begin with that most of the-people-who-have-the-power-to-
hire-you for the position that you want DO NOT like the word
"problems," as I said earlier. It reminds them that they are

mortal, have hangups, haven't solved something yet, or that they overlooked something, etc. "Smartass" is the word normally reserved for someone who comes in and *shows them up*. (This isn't true of every employer or manager, but it's true of altogether too many.) Since you're trying to use *their* language, speak of "an area you probably are planning to move into" or "a concern of yours" or "a challenge currently facing you" or *anything* except: "By the way, I've uncovered a problem you have." Use the word *problems* in your own head, but don't blurt it out with your prospective employer, *unless you hear them use it first*.

Beyond this, your goal is to be able to speak of Your Skills in terms of *The Language* of Their Problems. Here are some examples, in order to bring this all home:

The person who has the power to hire you, was bugged by or concerned about:	You therefore use language which emphasizes that you:
Your predecessor had all the skills, but was too serious about *everything*.	have all the skills (name them) *plus* you have a sense of humor.
This place is expanding, and now needs a training program for its employees.	have the skills to do training, and in the area they are concerned about.
All the picayune details they have to attend to, which they would like to shovel off on someone else.	are very good with details and follow-up. (That had better be true, or don't say it.)
Their magazine probably isn't covering all the subjects that it should, but that's just a gnawing feeling, and they've never had time to document it, and decide what areas to move into.	have done a complete survey of its table of contents for the last ten years, can show what they've missed, and have outlined sample articles in those missing areas.

While doing this research, please remember that the *woods are alive* with people who will solemnly tell you *something that ain't true* as though they were sure of it with every fibre of their being. So, check and cross-check and cross-check again the information that books, people, and experts give you. Let no one build any boxes for you; and watch that you don't hand them any wood with which to build one for you.

In the end, there is virtually no information you want that you cannot find. This is a *knowledge society,* and the only limits—really—lie within you, as to the commitment, diligence and perseverance you are willing to lavish on all this.

Well, that's it. Once you've found the answers to these four questions,

1. WHAT ARE THE NAMES OF JOBS THAT WOULD USE MY STRONGEST AND MOST ENJOYABLE SKILLS AND FIELDS OF KNOWLEDGE?
2. WHAT KINDS OF ORGANIZATIONS HAVE SUCH JOBS?
3. WHAT ARE THE NAMES OF THE ORGANIZATIONS THAT I PARTICULARLY LIKE, AMONG THOSE UNCOVERED IN QUESTION 2?
4. WHAT NEEDS DO THEY HAVE THAT MY SKILLS COULD HELP WITH?

you're done with your research.

Do remember, please, that during this research, *you* are the screener; *they* are the screenees. Except in the most difficult of job-hunting times, there are more places out there which could hire you, than you will ever imagine. The problem is, they don't know how to find you, and you don't know how to find them. But by doing this research thoroughly, you will make it possible for you both to find each other.

So, do remember during this research that you are examining careers, fields, industries, jobs, organizations, trying to decide which of them pleases *you*. They have to meet your criteria, or they get crossed off your list. You are gathering information in order to narrow things down. It is premature for you to be thinking about getting hired anywhere yet; you don't know where you want to be, until you've concluded this part of your research. If a job offer *accidentally* surfaces during this part of the process, it won't be because you were doing *anything* to encourage it. Your response, in fact, will reveal that. "Well, I'm tickled pink that you would want me to be working here. But, until I've finished my survey and am clearer about where my skills could best be used, in a way that would be most productive and give me the most satisfaction, I just can't say Yes or No to your kind invitation. But, when I've finished my personal survey, I'd sure be glad to get back to you about this, as this seems to me to be the *kind* of place I'd like to work in, and the kind of people I'd like to work with."

Over the years, I've asked job-hunters what was the most valuable part of this whole process. And they have responded again and again: "I learned to not just jump at the first offer I got, but to be more patient, and . . . well . . . more picky. I knew the right opportunity would come along, if I first took the time to find out what it was that I was truly looking for."

Yes. And that is why, during this phase of your research, you are *not* open to job offers. You are not looking for job offers. You are not yet thinking about job offers. You're visiting places to find out the information you need to know, in order to turn skills into a career, and a career into a job you would love. Whether the places you hit along the way happen to have a vacancy, or happen to want you, is—for the moment —premature and irrelevant. You have to first of all decide whether or not *you* want *them*.

*Y*ou're a bunch of jackasses. You work your rear ends off in a trivial course that no one will ever care about again. You're not willing to spend time researching a company that you're interested in working for. Why don't you decide who you do want to work for and go after them?

Professor Albert Shapero
(again) to his students

CHAPTER SIX

The Systematic Approach To The Job-Hunt and Career-Change:

PART III

How

Do You Find The Person Who Has The Power To Hire You For The Job That You Want?

The answer, in a nutshell, is:
through your research
and then through your contacts.

But let's back up for a moment. The three parts of any systematic approach to the job-hunt and career-change are, as we have seen, WHAT, WHERE, and HOW. Having traversed the WHAT and the WHERE, we come now to the HOW.

- Having found the career field you like best,
  - having found what sort of organization within that field appeals to you the most,
    - having found the names of specific organizations,
      - having found what kinds of needs they have and what sort of problems or challenges they are facing,
        - having narrowed down the possibilities to four or five places that truly interest you,

you now go—not as a "job beggar," but as a "resource person" —to talk to the person in each such organization who has the power to hire you.

The issue of HOW is
1. how do I find out who such a person is,
2. how do I get in for a job interview with that person?
3. and how do I convince them that they should hire me?

As I intimated above, the answer to the first question is: "Through the research you already did, and through your contacts." Contacts, you will recall, means every single person that you know, meet, talk to, blunder into, stumble across, or whatever. It does *not* mean "just business contacts." It means EVERYONE.

Let us say it is Capuchin Corporation that interests you, but you can't find out who has the power to hire you there. You use your library, all the directories we saw in the previous chapter, and your contacts. The question you ask of them all is, "Do you know anyone who works at Capuchin Corporation?" Once they say they do, you then of course ask them:

- What is their name?
- May I tell them you recommended that I talk with them?
- Can I use your name?
- Would you be willing to call ahead, so that they will know who I am when I go over there?

You go talk to that person, and just because they are already inside the organization, they are often able to give you the exact answer to your question, "Who would have the power to hire me, here, for this kind of position (which you then describe)?"

The presumed difficulty in finding out this sort of thing is predicated, of course, on the assumption that this is a large organization which interests you. If, however, the place that interests you is basically a "Mom-and-Pop" operation, then the issue of "who has the power to hire" is pretty obvious.

In all cases, it is likely that it is an individual you are seeking, or perhaps a committee, but not—in most cases—the Personnel Department.

The reason for this, as we saw in chapter 3, is that only 15% of all organizations even have personnel departments. And where they do, except for entry-level positions it is normally the function of the personnel department to *screen out* applicants and then send the ones who survive that screening on 'upstairs' to be interviewed by the person who actually has the power to hire. From the point of view of the organization, the personnel department is a great asset. It saves busy executives from being bothered by too many applicants, when it has come time to hire. But, from the point of view of the job-hunter or career-changer (namely, you or me) this passage

through the hands of the personnel department is not necessarily something to look forward to. We may get screened out at that level, by some overzealous and frightened clerk, and thus never get to see the person who has the power to hire—even though in fact we might be exactly the person he or she is looking for. But they will never get to see us, and they will never know.

To repeat the point of earlier chapters, the whole job-hunting process in this country is Neanderthal. *And,* that "Neanderthal-ness" hurts the employer as much as it does the job-hunter. In any event, all this that I have said concerning the personnel department dictates that the intelligent job-hunter (generally speaking) avoid that department. *Sometimes* that department will habor the kindest and warmest souls in the entire building; but, you never know. And by the time you find out, it may be too late. So it is better to try to get in directly to see the person who has the power to hire, without first going through this unnecessary extra step of possibly being screened out.

This leads us, then, directly into the second HOW question, how do I get in for a job interview with that person? The traditional answer, as you know, is "By sending a resume."

A CRASH COURSE IN RÉSUMÉS

My conversations with job-hunters, over the years, have convinced me that there is a passionate belief in the efficacy of resumes that is out of all proportion to how often they in fact ever get anyone an interview for a job. I think the faith placed in resumes is a very misplaced faith.

I said this once to a group of college placement people, many of whom were devoting large blocks of time to teaching students how to write a resume. When I sat down afterward, I found myself next to the personnel director for a huge public utility company, which employed thousands of people. He leaned across to me. "I listened to what you said about resumes," he began. I waited for the axe to fall. However he went on: "I've been trying to tell these counselors for years to get off this obsession they have with resumes. I'll interview anyone. But I don't read resumes. Haven't read one in five years. I can't tell a thing about a candidate from a resume. I was so glad you said what you did. Maybe they'll listen if they hear it from you."

The subject of resumes *is* loaded. So, perhaps we ought to briefly summarize what is known about resumes.

> **RÉ·SU·MÉ rez-ə-mā** n [F. *resume* fr. pp. of *resumer* to resume, summarize] SUMMARY *specif:* a short account of one's career and qualifications prepared typically by an applicant for a position.   —Webster's

Resumes can serve four different functions: they can be a SELF-INVENTORY, preparing you before the job-hunt to re-call all that you've accomplished thus far in your life; they can be an EXTENDED CALLING CARD, whose purpose is to get you invited in for an interview, by the employer(s) to whom you send that "calling card"; they can be an AGENDA FOR AN INTERVIEW, affording the interviewer a springboard from which to launch his or her inquiry about you, after you have been invited in; and, finally, resumes can be a MEMORY JOGGER for the employer after the interview, or for a whole committee—if a group is involved in the hiring decision.

It is as EXTENDED CALLING-CARD that the resume is most often used. Indeed, as calling-card it may be sent out to hundreds of prospective employers. Its lack of effectiveness in this role is well known. I cited the statistics in chapter 2. Only one job-offer is tendered for every 1,470 resumes that the average company receives. What is not so well known, is the tremendous damage which can be done to your self-

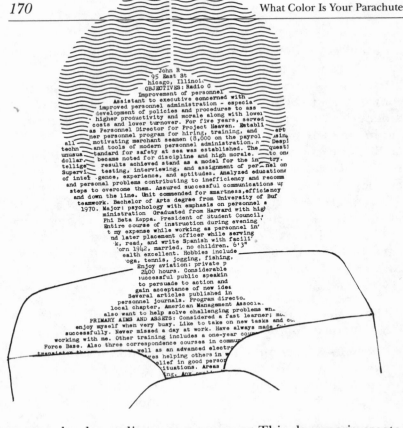

esteem by depending upon resumes. This damage is created by the following facts:

a) *Some* job-hunters do actually get an interview, and subsequently a job, because they sent out resumes.

b) *Many, many more* job-hunters do *not* get a job by means of a resume. In fact, many do not even get one invitation to an interview, in spite of sending out 800 or 900 resumes.

c) The ones who do get a job thereby, talk a lot about it; the ones who find their resumes don't work for them, rarely say much. Consequently, there is a widespread *mythology* in our culture that "resumes usually work."

d) When resumes don't work at all for a particular job-hunter, he or she usually assumes something is drastically *wrong with them*.

The result: plummeting self-esteem. It is not that a method has been tried, and failed. It is that a method *which you think works for almost everyone else* has failed for you. Hence, depression. Emotional paralysis, etc.

HOW TO GET IN

Well, you can see why I disbelieve in resumes as extended calling cards. How then *do* I think you are going to get in for an interview with the person who has the power to hire? I think you are going to get in by the methods that we KNOW are most effective:

a) *COMMITMENT. Devoting eight hours a day, five days a week, to the job-hunt.*

b) *GOING FACE-TO-FACE. Knocking on the door, personally, at every organization that looks the least bit interesting.*

c) *USING CONTACTS. When you find a place you like, or are curious about, but you can't get an interview there, asking every person you know if they know someone who works there, and can get you an invitation to an interview.*

I believe in these three strategies because I know they work.

RESUMES

Given the fact that the resume AS EXTENDED CALLING-CARD is not very effective, what can we say about its other three roles? Well, I believe the exercises in our previous chapters really supplant any need for the resume as SELF-INVENTORY. And your own research about organizations that interest you really supplants any need for the resume as AGENDA FOR AN INTERVIEW. But, after talking with countless numbers of successful job-hunters, I am bound to say that a resume may be very useful *after* the interview as A MEMORY-JOGGER FOR THE EMPLOYER.

It is an ancient saying in career-counseling: "A resume is something you should never send ahead of you, but always leave behind you." I believe that. Further, I believe it is often— if not always—wise *not* to carry a resume into an interview, but to say truthfully, "I don't have one with me, but I can mail one to you tonight." Then go home, construct a resume tailored exactly to the skills needed in the job you both just discussed, type it up *very* neatly, or run it over to a professional place post-haste, and then send it, along with a thank-you note as a cover letter.

I think there is a genuine need sometimes for this role of the resume as memory-jogger. Many hiring decisions are

made by a committee, and you do not always have a chance to meet them all. Oftentimes you may be called back for three or four more interviews, before they decide who they want. The resume, left behind from the first, will remind them of who you are.

FOR THAT FARAWAY CITY, YOU MAY HAVE TO SEND A RESUME

If you're interested in leaping across the country for your next job, it may of course be impractical for you at first to go there yourself. You may need to test the waters. I give detailed suggestions on page 292 on how you research a faraway city. But suppose that research is completed. You know some organizations that, at this distance, look like "possibles." You can't yet afford the money (or time, perhaps) to actually go there. What should you do?

Well of course you will begin by using every contact there, that you have developed. If a letter comes from you with the name of a mutual contact in that target city, the person to whom the letter is addressed is *always* going to pay more favorable attention to that letter, than would be the case if you were a total stranger. Unless—the job-hunter's nightmare —your mutual friend/contact has misrepresented how close he or she is to your target person, and as a matter of fact said person can't stand the sight of your mutual friend. It is to die.

Should you enclose a resume? Opinions vary widely. *Everything* depends on the nature of the resume, and the nature of the person you are sending it to. Resumes, after all, are a lot like dating. There is no man who is liked by all the women he dates. There is no woman who is liked by all the men she dates. Some employers like resumes; some hate them.

Some will like your resume; others, no matter what format or style it is in, won't like it. The question that concerns you the most, will inevitably be: never mind that not all employers will like my resume—will the employers *I care about the most* like it? Ah, that is the $64,000 question.

I used to have a hobby of collecting resumes that work. I delight in showing them to employers. Many of them don't like them at all. "That resume will never get anyone a job," they say. I delight in telling them, "Sorry, you're wrong. It already has. What you are saying is that it wouldn't get them a job *with you.*"

The resume reproduced on the next page is an example of what I mean. Jim Dyer, who had been in the Marines for twenty years, wanted a job as a salesman for heavy construction and mining equipment. He devised this resume, and had fifteen copies made. "I used," he said, "a grand total of seven before I got *the* job in *the* place I wanted!"

Like the employer who hired him, I *loved* this resume. Yet, when I've shown it to other employers, they criticized it for using a picture, for being two pages long instead of one, etc., etc. In other words, had Jim sent his resume to *them,* they wouldn't have been impressed enough to invite him in for an interview.

E.J. DYER   Street, City, Zip   Telephone No.

I SPEAK
THE LANGUAGE
OF
MEN
MACHINERY
AND
MANAGEMENT
...

OBJECTIVE: Sales of Heavy Equipment

QUALIFICATIONS   * Knowledge of heavy equipment, its use and maintenance.

                    * Ability to communicate with management and with men in the field.

                    * Ability to favorably introduce change in the form of new
                      equipment or new ideas... the ability to sell.

EXPERIENCE   * Maintained, shipped, budgeted and set allocation priorities for
Men and   85 pieces of heavy equipment as head of a 500-man organization
Machinery   (1975-1977).

                    * Constructed twelve field operation support complexes, employing
                      a 100-man crew and 19 pieces of heavy equipment (1965-1967).

                    * Jack-hammer operator, heavy construction (summers 1956-1957-1958).

Management   * Planned, negotiated and executed large scale equipment purchases
                      on a nation to nation level (1972-1974).

Sales   * Achieved field customer acceptance of two major new computer-
                      based systems:
                        - Equipment inventory control and repair parts expedite system
                          (1968-1971)
                        - Decision makers' training system (1977-1979).
                    * Proven leader ... repeatedly elected or appointed to senior posts.

EDUCATION   * B.A. Benedictine College, 1959. (Class President; Editor
                      Yearbook; "Who's Who in American Colleges").

                    * Naval War College, 1975. (Class President; Graduated "With
                      Highest Distinction").

                    * University of Maryland, 1973-1974. (Chinese Language).

                    * Middle Level Management Training Course, 1967-1968
                      (Class Standing: 1 of 97).

PERSONAL   * Family: Sharon and our sons Jim (11), Andy (8) and Matt (5)
                      desire to locate in a Mountain State by 1982, however, in
                      the interim will consider a position elsewhere in or outside
                      the United States ... Health: Excellent ... Birthdate: December
                      9, 1937 ... Completing Military Service with the rank of
                      Lieutenant Colonel, U.S. Marine Corps.

SUMMARY   A seeker of challenge ... experienced, proven and confident of
                    closing the sales for profit.

So, I repeat, matching your resume to the right employer is a lot like a dating game. Don't believe *anyone* who tells you there's one right format for a resume, or one way that's guaranteed to win.

If you decide you want to send your resume to a faraway place, and you want further guidance as to how to write one, I refer you to the books listed in section 24 of Appendix A, at the back of this book. The best of these, by a long shot, is Richard Lathrop's *Who's Hiring Who,* wherein he recommends (and describes) "a qualifications brief"—akin to John Crystal's idea of "a written proposal"—instead of a resume.

The most important quality needed in your resume, besides neatness and clarity, is that it should be a *living* resume, which it will be ONLY if YOU shine through it all. One job-hunter, for example, found this unique truthful way of describing her period of job-hunting: "Job-Hunter (Self-Employed) January 1982–January 1983.

- Developed and executed all phases of marketing and advertising for product.
- Targeted markets and identified the needs of diverse consumers.
- Developed sales brochure
- Designed packaging, and upgraded visual appeal of product
- Scheduled and conducted oral presentations"

So, *she* shined through it all.

But, back to our second HOW question: If resumes are not the preferred route to take, then how *do* you get in to see the person who has the power to hire? The answer of course is: Through your contacts. As before, you ask *everyone* you meet and everyone you know, "Do you personally know X, over at Capuchin Corporation, or do you know someone who does?" To the first person who says, "Yes," you say the by-now familiar refrain:

- May I tell them you recommended that I talk with them?
- Can I use your name?
- Would you be willing to call ahead, so that they will know who I am when I go over there?

If you persist with every contact you have, the odds are 20 to 1 that you are going to get in. And then, you will be face-to-face with the third HOW question, namely, how do I convince them that they should hire me? The answer is: read the rest of this chapter. We are going to go into this, in some detail.

But, briefly stated, the answer is that you sell yourself by finding out as much as you possibly can BEFORE YOU GO IN THERE FOR AN INTERVIEW. You lay your hands on everything you can that is in print about them. You read all their brochures, annual reports, addresses of the chairman or boss—whatever. You talk to everybody you know, to find out everything you can about them: the good and the bad.

Organizations, including hospitals, colleges, and everything else, love to be loved. You are going to be a very rare bird when you walk in their front door. You loved them enough to find out a lot of information about them. *You know far more than you are ever going to have to use,* at least during the hiring process. But the depth of your knowledge will pay off in your quiet sense of competence.

WELL, YOU WANT TO SEE THEM,
BUT DO THEY WANT TO SEE YOU?

This is the question which bothers almost everyone new to the job-hunt. We sort of just assume the answer is "No." And particularly so, if we have some very obvious job-market handicap, such as age, or a psychiatric history, or a prison record, or whatever.

You need to remember, no matter what your job-market handicap may be, this simple but profound truth:

ALL EMPLOYERS DIVIDE INTO TWO GROUPS: 1) THOSE WHO WOULD BE PUT OFF BY YOUR HANDICAP. And 2) THOSE WHO WOULD NOT BE AT ALL PUT OFF BY YOUR HANDICAP. YOUR JOB IS TO FIND THE SECOND KIND OF EMPLOYER, AND NOT PAY ANY ATTENTION TO THE FIRST.

This is true, no matter what the odds. If out of every 100 employers, 75 would be bothered by your history, but 25 wouldn't care about it in the slightest, YOUR JOB IS TO MAKE YOUR WAY QUICKLY THROUGH THE 75, AND FIND THOSE OTHER 25. THEY ARE THE ONLY ONES YOU REALLY WANT TO SEE, ANYWAY.

I can hear your objections, right now. "But, hey, I'm over 60 years old. Employers don't want someone that old."

Now, you *know* what I'm going to tell you: "All employers divide into two groups: 1) those who would be put off by your age, and 2) those who would not be at all put off by your age. Your job is to find the second kind of employer, and not pay any attention to the first."

Please! Make no generalizations about "employers." There ain't no such animal. In any and all circumstances that you can possibly come up with, there are *always* at least two kinds of employers. Your job is to find the second kind, and pay no never mind to the first. You wouldn't want to work for them anyway, now would you?

Having said that, remember this. You're not visiting an employer in order to get him or her to do something for *you* —like it was a big favor, or something. If you've done your homework so that you *know* you can be part of the solution there, and not part of the problem, then you're going in to see this employer in order to do a favor *for them*. That's not an arrogant posture for you to take. It can be stated very quietly and confidently. But, it *is* the truth.

You are coming to see this employer, in order to make an oral proposal, followed hopefully by a written proposal, of what *you* can do for *them*.

What a switch from the way *most* job-hunters approach an employer! And will he or she, in such a case, be glad to see you? In most cases, you bet they will.

Once you get in to see her or him, the interview has begun. The term "interview" shouldn't frighten you by this time. You will have had rich experience in interviewing people all along the way, prior to this moment. But truth to tell, the Employment Interview does feel different from all previous interviews—so let's see what its special characteristics are. For, if you understand what an interview is, you will be ahead of 98% of all other job-hunters who go into the Interview as a lamb goes to the slaughter.

You will understand what an interview is, if you simply remember two fundamental truths about it.

FIRST FUNDAMENTAL TRUTH ABOUT THE INTERVIEW:

You and the employer are sitting there. Each of you has questions, and the essence of the interview is that each of you is trying to find out the answers to those questions.

YOUR QUESTIONS ARE:

First you report to them just exactly how you've been conducting your job-hunt, and what impressed you so much about their organization during your research, that you decided you wanted to come in and talk to them about a job.

Then, if this is a job that already exists, your questions are:
1. What does this job involve?
2. Do my skills truly match this job?
3. Are you the kind of people I would like to work with?
4. If we do match, can I persuade you to hire me?

You will rarely, if ever, say these questions out loud during the interview; but you will keep them in the front of your mind (or written on a pad) because these *are* the questions you came there to find the answers to.

If on the other hand the job in question is a job that you want them to create for you, then your four questions get changed into four statements:

1. What you like about this organization.
2. What sorts of *needs* you find intriguing in this field and in this organization (don't *ever* use the word "problems," as most employers resent it—unless you hear the word coming out of their mouth, first).
3. What skills seem to you to be needed in order to meet such needs.
4. Your presentation of your claim, backed by evidence, that you have the very skills in question.

THEIR QUESTIONS ARE:

1. Why are you here? They mean by this, why did you pick out our organization?
2. What can you do for us? They mean by that, what are your skills and your special knowledges?
3. What kind of person are you? They mean by that, do you have a personality that they will enjoy working with, or not? What are your values and how do you get along with people?
4. Can they afford you? They want to know what your minimum salary needs are, and what your maximum salary hopes are.

Now, the object of the interview is to find out the information that you need to know; and to help the employer find

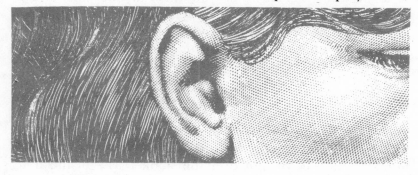

out the information that he or she needs to know, in order to make a competent decision about whether to hire you or not. Even if these questions are *never* put into words, during the interview.

HOW DO YOU ANSWER
THEIR QUESTIONS?

1. "WHY ARE YOU HERE?" *If* you did all your research, as described in the previous chapter, you'll know the answer. If you didn't, you won't. The essence of a good answer to this question is some variation on: "I have been interested in organizations which are _____, and yours particularly attracted me because _____."

2. "WHAT CAN YOU DO FOR ME?" *If* you did all your research, you will know that what the employer is essentially asking, here, is: "Will you help this organization to better do its work, and achieve its goals, and if so, in what way?" If you did your research, you will know what that company's work and goals are, what their problems and challenges are, and how you would be an asset toward the accomplishing of that work, the achieving of those goals, and the overcoming of those problems and challenges.

3. "WHAT KIND OF PERSON ARE YOU?" You will answer this question by *everything* you say during the interview, and everything you do during the interview. It is likely that *nothing* will escape the scrutiny of the person across the desk from you. And I mean: your haircut or hairdo; your manner of dress; your posture; your use of your hands; your body odor or perfume; your breath; your fingernails; the sound of your voice; the way in which you do or don't interrupt; the hesitant or assured manner in which you ask your questions or give your answers; your values as evidenced by the things which impress you or don't impress you; the carefulness with which you did or didn't research this company before you came in; the thoroughness with which you know your skills and strengths; your awareness of what you are willing to sell in order to get this job *and* what you aren't willing to sell in order to get this job; your enthusiasm for your work; and— that's just for openers. We can throw in whether or not you smoke (in a race between two equally qualified people, the non-smoker will win out over the smoker 94% of the time, according to a study done by a professor of business at Seattle University); whether, if at lunch, you order a drink or not; whether you show courtesy to receptionist, secretary, waiter or waitress, or not; and—like that. Everything is grist for the

mill, as the employer tries to divine "what kind of person is this?" What the employer, if he or she be an average employer, is looking for, are:

- any signs of dishonesty or lying;
- any signs of irresponsibility or tendency to goof off;
- any sign of arrogance or excessive aggressiveness;
- any sign of tardiness or failure to keep appointments and commitments on time;
- any sign of not following instructions or obeying rules;
- any sign of complaining or blaming things on others;
- any sign of laziness or lack of motivation;
- any sign of a lack of enthusiasm for this organization and what it is trying to do;
- any sign of instability, inappropriate response, and the like.

Since the employer will probably end up having to fire anyone with these signs, the employer would like to find these things out *now* rather than later.

Beyond these tangibles, there are the intangibles of *making a good impression*. Study after study has confirmed that if you are a male, you will make a better impression if:

- your hair or beard is short and neatly trimmed;
- you have freshly bathed, use a deodorant and mouth-wash, and have clean fingernails;
- you have freshly laundered clothes on, and a suit rather than a sports outfit, and sit without slouching;
- your breath does not dispense gallons of garlic, onion, stale tobacco, or strong drink, into the enclosed office air;
- your shoes are neatly polished, and your pants have a sharp crease;
- you are not wafting tons of after-shave cologne fifteen feet ahead of you.

And, if you are a female, you will make a better impression if:

- your hair is newly 'permed' or 'coiffed';
- you are freshly bathed, use a deodorant
  and mouthwash, and have clean or
  nicely manicured fingernails;
- you wear a bra, freshly cleaned clothes,
  a suit or sophisticated-looking dress,
  and sit without slouching;
- your breath does not dispense gallons
  of garlic, onion, stale tobacco, or strong
  drink, into the enclosed office air;
- you wear shoes rather than sandals;
- you are not wafting tons of perfume
  fifteen feet ahead of you.

Now please, dear reader, do not send me mail telling me how asinine you think some of these 'rules' are. I *know* that. I'm only reporting, here, that study after study reveals these things do affect whether or not you get hired. There are *of course* employers who care about none of these things, and will hire you if you can do the job. Most such jobs, however, are in back rooms, away from people, staring at little computer chips, or such like.

You *are* on trial, in a sense, during this interview. All of the above factors are a part of that trial.

Of course, what makes the job interview tolerable or even *fun,* is that *you* are studying *everything* about this employer, at the same time that they are studying everything about you. You are just as much in need of making up your mind about what kind of person *they* are, and whether or not you would like to work with them, as they are doing with you. Two people, both sizing each other up. Well, you know what that reminds you of. The dating game. The job interview is indeed every bit like 'the dating game.' *Both* of you have to like the other, before you can get on to the question of 'going steady.' Thus the employer is just as much 'on trial' during the job interview as you are. Realizing *that,* can take some of the stress away.

4. "HOW MUCH ARE YOU GOING TO COST ME?" Until they have said "We *want* you," *and* you have decided, "I want them," all discussion of salary tends to be inappropriate. You

may think to yourself, "Yes, but what if they have a fixed salary figure in mind, and it is way below what I could accept— shouldn't I find that out as early as possible, so that I can graciously excuse myself, and go elsewhere?" That's logical, except for one minor little point: if you're the first person they've interviewed, and they haven't yet had a chance to get to know you very well, they may assume you are 'average material' and so mention merely an average kind of salary. But if they have seen a lot of people, *and* have had a chance to get to know you over two or three interviews, say. And if they are *very* impressed with you by this time and by contrast, *obviously* they are now going to be willing to do whatever they can to get a hold of you. And if *that* takes more money than they were originally prepared to offer, they may push themselves to find it. This happens *very* often.

TIMING IS EVERYTHING *

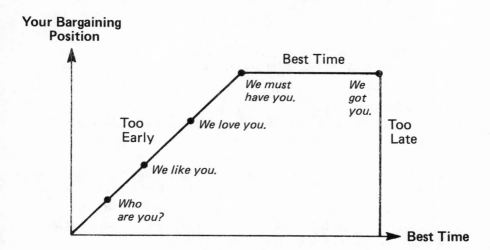

If you allow discussion of salary to take place prematurely, you will be told *the lowest* figure they had in mind, but it will be presented as though it were *the highest* they could go. They haven't seen you yet in all your splendor. They don't

---

know what they would be getting if they got you. Or, what they would be losing, if they let you go. Therefore, generally speaking until a firm offer has been made, postpone all discussion of salary.

TWENTY SECONDS TO
TWO MINUTES

Beyond the issue of *what* to say, is the issue of *how* to say it. Studies have revealed that generally speaking the people who get hired are those who speak half the time in the interview, and let the employer speak the other half of the time. Fifty-fifty. Furthermore, studies have revealed that generally, when it is your turn to speak, you should speak no shorter than twenty seconds and no longer than two minutes—at any one time. This is very useful information for you to know, in conducting a successful interview—as you certainly want to do.

Well, I said earlier that there are two fundamental characteristics to the Employment Interview. We come now to the

SECOND FUNDAMENTAL TRUTH
ABOUT THE EMPLOYMENT INTERVIEW:

Beneath the questions, each of you—Employer and Job-Hunter—has a number of anxieties and fears.

You know what yours are: that you will really like the place, really want to get hired there, and they will decide not to hire you.

What is rarely discussed is the fact that the Employer, sitting across the desk from you, has as many fears as you do.

Suppose you have come to see me, after being with an Employer in an interview, and you and I are having a friendly little discussion about this matter. You begin:

■ "INTERVIEWING FOR A JOB IS JUST THE PITS.
I'M SITTING THERE SWEATING TO BEAT THE BAND,
WHILE THE EMPLOYER IS THIS COOL CUSTOMER
WHO SEEMS TO BE ENJOYING MY DISCOMFORT."

Well, I reply, I think the Employer is just as fearful of the interview as you are.

■ "WHAT DO YOU MEAN?" YOU RETORT.
"I DON'T SEE ANY FEAR BEHIND THEIR QUESTIONS.
WHAT FEARS COULD AN EMPLOYER POSSIBLY HAVE?"

That's easy. They run the gamut. For openers, the Employer has the following ten major fears when You, the Job-Hunter, are face-to-face with him or her:

1. That You Won't Be Able to Do the Job: That You Lack the Necessary Skills or Experience

2. That If Hired, You Won't Put In a Full Working Day

3. That If Hired, You'll Be Frequently "Out Sick," or Otherwise Absent Whole Days

4. That If Hired, You'll Only Stay Around for a Few Weeks or at Most a Few Months

5. That It Will Take You Too Long to Master the Job, and Thus Too Long Before You're Profitable to That Organization

6. That You Won't Get Along with the Other Workers There, or That You Will Develop a Personality Conflict with the Boss Himself (or Herself)

7. That You Will Do Only the Minimum That You Can Get Away With, Rather Than the Maximum That You Are Capable Of

8. That You Will Always Have to Be Told What to Do Next, Rather Than Displaying Initiative; That You Will Always Be in a Responding Rather Than an Initiating Mode (and Mood)

9. That You Will Have a Work-Disrupting Character Flaw, and Turn Out to Be:

    Dishonest, OR   A Spreader of Dissention at Work, OR
    Lazy, OR   An Embezzler, OR
    A Gossip, OR   Totally Irresponsible, OR
    A Liar, OR   Incompetent

    In a word: No Fun to Have Around

10. (If This Is a Large Organization, and Your Would-Be Boss Is Not the Top Person) That You Will Bring Discredit upon Them, upon His or Her Department/Section/Division, etc. for Ever Hiring You in the First Place—Possibly Costing Your Would-Be Boss a Raise or Promotion

■ **"WELL, IF WHAT YOU'RE SAYING IS TRUE, THEN DURING THE JOB-INTERVIEW THE WOULD-BE EMPLOYER MAY BE AN ABSOLUTE BUNDLE OF FEARS."**

Yes, and it's not something he or she can really talk about. It's the job-hunter who is *supposed* to be afraid of the interview; *not* the employer. Moreover, employers don't usually talk with each other about this sort of thing. So, oftentimes an employer is facing the job-interview thinking that he or she is the only employer in the world with sweaty palms. They've never had a chance to check it out, and discover if other employers feel the same way.

■ **"THAT MUST MAKE FOR LONELINESS, AS AN EMPLOYER WITH SWEATY PALMS APPROACHES THE JOB-INTERVIEW PROCESS."**

Yes, he or she often feels extremely isolated and alone. That's why, in larger organizations, the hiring decision is often shared with a committee or a veritable army of his or her peers, within that organization. The rationale for this style of hiring might well be stated as: "Deliver me from my fears."

"AND MY LONELINESS."

Yes.

■ **"WELL, SURELY AN EMPLOYER CAN'T KEEP THEIR FEARS ENTIRELY HIDDEN. THEY MUST SURFACE DURING THE INTERVIEW, IN SOME FASHION."**

Absolutely. Fear is behind almost *every* question that an employer asks. Indeed, any job-hunter will be able to "field" the employer's questions, during the interview, if the job-hunter just keeps in mind that behind every question is some Fear.

■ **"CAN YOU GIVE ME SOME EXAMPLES?"**

Of course. But first let me say that the most important thing to keep in mind is that no Employer cares about your past. The only thing the employer can possibly care about is your future. Therefore, the more a question *appears* to be about your past, the more certain you may be that some Fear is behind it. And that Fear is about your future—i.e., what will you be like, *after* the employer decides to hire you, if they decide to hire you.

So, let's run down typical employer interview questions—see what they are, then what the fear behind those questions is, and perhaps some key phrases that can be used in answering the questions—so as to allay the Fear.

THE INTERVIEW QUESTION:
"Tell me about yourself."

• The Fear Behind the Question: The Employer is afraid they won't ask the right questions during the interview.

The Employer is afraid there's something in your background or in your attitude toward your work that will make you a Bad Employee.

• The Point You Try to Get Across to Answer Their Fear: You would make a good employee, and you have proved that by your past.

• Ideas or Phrases You Might Use: The briefest history in the world, of where you were born and raised, hobbies, interests, etc.

The briefest description of where you have worked or the kind of work you have done. ANY sentence or phrase which describes your past attitude toward your work in a positive way:

"Hard worker"
"Came in early, left late"
"Always did more than was expected of me"
Etc.

THE INTERVIEW QUESTION:
"What kind of work are you looking for?"

• The Fear Behind the Question: That it isn't the same kind of job the employer needs to fill—e.g., they are looking for a secretary, you are looking to be office manager; they are

looking for somebody who can work alone, you are looking
for a job where you would be rubbing shoulders with other
people.

• The Point You Try to Get Across to Answer Their Fear:
You have picked up many skills, which are transferable from
one field to another.

• Ideas or Phrases You Might Use: You are looking for work
where you can use your skills with People (specify what those
skills are—that you most enjoy).
AND/OR
You are looking for work where you can use your skills with
Data or Information (specify what those skills are—that you
most enjoy).
AND/OR
You are looking for work where you can use your skills with
Things/Machines/Tools/Plants etc. (specify what those skills
are—that you most enjoy).

P.S. If you are applying for a known vacancy, you can *first*
respond to this question by saying, "I'd be happy to answer
that, but first it seems to me it's more important for you to
tell me what kind of work this vacancy entails."

Once the employer has told you, *don't forget* to then answer
their question. But now you can couch your answer in terms
of the skills you genuinely have, which are *relevant* to the work
the employer has described.

THE INTERVIEW QUESTION:
"Have you ever done this kind of work before?"

• The Fear Behind the Question: The Employer is afraid
you can't do the work, that you don't possess the necessary
experience or skills.

• The Point You Try to Get Across, to Answer This Fear:
You have transferable skills.

• Ideas or Phrases You Might Use: The same ones as in the
last question. Plus:

"I pick up stuff very quickly."

"I have quickly mastered any job I have ever done."

"Every job is a whole new universe, but I make myself at
home very quickly."

THE INTERVIEW QUESTION:
"Why did you leave your last job?"
OR
"Why did your last job end?"
OR
"How did you get along with your former boss
and co-workers?"

• The Fear Behind the Question: The Employer is afraid that you don't get along with people. Especially Bosses.
• The Point You Try to Get Across, to Answer This Fear: That you do get along well with people, and your *attitude* toward your former boss(es) and co-workers proves it.
• Ideas or Phrases You Might Use:
  "My *job* was terminated" (if you were fired)
  "My boss *and I* both felt . . ."
  "I would be *happier* and *more effective* in a job where (here describe your strong points: e.g., I would be under less supervision and have more room to use my initiative and creativity)"

Say as many positive things as you can about your boss and co-workers (without telling lies).

THE INTERVIEW QUESTION:
"How much were you absent from work during
your last job?"

• The Fear Behind the Question: The Employer is afraid that you will be absent from work a lot, if they hire you.
• The Point You Try to Get Across, to Answer This Fear: You Will Not Be Absent from Work.
• Ideas or Phrases You Might Use: If you *were* absent quite a bit on a previous job, say why and stress that it is a *past* difficulty (if it is).

If you were *not* absent on your previous job, stress your good attendance record, and *the attitude* you have toward the importance of always being at work.

THE INTERVIEW QUESTION:
"How is your health?"

• The Fear Behind the Question: The Employer is afraid that you will miss work because of sickness.
• The Point You Try to Get Across, to Answer This Fear: You are a hard worker, and you have no health problem that keeps you from being at work daily.
OR
(If you do) you stress your attendance average in terms of how many days *per month* you have been absent at previous jobs, and you stress how *hard* you work on the days that you *are* there.
• Ideas or Phrases You Might Use: Your productivity, compared to other workers, at your previous jobs.

Your determination to *produce* more than other workers, if you get this job (or more than your predecessor did).

THE INTERVIEW QUESTION:
"Can you explain why you've been out of work so long?"
OR
"Can you tell me why there are these gaps in your work record or work history?" (Usually asked, after studying your resume)
OR
"How long have you been out of work?"

• The Fear Behind the Question: The Employer is afraid that you don't really like to work, and will quit the minute things aren't going "your way."
• The Point You Try to Get Across, to Answer This Fear: You like to work.
AND
You regard times when things aren't going well as Challenges.
• Ideas or Phrases You Might Use: You were working hard during the times when you weren't employed. Either: studying, doing volunteer work, sitting down to do lots of hard thinking about how you could most effectively use the talents you have been given, trying to get beyond merely "keeping busy" to finding some sense of mission for your life.

THE INTERVIEW QUESTION:

"Doesn't this work (or this job) represent a step down for you?"

OR

"Don't you think you would be underemployed if you took this job?"

OR

"I think this job is way beneath your talents and experience."

• The Fear Behind the Question: The employer is afraid that you *could* command more salary and more responsibility, that you are only taking *this* job as a stopgap measure, and that you will leave him (or her) as soon as something better turns up.

• The Point You Try to Get Across, to Answer This Fear: You will stick with this job just as long as you possibly can, so long as you *and the employer* agree this is where you should be.

• Ideas or Phrases You Might Use: "This job isn't a step down for me. It's a step *up*—from being on welfare."

"I like to work, and I give my best to every job I've ever done."

"Every employer is afraid the employee will leave too soon, and every employee is afraid the employer might fire him (or her). We have mutual fears. I'll do a crackerjack job here, and I'll stay as long as we both agree this is where I should be."

THE INTERVIEW QUESTION:

"Tell me, what is your greatest weakness?"

• The Fear Behind the Question: The Employer is afraid you have some work-flaw or character-flaw—and is hopeful you will confess to it, now.

• The Point You Try to Get Across, to Answer This Fear: You have limitations just like any other person but you work constantly to improve them and make yourself into a more effective worker.

• Ideas or Phrases You Might Use: Mention some weakness of yours that has a positive aspect to it. Stress the positive aspect, e.g., "I don't respond well to being over-supervised, because I have a great deal of initiative, and I like to use it—anticipating problems before they even arise."

Well, there are many other interview questions we could look at; but I think you get the idea.

"I'll tell you why I want this job. I thrive on challenges. I like being stretched to my full capacity. I like solving problems. Also, my car is about to be repossessed."

From all of the foregoing you will see: The essence of the Employment Interview is two fearful people talking to each other, each one trying to allay their own fears.

If it is a successful interview, the fears of each of you *will* get allayed, and you will both feel pretty good about each other. But they may not yet have said the job is yours—there may be more interviews in store for you, either with the same person, or with a larger committee. But for now, the first interview is over, and you are free to go home.

BACK HOME AFTER THE FIRST INTERVIEW AT THAT PLACE

That evening, you put your feet up, turn on the TV, and have a pleasant evening to yourself or with your loved one, right? Wrong. That evening *you work*. You've got to send them something in writing. At the very least, you are going to send them:

THE ABSOLUTELY CRUCIAL
THANK-YOU NOTE

Each evening, you MUST take time to sit down and write (pen or typewriter) a brief thank-you note to *each person that you saw that day*. That includes executives, secretaries, people who gave you helpful information, or anyone else who gave you a helping hand in any way. It should be regarded as basic to the simplest dictates of courtesy and kindness, that you write such notes. After all, you are presenting yourself as one who has skills at treating people as people. Prove it. *Your actions must be consistent with your words.*

This thank-you note serves several purposes. First of all, it helps them to remember you. Even if the interview did not go well, and you have lost all interest in working there, they (executive and secretary or receptionist) may still hear of *other* openings, that might be of interest to you. In the thank-you note, you can mention this, and ask them to keep you in mind.

If the interview went rather well, and you are hopeful of being invited back, then the thank-you letter can reiterate your interest in further talks. You can also correct any impression you left behind you. Add anything you forgot to tell them. Underline anything that you want to emphasize from among those things discussed.

The importance of sending a thank-you letter to *everyone* is one of the most essential steps in the entire job-hunt. *Yet it is the most overlooked step in the entire process.* We know of one woman who was told she was hired because she was the *only* interviewee, out of thirty-nine, who sent a thank-you letter after the interview.

That's right, the thank-you letter may actually get you the job. *You cannot afford to think of this as simply an optional exercise. It is critical to your getting hired.*

If you are still interested in that place, with the thank-you letter you may want to include two other documents. The first, and preferred piece of paper, would be a written proposal from you as to what it is you would like to be able to do for that organization, what it is you hope you could accomplish for them. As evidence, you will want to cite *relevant* past accomplishments of yours, taking care *in each case* to cite:

a) what the problem was
b) what you did to solve it

c) what the results were, of your actions

The virtue of such a written proposal is that it looks forward rather than backward, as the resume does. And it puts into writing the essence of the hiring interview: you are not asking them merely to do something for you. More importantly, you are offering to do something for them.

The second piece of paper to be included with your thank-you letter, if you are still interested in that place, is a resume —*carefully* tailored to that particular place and that particular job. Composed, and neatly typed, that very evening if necessary. Don't mention any skill, any experience, or any personal data that isn't *absolutely relevant* to that particular job.

If you have included a proposal, the resume is really unnecessary. If you haven't included a written proposal, then some kind of summary of your background and history *should* be included, to remind them of who you were in that parade of people that they interviewed.

MEANWHILE, BACK AT THE RANCH

While you are sitting there, writing out your thank-you letter and proposal, the employer you saw that day is also sitting at home, reflecting on the interview. What's going on in his or her head, do you suppose? Well, you know. They are sifting through all the candidates they saw, trying to decide who stands out, so far. *Usually,* they've seen a number of candidates who—in terms of skills—are equally qualified. We will assume you are among those. But the problem the employer faces is *trying to decide who stands out, on other grounds.* How do you think they decide that? On what grounds do they give the nod to one person over seventeen others, equally qualified? The answer will vary from employer to employer, but most often, according to a survey we did, this is how the employer chooses you over other candidates, equally qualified:

1) They ask themselves, does this prospective employee *fit in* with the people who are already here? Does this person share compatible perspectives, exhibit integrity, manifest a desire to work as part of a team, and have similar values and sense of humor?

2) They ask themselves, does this prospective employee give the feeling of great *enthusiasm for this particular job?* How much does he or she seem to *want* it?

3) They ask themselves, does this prospective employee have an *appearance* that I like? This is an intangible thing, and I can't define it, but it has to do with my intuition about the person, their face, the way they dress, and how reliable or stable I feel them to be, beneath all the externals. I look for a quiet self-confidence.

4) They ask themselves, does this prospective employee give me the feeling that he or she would give that *extra boost of energy* to their work that I like to see, rather than just trying "to get by." I think this is dependent on how much the prospective employee truly has their own individual goals, toward which they are striving.

5) Finally, they ask themselves, does this prospective employee seem to have a genuine *enthusiasm for our organization* and what it is trying to do? Does he or she seem to like its goals, appreciate its style, and want to work for its success?

If you get chosen, it will probably be because you *stood out* from the other applicants, in these five areas. Therefore, in your thank-you note, and in your written proposal, *anything* you can point to that demonstrates you stand out in these arenas, will be very much in your favor: particularly, your enthusiasm for that place and for that job.

WHEN YOU GET INVITED BACK

Assuming things are going favorably, you will be invited back for another interview, or interviews. If you still like them, and they increasingly like you, an offer will be made. *That's*

the time to deal with the fourth question that we saw earlier
has got to be on the employer's mind:

"How much are you going to cost me?" As I said before,
if this matter gets raised before you have each decided you
want to work together, turn the question gently aside. If the
employer says, "How much salary are you looking for?" early
on in the game, you can respond with gentleness and grace:
"I think that's a fair question once we have both decided that
this is where I should be working. First, however, there are
other areas we need to explore."

But if you have explored those areas, and are agreeing
'to go steady,' *then* the subject of "how much are you going to
cost me?" is not only legitimately raised, it is crucial that it be
raised. "The laborer is worthy of his (or her) hire," says the
Scriptures. Which, roughly translated, means: "You are entitled to get what you are worth, and not a penny less."

Unhappily, you and the employer are likely at this point
to be at odds with each other. Your would-be employer is
interested in saving money as much as possible—therefore, in
getting you for as little as possible.

There are exceptions, to be sure. Times when the employer
offers you so much more than you were expecting, that your
jaw drops open. This happens, but my advice would be not
to count on it.

"Let's talk salary. How does 'astronomical' sound to you?"

Count rather on the fact that you will need to do some negotiation. Salary negotiation it is technically called, as you probably know. And few of us are born knowing how to go about this. We need some instruction in the technique. So, here is some help:

SALARY NEGOTIATION

A woman was once describing her very first job to me. It was at a soda fountain. I asked her what her biggest surprise at that job was. "My first paycheck," she said. "I know it sounds incredible, but I was so green at all this, that during the whole interview for the job it never occurred to me to ask what my salary would be. I just took it for granted that it would be a fair and just salary, for the work that I would be doing. Did I ever get a shock, when my first paycheck came! It was so small, I could hardly believe it. Did I ever learn a lesson from that!" Yes, and so may we all.

AT ITS SIMPLEST LEVEL

To speak of salary negotiation is to speak of a matter which can be conducted on several levels. The simplest kind—as the above story reminds us—involves remembering to ask during the job-hiring interview what the salary will be. And then stating whether, for you, that amount is satisfactory or not. *That* much negotiation, everyone who is hunting for a job must be prepared to do.

It is well to recognize that you are at a disadvantage if salary negotiation is approached on this simplest level, however. A figure may be named, and if you have not done any research, you may be totally unprepared to say whether or not this is a fair salary for that particular job. You just don't know.

AT ITS NEXT HIGHEST LEVEL

Hence, you may prefer to do a little research ahead of time. The books which will prove useful to you are listed in section 24 of Appendix A, on page 238. Try to find these, first of all, in your local library.

• If it's a non-supervisory job you are interested in, you can find out a 'ballpark figure" for that industry, by having your library unearth for you the latest monthly issue of the U.S. Department of Labor's *Employment and Earnings.*

If it's a manager's or supervisory job you are interested in, you will find many of the directories listed in our previous chapter will unearth the information you want. For those graduating from college, some of this information is to be found in the "Salary Surveys" put out by the College Placement Council, from Bethlehem, Pennsylvania. See your library, or the career counseling/placement office of a nearby college.

• *The Occupational Outlook Handbook* will also give you ballpark figures for a selected list of jobs. The job you are interested in *may* be included.

In all dealings with this kind of information, you must keep in mind that there are often *serious* variations in salary from region to region.

Such regional differences in salary reflect, of course, a variety of factors, such as differences in cost of living, differences in supply and demand, etc.

If your librarian simply cannot find or help you find the salary information that you want, do remember that almost every occupation has its own association or professional group, whose business it is to keep tabs on what is happening salary-wise within that occupation or field. To learn the association or professional group for the field or occupation you are interested in, consult the *Encyclopedia of Associations, Vol. 1,* at your library.

WHAT DO THEY PAY?

Here are average annual salaries for selected jobs, paid in 1984 for persons in the following occupations. Unless otherwise specified, the figure is the national average for all workers.

Less than $20,000

Senior key entry operator $12,500
Bank assistant branch manager $18,000
Waiter/Waitress (Las Vegas)
    $14,000-$17,000
Armed security guard $17,297
File clerk $10,712
College bookstore director $19,913
Police "911 Line" operator, NY $13,180
Radio news reporter $13,000
Licensed practical nurse (Washington
    State) $12,360
Manufacturing production worker $18,886

Secretary (high school grad) $16,000
Turkey cleaner (East) $11,270
Messenger $11,230
Typist $13,041
Roman Catholic nun (East) $6,000 + housing
Minor pro league basketball player $15,000
Accounting clerk $16,077
Correctional officer (Washington State)
    $17,232
Typing pool supervisor (Minnesota) $16,476
Grocery produce clerk $10,100

$20,000 to $29,000

Airline flight attendant $27,000
Bank cashier $28,000-$38,000
Federal government (all jobs) $25,354
Fire fighter $24,000
Data processing specialist $22,500
Cook (Las Vegas) $20,000-$25,000
Word processing manager $22,400
Buyer, 2-4 yrs. exp. $27,600
Association exhibits manager $28,200
Accountant, 5-8 yrs. exp. $26,500
College assistant professor $22,000
Auditor $29,005

Technical recruiter $24,300-$35,900
Registered nurse (Minnesota) $20,672
Bank branch manager $27,500
Postal service worker $23,058
Secretary (Bachelor's degree) $20,000
Publications editor, 5+ yrs. exp. $29,400
Radio news director $24,000
Painter (Minnesota) $20,484
Recruiter, managerial employees $26,460
State & local government—all employees
    $21,000
Vocational ed. teacher (Minnesota) $27,120

$30,000 to $49,999

Agricultural engineer $38,740
Electrical engineer $42,290
Captain, US Army $30,400
College professor $33,000
Personnel director $47,745
Senior computer systems analyst $33,000
Bank real estate lending officer $41,200
Steel mill production worker $45,023
Market research manager $44,664

Nuclear engineer $47,640
State geological survey director $43,900
Plant manager $41,900
Recruitment manager $37,000-$42,400
Sanitary engineer $39,000
TV news director $31,200
EDP operations manager $36,500
Lawyer $49,022

$50,000 and over

Public accounting firm partner $64,500
Petroleum engineer $51,000
Judge (Cleveland) $57,000
Airline captain $95,000
Dean, engineering college $55,824
Federal civil service (top salary) $68,700
Vice-president, marketing $63,000
Investment banker $200,000

Association, top exec. (Washington) $98,500
Physician (East) $97,700
College president, large school $70,000
    plus $37,000 benefits
Major league baseball player $289,194
US Cabinet officer $86,200
Chief justice, US Supreme Court $104,700

Sources: Association salary studies, *National Business Employment Weekly,* Scientific Manpower Commission, Abbott Langer and Associates, and many others. Minichart prepared by the *Career Opportunities News,* Garrett Park Pres, Garrett Park, Maryland 20896. Used by permission.

MORE SOPHISTICATED YET

Some job-hunters may want to get beyond these "ballpark figures" into more detailed salary negotiation. You may want to walk in on an interview knowing exactly what That Place pays for a job. Why? Well, for one thing, it may be too low for you—and thus you are saved the necessity of wasting your precious time on that particular place. Secondly, and more importantly, many places have—as John Crystal has so insistently pointed out—a *range* in mind. And if you know what that range is, you can negotiate for a salary that is nearer the *top* of the range, than the *bottom*.

By way of example, let's assume you did all the homework outlined in the previous two chapters. You have done your research, going out and knocking on doors, as well as visiting libraries. And you have gotten your search down to three or five places that really interest you. You know in general what sort of position you are aiming at, in those particular places— and you are ready to go visit them in The Interview for Hiring —*as soon as you know what the salary range is for the position that interests you* (whether that position already exists, or is one you are going to ask them to create). How do you find out what the salary is, or should be, by way of range?

It's relatively easy to define. The rule of thumb is that you will, generally speaking, be paid more than the person who is below you on the organizational chart, and less than the person who is above you. There are—needless to say—exceptions to this rule: people who don't quite fit in the organizational chart, such as researchers financed by a grant, or consultants. But In General, the Rule of Thumb is true.

This makes the matter of salary *research* which precedes salary negotiation relatively (I said "relatively") simple. If through your own information search you can discover who is or would be above you on the organizational chart, and who is or would be below you, and what they are paid, you would know what your salary range is, or would be.

a) If the person above you makes $27,000, and the person who would be below you makes $22,000, your range will be something like $23,000 to $26,000.

b) If the person above you makes $13,500, and the person who would be below you makes $10,000, then your range will be something like $10,500 to $12,500.

c) If the person above you makes $7,800, and the person who would be below you makes $6,240, your range would be $6,400 to $7,600.

That's not so hard to figure out, is it? Not as hard as you thought it was going to be, at any rate!

Now, how do you find out what those who would be above and below you, make? Well, first—to emphasize the obvious—you have to find out the *names* of those who would be above or below you. If it is a small organization you are going after—one with twenty or less employees—finding this information out will be duck soup. Since two-thirds of all new jobs are created by companies of that size, you would be *wise beyond your years* to be looking at such sized organizations, anyway.

But if you still like "the Big Guys," the large corporations with row upon row of cubicles, and floor after floor of offices, laboratories, or classrooms, then you need to resort with mercy and pleading to our two familiar standbys:

your local reference librarian

every contact you have (family, friend, relative, business or church acquaintance) who might know the company, and therefore, the information you seek.

You will be surprised at how much of this information *is* in the annual report, or in books available at your library. When those sources produce all they can for you, and you are still short of what you want to know, go to your contacts. You are looking for Someone Who Knows Someone who either is working, or has worked, at that particular place or organization that interests you.

If you absolutely run into a blank wall on that particular organization (everyone who works there is pledged to secrecy, and they have shipped all their ex-employees to Siberia), then seek out information on their nearest *competitor* in the same geographic area (e.g., if Bank of America is inscrutable, try Wells Fargo as your research base; or vice-versa).

You will be surprised at how often perseverance and leg-work pay off, in this. And if your enthusiasm flags along the way, just picture yourself sitting in the interview for hiring, and now you're at the end of the interview. The prospective employer likes you, you like them, and they say: "How much salary were you expecting?" Because you have done your homework, and you know the range, you can name a figure

near or at the *top* of the *range*—based on your anticipated performance in that job: i.e., "Superior."

But suppose you *didn't* do your research. Then you're Shadow-Boxing in the Dark—as they say. If you name a figure way too high, you're out of the running—and you can't backtrack, in most cases. ("Sorry, we'd like to hire you, but we just can't afford you.") If you name a figure way too low, you're also out of the running. ("Sorry, but we were hoping for someone a little more, ah, professional.") And if you're in the right range, but at the bottom of it, you've just gotten the job—*but needlessly lost as much as $2,000 a year that could have been yours.*

So, salary research/salary negotiation—no matter how much time it takes—pays off handsomely. Let's say it takes you a week to ten days to run down this sort of information on the three or four organizations that interest you. And let us say that because you've done this research, when you finally go in for the hiring interview you are able to ask for and obtain a salary that is $2,000 higher in range, than you would otherwise have known enough to ask for. In just three years, you'll have earned $6,000 extra, because of that research. Not bad pay, for ten days' work!

AT ITS MOST SOPHISTICATED LEVEL

Job-hunters with incredibly developed bargaining needs, always ask how salary negotiation is conducted at the most sophisticated level. It is my personal conviction that Most Job-Hunters will not operate at this level, and therefore do not need this sort of information. But in case you do, or in case you are simply dying out of curiosity, it is completely described in *Where Do I Go From Here With My Life?* pages 140-142. As honed to a fine point by John Crystal, the most sophisticated salary negotiation goes like this:

You do all the steps described previously, so that you discover what the employer's range would likely be. Let us say it turns out that the range is one that varies two thousand dollars. You then "invent" a new range, for yourself, that "hooks" on the old one, in the following fashion:

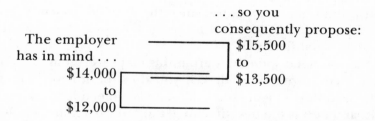

The employer has in mind . . .
$14,000
to
$12,000

. . . so you consequently propose:
$15,500
to
$13,500

And when the employer says, "What kind of a salary did you have in mind?" you respond, "I believe my productivity is such that it would justify a salary in the range of $13,500 to $15,500." This keeps you, at a minimum, near the top of their range; and, at a maximum, challenges them to go beyond the top that they had in mind, either immediately—or in terms of future raises. (Don't be afraid to ask "When?")

FRINGES

In your salary negotiation, do not forget to pay attention to so-called "fringe benefits." Such 'fringes' as life insurance, health benefits or plans, vacation or holiday plans, and retirement programs add up to 25% of many manufacturing workers' salary. E.g., if an employee receives $800 salary per month, the fringe benefits are worth another $200 per month. So, if the employee who is beneath you on the organizational chart gets $700 plus benefits, and the employee who is above you gets $1,100 plus benefits, while you are offered $800 and no benefits, you are being bought rather cheaply. Ask for similar benefits to those above and below you. OR, if no benefits are possible, ask for a higher salary—say, $1,000, in this case.

FINALLY, THE MATTER OF A RAISE AND OR PROMOTION

If during your salary negotiations you deal only with your initial position and salary, you will have been very short-sighted. Your initial "good salary" will annually decline in value, as inflation takes its toll. In 75 out of the last 100 years, the cost of living increased.

The urgency of protecting your initial salary against erosion, is further compounded for women by the fact that so many of you *start out* at too low a salary. You need raises and promotions even more, since the average woman would need pay raises of 70% just to bring her up to the level of a similarly qualified man.

So, you need something from this employer: some kind of assurance or guarantee that, if you do superior work, there will be raises and on some kind of a timetable. You need this, and *now* is the best time to get it. Your bargaining power inevitably diminishes once they've 'got you.'

Therefore, this question should be a part of your salary negotiation without fail: "If I accomplish this job to your satisfaction, as I fully expect to—and more—when could I expect to have my salary raised, and to what degree? Would there be a promotion in this job, and if so, on what kind of timetable?" If you have certain desires in this area, you may or may not wish to mention them at this point. But none of this discussion, as I have repeatedly said, should take place until they have made you a firm offer and said in no uncertain terms: "We want you."

Once this part of the salary negotiation is concluded, to your satisfaction, do ask to have it included in any letter of agreement or employment contract that they may be sending you. It may be you cannot get it in writing, but *do try!* The Road to Hell is paved with Promises that went unwritten. Too many executives conveniently "forget" what they told you.

Too many executives leave the company for another position and place. And their successor or the one over you all may disown any unwritten promises: "I don't know what caused them to say that to you, but they clearly exceeded their authority, and of course we can't be held to that."

Raises and promotions are something you may have to continually justify, not just during the hiring interview, but throughout your time of work there. You will be amazed sometimes at how little attention your superiors pay to your noteworthy accomplishments. Noteworthy they may be, but no one is taking notes. They're too absorbed with their own problems. Accordingly, career experts such as Bernard Haldane have suggested that you should keep a weekly diary of your accomplishments, once you are on the job. Take time each Sunday to chronicle what you accomplished that past week, or helped others to accomplish, if you were part of a team effort. That way, when the yearly anniversary of your being hired comes around, you can read through the diary, make up a one-page summary of its contents, and take that summary in with you when you discuss why you deserve a raise.

SUMMARY

If you have done the exercises in the last two chapters, you will have mastered the systematic techniques job-hunters use.

There may be others out there who could have done the job better than you. But it is true today, and it will ever be true:

> The person who gets hired is not necessarily
> the one who can do that job best; but, the one
> *who knows the most about how to get hired.*

CHECKLIST WHEN THINGS
AREN'T GOING WELL

1. Are you devoting at least six hours a day, five days a week to your job-hunt?

    IF NOT, *THAT* IS YOUR DIFFICULTY. GO DO IT.

2. If you're having trouble in getting going, are you recruiting some other job-hunters to meet with you regularly, in a group?

    IF NOT, *THAT* IS YOUR DIFFICULTY. GO DO IT.

3. Are you clear exactly what your skills are?

    IF NOT, *THAT* IS YOUR DIFFICULTY. GO DO IT.

4. Have you put your skills in their order of priority for you?
   IF NOT, *THAT* IS YOUR DIFFICULTY. GO DO IT.

5. Have you got your skills described with more than one word—e.g., not just "organizing" but, say, "organizing data into meaningful groups" or "organizing people into motivated small groups"?
   IF NOT, *THAT* IS YOUR DIFFICULTY. GO DO IT.

6. Have you decided just exactly where it is you want to use your skills, in terms of factors?
   IF NOT, *THAT* IS YOUR DIFFICULTY. GO DO IT.

7. Have you gone out and done intensive research, devoting at least two or three hours a day to it, for twenty days?
   IF NOT, *THAT* IS YOUR DIFFICULTY. GO DO IT.

8. Are you looking for exceptions, rather than the rule (e.g., most employers may be prejudiced against someone over forty, but are you looking for those who *aren't*)?
   IF NOT, *THAT* IS YOUR DIFFICULTY. GO DO IT.

9. If you're getting in to be interviewed for hire, after finishing your research, and getting turned down, are you going back to ask them for helpful feedback as to how you could improve the way in which you are presenting yourself?
   IF NOT, *THAT* IS YOUR DIFFICULTY. GO DO IT.

10. Are you really determined to find that job that fits you, no matter what, rather than just giving this an idle push, so you can say, Well, I knew it wouldn't work?
    IF NOT, *THAT* IS YOUR DIFFICULTY. GO DO IT.

POSTSCRIPT—
DOES THIS CREATIVE METHOD OF
THE JOB-HUNT ALWAYS WORK?

Ah, dear reader, how I wish I could assure you that it does. It would be nice if there were magic in our life. The desire to see Merlin, and unicorns, and trees that talk, lives in the child in us all.

But there is no magic in the job-hunt. There is no formula which, if you follow it scrupulously, will lead irresistibly to your finding a job. Or *the* job.

The picture of the job-hunt remains as we saw it earlier:

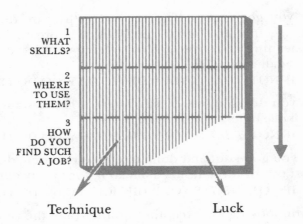

Technique   Luck

When you are down in this "How" part of the process, technique—such as we have described in this chapter—is terribly important. But so is *luck*. The best technique on your part will not get you a job, if luck is not also on your side. By luck, I mean that accidental meeting with *just* the right person, to open a door for you that leads to a job.

The 'numbers game' is almost *all* luck. What this alternative method of the job-hunt does, is to try to reduce the importance of luck. But it can never eliminate its place in the job-hunt, entirely.

Follow every instruction in this book *precisely*, do every exercise *slavishly*, follow every prescription *religiously*, you still may not find the job you are looking for. Or at least not right away. Over and above everything else, *luck* must be on your side if you are to find a job.

But, we know several things about luck. We know that:

(1) *Luck favors the prepared mind.* If you've done all the homework on yourself, diligently identified your favorite skills, and *in order,* and if you've gotten a pretty complete picture of the kind of job you are looking for, *you will be more sensitive and alert to luck, when it crosses your path.*

(2) *Luck favors the person who is working the hardest at the job-hunt.* In a word, the person who is devoting the most hours

to getting out there and pounding the pavement, doing their research, making contacts. Luck favors the person who is putting in thirty-four hours a week on their job-hunt much more than it favors the person who is putting in five hours a week.

(3) *Luck favors the person who has told the most people clearly and precisely what he or she is looking for.* The more ears and eyes you have out there, looking on your behalf for the kind of job you want, the more likely that you will 'get lucky.' Forty eyes and ears are 'luckier' than two. Eighty, a hundred and twenty, are 'luckier' still. But before you get 'this lucky,' you *must* have done your homework so carefully that you can *tell* those other eyes and ears just exactly what it is you want. Luck does *not* favor the vague.

(4) *Luck favors the person who has alternatives up his or her sleeve,* and doesn't just *bull-headedly* persist in following one method, or going after one place, or one kind of job.

(5) *Luck favors the person who WANTS WITH ALL THEIR HEART to find that job.* The ambivalent job-hunter, who is looking half-heartedly, for a job that inspires no enthusiasm in them, is rarely so 'lucky.'

(6) *Luck favors the person who is going after their dream— the thing they really want to do the most in this world.* When you

want something so much that it brings tears to your eyes at the thought of getting it, you will always be 'luckier' than the person who is *settling* for 'what's realistic.'

(7) *Luck favors the person who is trying hard to be 'a special kind of person' in this world, treating others with grace and dignity*

and courtesy and kindness. The person who runs roughshod over others in their race to 'get ahead,' usually is not so 'lucky.' During the job-hunt you need 'favors' from others. If you treated them cavalierly in another day and age, now is their time to say, "Sure, I'll help you out," and then do nothing. Getting even is more popular than forgiveness, when there is a score to be settled.

So, if you would have 'luck' on your side during this phase of the job-hunt, *do* take seriously the above *ways of improving your luck.*

I am glad to have been able to hold your hand through this process. I wish you a successful job-hunt. I wish you perseverance in the hard work and time that a successful job-hunt requires. I wish you good luck.

WHAT IS SUCCESS?

To laugh often and much;

To win the respect of intelligent people
and the affection of children;

To earn the appreciation of honest critics and
endure the betrayal of false friends;

To appreciate beauty;

To find the best in others;

To leave the world a bit better, whether by
a healthy child, a garden
patch or a redeemed social condition;

To know even one life has breathed
easier because you have lived;

This is to have succeeded.

—Ralph Waldo Emerson

My son, be admonished:
of making many books there is no end;
and much study is a weariness of the flesh.

Ecclesiastes

Appendix A

Special Problems and Interests
For Further Exploration:

Books
And Other Resources

BOOKS

Every book has a different voice. That's fortunate. No one book (least of all this one) can reach every reader. If you find *Parachute* didn't give you what you needed or wanted, here are some other books that may succeed for you. Different voices.

It may also be that while *Parachute* helped you, there are still some areas where you need or want more light shed. These books should help. Different lights.

HIGHLY RECOMMENDED

Lathrop, Richard, *Who's Hiring Who?* Ten Speed Press, Box 7123, Berkeley, CA 94707. 1977. Simply excellent resource. Used more often by our readers than any other book (besides *Parachute*).

Holland, John L., *Making Vocational Choices. A Theory of Vocational Personalities and Work Environments*, 2nd ed., Prentice-Hall, Inc., Englewood Cliffs, NJ 07632. 1985. This book continues to be one of the most useful supplementary books for all of our readers. It is mandatory reading for anyone who is thinking of becoming a career counselor. It contains the immensely useful *Self-Directed Search*, an instrument for figuring out what occupations you might *start* your personal research with. Once you have found your "Holland code" I would recommend however that you not use the *Occupations Finder* there, which is a very limited list of possible occupations. Instead, get your hands on (from the library or from the publisher, directly): Gottfredson, Gary D., and Holland, John L., and Ogawa, Deborah Kimiki, *Dictionary of Holland Occupational Codes: A Comprehensive Cross-Index of Holland's RIASEC Codes with 12,000 DOT Occupations*. Consulting Psychologists Press, Inc., 577 College Avenue, Palo Alto, CA 94306. 1982. 520 pp. This invaluable book essentially does two things. 1) When you know your "Holland code", it then gives you a *comprehensive* list of occupations which may be "possibles" for you. You thus gain a better idea of where to start your research. The list is *much* broader and more comprehensive than that found in the little *Occupations Finder* at the back of *Making Vocational Choices*. 2) It gives you the DOT number for each occupation (the code number of that occupation, as found in the Dictionary of Occupational Titles); thus enabling you to go look up more comprehensive information about each possible occupation, for you, before or as you begin your own personal research. Another book serving essentially the same function is:

Holland, John L., Ph.D., *The Alphabetized Occupations Finder.* For use with the Self-Directed Search. Psychological Assessment Resources, Inc., Box 998, Odessa, FL 33556. 1-800-331-TEST. In Florida 1-813-968-3003. 1986.

Crystal, John, and Bolles, Richard N., *Where Do I Go From Here With My Life? The Crystal Life Planning Manual.* 1974. A more detailed step-by-step explanation of the process described in chapters 5-7 of *Parachute*. From Ten Speed Press, Box 7123, Berkeley, CA 94707.

Wallach, Ellen J., and Arnold, Peter, *The Job Search Companion: The Organizer for Job Seekers*. The Harvard Common Press, 535 Albany Street, Boston, MA 02118. 1984. Primarily a book of very useful "forms" for keeping track of your job search. Intended as a supplement to other job-hunting books. If I myself were going job hunting tomorrow, I would definitely use the forms in this book to help organize my job hunt.

Jackson, Tom, *Guerrilla Tactics in the Job Market* (revised). Bantam Books, 666 Fifth Ave., New York, NY 10103. 1980. A popular and useful book.

Figler, Howard E., *The Complete Job Search Handbook: Presenting the Skills You Need to Get Any Job, And Have A Good Time Doing It.* Holt, Rinehart and Winston, 383 Madison Ave., New York, NY 10017. 1979. Tries to identify twenty skills the job-hunter needs in order to pull off a job hunt *successfully.*

Germann, Richard, and Arnold, Peter, *Bernard Haldane Associates' Job and Career Building.* Ten Speed Press, Box 7123, Berkeley, CA 94707. 1981, 1980. A detailed description of how to find a job, once you know what it is you want to do.

Miller, Arthur F., and Mattson, Ralph T., *The Truth About You: Discover What You Should Be Doing with Your Life.* People Management Incorporated, 10 Station Street, Simsbury, CT 06070. 1977. The former publisher, Fleming H. Revell Co., lists this book as out of print, but it is still available from the authors, at the address listed above. A first class book, very helpful. I like it a lot.

Haldane, Bernard, *How to Make a Habit of Success.* Acropolis Books, Ltd., 2400 17th St. NW, Washington, DC 20009. One of the pioneer books in this field, first published in 1960.

Haldane, Bernard, and Jean, and Martin, Lowell, *Job Power: The Young People's Job Finding Guide.* Acropolis Books Ltd., 2400 17th St. NW, Washington, DC 20009. 1980. Undoubtedly the best book available for high school students.

Campbell, David P., *If You Don't Know Where You're Going, You'll Probably End Up Somewhere Else.* Argus Communications, Niles, IL. 1974. Useful for those who need to be convinced of the need for career planning.

Edlund, Sidney and Mary, *Pick Your Job and Land It.* Sandollar Press, Santa Barbara, CA 93101. 1938. A classic among job-hunting books, still (mercifully) available.

If you dislike books, but like to listen to audio-cassettes, you may want to know that an overview (nothing more) of *Parachute* is available on cassette:

Bolles, Richard N., *How to Choose and Change Careers,* #20247. Psychology Today Cassettes, Box 278, Pratt Station, Brooklyn, NY 11205.

ADDITIONAL RESEARCH

Some of you will find that *Parachute* gives you everything you need to successfully conduct your job-hunt. Others of you, however, may feel the need for some additional comments, help, or research, in particular areas. The areas most often mentioned by our readers, over the past ten years, have been:
1. If you want Alternative Patterns of Work
2. If you want Volunteer Opportunities or Internships
3. If you want Self-employment or Part-time Work or Work at Home
4. If you want Work Dealing with Social Change
5. If you want to Make Your Living by Writing and Getting Published
6. If you want to Get Work with Arts and Crafts
7. If you want to Get a Government Job
8. If you want Overseas Work
9. If you want help with the Special Problems of Women
10. If you want help with the Special Problems of Minorities
11. Help with the Special Problems of Handicapped Job-Hunters
12. Help with the Special Problems of Ex-Offenders
13. Help with the Special Problems of Executives and the Business World
14. Help with the Special Problems of Couples
15. Help with the Special Problems of Clergy and Religious

16. How to Hang On to Your Present Job
17. Help with Being Fired, Riffed, or Laid Off
18. Help with Mid-Life, Second Careers or Retirement
19. Help with Going Back to School or Getting an External Degree
20. Help with the Special Problems of College Students
21. Help with the Special Problems of High School Students
22. Help with Getting a Job in Education
23. Help with Analysis of Skills
24. Help with Interviewing, Salary Negotiation, Resumes
25. Help with Job-Hunting in General, Places to Live
26. If you are a Career Counselor, or Want to Be
27. Perspectives on the World of Work Today
28. Perspectives on Creativity and the Brain

Accordingly, these are the sub-headings in the remainder of this Appendix. For the past ten years, I have tried to make this the most comprehensive career counseling bibliography to be found in any book I know of. Unhappily, this noble pursuit has run into two major obstacles:

1) There has been an explosion of books in this field. When *Parachute* was first published (1970), I had no difficulty whatsover keeping up with the other books in the field. A good bookstore would have only about seven titles, at that time; a good library, only twenty, at best. Now, there are so many titles *no one* can keep track. Career counseling books, in a large bookstore, have—until recently—occupied 40 feet of shelf space. (Now, a decline in their number appears to be going on. But still, the number of such books is LARGE.)

2) Most of these books have *a very short* "shelf life." Even though we rush the newest edition of *Parachute* into print, half of the books on this list have already disappeared (read: out of print), forever. Indeed, 90% of *all* books disappear from bookstores in less than 11 months. And, if the book is a paperback, the "shelf life" may be much shorter. One expert claims that in computerized bookstores, the shelf life of a paperback that doesn't start to sell is about two weeks. It is not surprising therefore that I have been receiving a great many letters from readers trying to use this bibliography, who can't find *many* of the books listed herein. There is no point to a bibliography that is little more than a tombstone for the books that *used* to be.

Accordingly, from now on I am greatly restricting this bibliography, to:

1) Those books which have become classics, and are therefore available in most decent libraries. If you want any of these, *please* check them out at your local library. That's where many books go, after they're no longer in any bookstore.

2) Those books which are newly in the bookstores, and therefore deserve a hearing. A listing of a book in this section is *not* a recommendation of it. It is merely a listing of the kind of books that are available.

3) Books which are self-published, and not in any bookstore. *Parachute* is one of the few national "bulletin boards" where such books can find their audience.

If you have a particular interest, and you don't find here any book that helps, there are two alternative routes still open to you: one is your local bookstores—go there, browse, and see what they have that is even newer than those listed in this bibliography. The other is your friendly local reference librarian. If your library has such a person, he or she can often be worth their weight in gold to you. Tell them your problem or interest, and see what they can dig up. They often know of hidden treasures, buried in books, articles and clippings, which will be an answer to your prayers.

1. IF YOU WANT ALTERNATIVE PATTERNS OF WORK

People are discovering there are all kinds of alternatives to the traditional nine to five, Monday through Friday job. Job-sharing with another worker, flex-time, where you decide which hours of the day you want to work, the four-day work week, holding down three to five small jobs rather than one full-time job, working long and hard two or three days a week, then having the other days to yourself, etc. If such alternatives appeal to you, do your informational interviewing with people who have already gone that route, first; and then with smaller employers, who are often more open than are larger employers, to new patterns of work.

Lee, Patricia, *The Complete Guide to Job Sharing*. Walker and Co., 720 Fifth Ave., New York, NY 10019. 1983.

Olmstead, Barney, and Smith, Suzanne, *The Job Sharing Handbook*. Ten Speed Press, Box 7123, Berkeley, CA 94707. 1983. How to share a full-time job with another person, if you don't want to work full-time.

Mayall, Donald and Nelson, Kristin, *The Temporary Help Supply Service and the Temporary Labor Market*, Olympus Publishing Co., Box 9362, Salt Lake City, UT 84109. 1982.

Work Times Newsletter, published by New Ways to Work, 149 Ninth St., San Francisco, CA 94103. An international information exchange on alternative work time.

Levinson, Jay Conrad, *Earning Money Without a Job: The Economics of Freedom*. Holt, Rinehart, and Winston, 521 Fifth Ave., New York, NY 10175. 1979. The first part of this book is the best, as Jay sets forth his idea of "modular economics"—putting together several small jobs, rather than one big one—and having plenty of time left over for leisure. (One in every 20 workers, currently, holds two or more jobs.)

There are centers dedicated to helping people who want to find flexible work-time options, such as job-sharing. They often have helpful pamphlets and other publications. Among them are:

Work/Life Options
5004 W. Tierra Buena
Glendale, AZ 85306
602-938-2351

New Ways to Work
149 Ninth St.
San Francisco, CA 94103
415-552-1000

Flexible Career Associates
Box 6701
Santa Barbara, CA 93111
805-687-2575

Innovative Career Options
School of Business—Box 13
Metropolitan State College
1006 Eleventh St.
Denver, CO 80204
303-629-3245

Family and Career Together
(FACT)
Eight N. Main St., Ste. 143
W. Hartford, CT 06107
203-521-1603

Association of Part-Time
Professionals
Atlanta Chapter
c/o Debbie Weil
77 28th St. NW
Atlanta, GA 30309
404-351-6637

Division of Women's Programs
Alternative Working Arrangements
Project
27000 University Ave.
Drake University
Des Moines, IA 50311
515-271-2181

Work Options for Women
1358 N. Waco
Wichita, KS 67203
316-264-6604

Work Options Limited
645 Boylston St.
Boston, MA 02116
617-247-3600

Nancy Viehmann
Pier Rd., Box 78
Cape Porpoise, ME 04014
207-967-3462

Lansing Women's Bureau
Human Resources Dept.
City of Lansing
119 N. Washington Sq.
Lansing, MI 48933
517-483-4479

Adult Career Exploration Center
Counseling Center—Memorial Hall
Glassboro State College
Glassboro, NJ 08028
609-445-5378

Workshare
311 E. 50th St.
New York, NY 10022
212-832-7061

Flexible Ways to Work
c/o YWCA
1111 SW Tenth Ave.
Portland, OR 97205
503-241-0537

Center for Flexible Employment
3060 Bristol Rd.
Box 404
Bensalem, PA 19020
215-757-3328

Work Time Options, Inc.
966 Summer Pl.
Pittsburgh, PA 15243
412-261-0846

Austin Women's Center
2700 S. 1st St.
Austin, TX 78704
512-447-9666

Phoenix Institute
383 S. 600 E.
Salt Lake City, UT 84102
801-532-5080

Association of Part-Time
Professionals
Box 3419
Alexandria VA 22302
202-734-7975

Focus
509 Tenth Ave. E.
Seattle, WA 98102
206-329-7918

2. IF YOU WANT VOLUNTEER
OPPORTUNITIES OR INTERNSHIPS

Hulse, Lisa S., ed., *1987 Internships*, Writer's Digest Books, Published by F&W Publications, 9933 Alliance Rd., Cincinnati, OH 45242. 1985.

I CAN Volunteer Development Workbook. National Center for Citizen Involvement's Volunteer Readership Service, Box 1807, Boulder, CO 80306. There is also an *I CAN Advisor's Manual* and *I CAN Administrative Guidelines*, for those wishing to help recruit or train volunteers. The I CAN program, which helps volunteers identify the basic skills they are using in their volunteer work, was developed by the Council of National Organizations for Adult Education, and by the I CAN Interagency Collaboration for Volunteer Development (which included such organizations as the American Red Cross, the Girl Scouts of the U.S.A., the YWCA, the YMCA, the Junior Leagues, and the National Council of Jewish Women).

Hughes, Kathleen, ed., *Good Works: A Guide to Social Change Careers*. Center for Study of Responsive Law, Box 19367, Washington, DC 20036. 1982.

Community Jobs, 1319 18th St., NW, Washington, DC 20036. Published monthly by Community Careers Resource Center. Will list jobs and internships in nonprofit, community organizations. Send job descriptions and announcements to them.

Shenk, Ellen J., ed., *Directory of Volunteer Opportunities*. Career Information Centre, University of Waterloo, Waterloo, Ontario, N2L 3G1 Canada. 1986.

Stanton, Timothy, and Ali, Kamil, *The EXPERIENCED HAND: A Student Manual for Making the Most of an Internship*. Carroll Press, 43 Squantum St., Cranston RI 02920-9990. 1982.

National Directory of Internships, published by the National Society for Internships and Experiential Education (NSIEE), 122 St. Mary's St., Raleigh, NC 27605.

Directory of Internships, Work Experience Programs, and On-the-Job Training Opportunities. Ready Reference Press, Box 5169, Santa Monica, CA 90405. Also available— *The First Supplement to the Directory*.

Center for Environmental Intern Programs, 25 West St., Boston, MA 02111, 617-426-4375.

The San Francisco Bay Area People's Yellow Pages, Box 31291, San Francisco, CA 94131. Alternative services catalog.

3. IF YOU WANT SELF-EMPLOYMENT
OR PART-TIME WORK OR WORK AT HOME

The self-employment route is exceedingly attractive to the unemployed, because it is a beautiful way to avoid the job-hunt. Unable to find work, we figure we have nothing to lose.

But of course you do. Your shirt (or blouse). The statistics on new businesses are depressing. You've probably heard them already, but just in case you haven't: 65% of all new businesses fail within five years. That's the bad news.

The good news, if you want the bright side of things, is that there are about 28 old businesses in this country, for every new business that starts up. This keeps the bankruptcy/failure rate *for the country* much lower than most people think. In Good Times, out of every 10,000 businesses, only 62 fail in a given year. In Hard Times, out of every 10,000 businesses, 186 fail. That means 9,814 out of every 10,000 survive even during a tough Recession year. So, *if* you make it through the first few very difficult years in your new business you'll probably survive.

EVERYTHING therefore depends on how you start up. That's why you must not even for a moment think that the self-employment route is a good way to avoid the job-hunt. On the contrary, you'll have to work harder at your research, harder

at setting up your business, harder at finding customers (should you be offering a service or product) than you ever would in a normal job-hunt if your experience is at all like the self-employed from whom I regularly hear. You will look back at the job-hunt as an elementary school exercise by comparison.

The ten riskiest small businesses, according to experts, are local laundries and dry cleaners, used car dealerships, gas stations, local trucking firms, restaurants, infant clothing stores, bakeries, machine shops, grocery or meat stores, and car washes.

If I could move *gradually* into self-employment, doing it as a moonlighting activity first of all, I certainly would. Test out your enterprise, as you would a floorboard in a very old run-down house, stepping on it cautiously without putting your full weight on it, at first, to see whether or not it will hold you. If you're not presently employed, and you're determined to go the self-employment or franchise route, for heaven sakes have a plan B. "I'm going to try out this self-employment, and my plan B is that if after a certain number of months it doesn't look like it's going to make it, then I'm going to. . . . (fill in the blank)." And give some time to the exploration of that alternative before you start your self-employment thing, so that plan B is "all in place," as they say.

No matter how inventive you are about self-employment, you're probably *not* going to create a job no one has ever heard of; in all likelihood you're only going to create a job that *most* people have never heard of. But someone, somewhere, in this world of endless creativity, has probably already put together the kind of job you're dreaming about. Your task: to go find her, or him, and interview them to death. Why should you have to invent the wheel all over again? They've already stepped on all the landmines for you. They know where all the pitfalls are in this business you're dreaming of starting.

But suppose you can't find such a person? Well, then, figure out who is doing something that is *close* to what you're dreaming of doing, and go interview *that* person. For example, let's suppose your dream is to use computers to monitor the growth of plants at the Arctic. And you can't find anybody who's ever done such a thing. Well, then, break it down into its parts: computers, plants, and Arctic. Try combining *two* parts with each other, and you'll see what your research task is: to find someone who's used computers with plants, or computers at the Arctic, or someone who's worked with plants at the Arctic (yes, I know this is a moderately ridiculous example, but I wanted to stretch your imagination). My point is a simple one: you can ALWAYS find someone who has done something that approximates what it is you want to do, and from her or him you can learn a great deal. Better yet, they may lead you to others who have done something even closer to what it is you want to do.

How do you get funded for a new job no one has ever heard of? Well, if it's a product or service you are offering, you get funded by convincing people to buy it. (And you ask people already offering a similar product or service how they got people to buy theirs, so you'll know what the general principles are, regarding what works and what doesn't work.)

But admittedly, this *can* be "the pits" if you have to go out and convince people, one by one, to buy your product, services, or whatever. No wonder, then, that a number of (hopefully) soon-to-be self-employed persons find the idea of a foundation grant or government grant tremendously attractive and winsome. How, they ask—in letter after letter—can I find such a grant? Well, basically the same way you find a job. Thorough-going research. To get you started, consult your library (or else your banker) for one of the directories of grants (already) given. Such directories as:

Annual Register of Grant Support, published by Marquis Academic Media, 200 E. Ohio St., Room 5608, Chicago, IL 60611. The directory or register covers 2300 current grant programs, and has four helpful indexes.

The Foundation Center, 79 Fifth Ave., New York, NY 10003, is an independent, nonprofit organization offering assistance in locating grants. It publishes *The Foundation Directory*, which lists over 4,400 U.S. foundations, whose grants accounted in toto for 92% of all U.S. dollars awarded in 1983 and 1984. 1985. (If you're searching for this in your local library, you're looking for the tenth edition.) There are four reference collections operated by the Center, in New York, Washington, DC, Cleveland, and San Francisco. There are also dozens of cooperating collections nationwide. For information on locations nearest you, call 800-424-9836.

If you decide that applying for a grant is the way in which you would like to try to get funded, there are some rules. As Matthew Lesko (author of *Getting Yours*) points out:

1. If it is a government grant you seek, look at state and local governments as well as the Federal.
2. The money may not be where logic would suggest it should be. For example, the Department of Labor funds doctoral dissertations, the Department of Agriculture funds teenage entrepreneurs, and the like.
3. Talk to the people at the agency who are in charge of dispersing the grant funds.
4. When you have located an appropriate agency for what you want to do, ask to see a copy of a successful application (under the Freedom of Information Act).
5. If they make clear that they will not give you a large amount, ask for a small amount for a year; and let them get to know you.

Kiam, Victor, *Going For It! How to Succeed as an Entrepreneur*. William Morrow and Co., Inc., New York, NY 1986.

Levinson, Jay Conrad, *Guerrilla Marketing: Secrets for Making Big Profits from Your Small Business*, Waldentapes, Box 1084, Stamford, CT 06904. 1985. Listen & Learn Cassettes, ISBN 0-681-30739-0.

Pinchot, III, Gifford, *Intrapreneuring: Why You Don't Have to Leave the Corporation to Become an Entrepreneur*. Harper & Row, 10 E. 53rd St., New York, NY 10022. Published in Canada by Fitzhenry & Whiteside, Ltd. Toronto. 1985.

Rothberg, Diane S. and Cook, Barbara Ensor, *Part-Time Professional*. Acropolis Books Ltd., Colortone Bldg., 2400 17th St., NW, Washington, DC 20009. 1985.

Kamoroff, Bernard, *Small-Time Operator: How to Start Your Own Small Business, Keep Your Books, Pay Your Taxes & Stay Out of Trouble*. Bell Springs Publishers, Box 640, Laytonville, CA 95454. 1984.

Lant, Dr. Jeffrey L., *The Consultant's Kit*. JLA Publications, a division of Jeffrey Lant Associates, Inc., 50 Follen St. Ste. 507, Cambridge, MA 02138. 1984.

Esperti, Robert A., and Peterson, Renno L., *Incorporating Your Talents, A Guide to the One-Person Corporation*. McGraw-Hill Book Company, 1221 Avenue of the Americas, New York, NY 10020. 1984.

Edwards, Paul and Sarah, *Working from Home: Everything You Need to Know about Living and Working under the Same Roof.* J. P. Tarcher, Inc., 9110 Sunset Blvd., Los Angeles, CA 90069. 1985. 420 pages. Has a long section on computerizing your home business, and on telecommunicating.

Drucker, Peter F., *Innovation and Entrepreneurship: Practice and Principles.* Harper & Row, 10 E. 53rd St., New York, NY 10022. 1985. 277 pages.

Brabec, Barbara, *Homemade Money: The Definitive Guide to Success in a Home Business.* Betterway Publications, Inc., White Hall, VA 22987. 1984. 272 pages. A very fine book, with an A to Z business section, and a most helpful summary of which states have laws regulating (or prohibiting) certain home-based businesses.

Feldman, Beverly Neuer, *Homebased Businesses.* Till Press, Box 27816, Los Angeles, CA 90027. 1983. Revised.

Hoge, Cecil C., Sr., *Mail Order Know-How.* Ten Speed Press, Box 7123, Berkeley, CA 94707. 1982.

Lesko, Matthew, *Getting Yours: The Complete Guide to Government Money.* Penguin Books, 40 W. 23rd St., New York, NY 10010. 1982.

Moscowitz, Milton; Levering, Robert; and Katz, Michael, *The Computer Entrepreneurs.* New American Library, 1633 Broadway, New York, NY 10019. 1985. 481 pages.

Mancuso, Anthony, *How to Form Your Own California Corporation.* Nolo Press, Box 544, Occidental, CA 95465. 1977.

Hoge, Cecil C., Sr., *Mail Order Moonlighting.* Ten Speed Press, Box 7123, Berkeley, CA 94707. 1976.

Nicholas, Ted, *How to Form Your Own Corporation Without a Lawyer for Under $50.00. Complete with Tear-Out Forms, Certificate of Incorporation, Minutes, By-Laws.* Enterprise Publishing Co., Inc., 1000 Oakfield Le., Wilmington, DE 19810. 1973.

There are, incidentally, 15 million small business enterprises in the U.S. Women own 25% of them (but only take in 9% of all small business income). That's mostly because they price goods and services too low, are not able to take risks to the same degree as men are, and often get turned down for financing because of their sex.

Behr, Marion, and Lazar, Wendy, *Women Working Home: The Homebased Business Guide and Directory.* Women Working Home, Inc. 24 Fishel Rd., Edison, NJ 08820. 1983. An estimated 9 to 11 million people work out of their homes—many if not most of them women. The authors were co-founders of the National Alliance of Homebased Businesswomen, a New Jersey based group, with 1500 members currently.

The Home Office Newsletter. A monthly publication for individuals who run businesses from their homes. Newsletter is also available in electronic database form through Genie and Delphi information services. Subscribe to Compusystems Management, 4734 E. 26th St., Tucson, AZ 85711. 602-790-6333.

Homeworking Mothers, a quarterly newsletter for women who want to start their own businesses and work from their homes. Mother's Home Business Network, Box 423, East Meadow, NY 11554.

Women who are thinking of starting their own business can get counseling over the phone, from the American Women's Economic Development Corporation (AWED), Monday through Friday, between 10 a.m. and 5 p.m. eastern time, at a cost of $5 for up to ten minutes. The hotline offers an expert in the area in which the caller needs help. Longer counseling, up to one and a half hours, is also offered, at a cost of $25. If calling from New York City, Alaska or Hawaii, call 212-692-9100. If calling from New York State, call 1-800-442-AWED. If calling from any other area, call 1-800-222-AWED. Both services may be charged to major credit cards.

4. IF YOU WANT WORK DEALING WITH SOCIAL CHANGE

Careers in this arena are often called "public service careers."

Public service careers may be with *government* (federal, state, or local), with *non-profit organizations*, with *agencies* (independent of state or local government, but often cooperating with them) or with *colleges* (particularly community colleges), etc.

Public service careers include such varied occupations as *Community Services Officer* at a community college, *recreation educator, city planner, social service technician* (working with any or all agencies that deliver social services), *welfare administration, gerontology specialist* (for further information, contact—among others—your State Commission on Aging), etc.

Other public service careers: *Workers with the handicapped, public health officials* (see your State Department of Public Health, or the Chief Medical Doctor at the county Public Health Agency—the Doctor often being the best informed person about *opportunities), officials dealing with the foster parent program for mentally retarded persons, workers in the child welfare program,* and so forth.

If you are interested in this general field of social service, you ought to do extensive research, including talking with national associations in the fields that interest you, state departments, county, city.

Potential employers for social or public service occupations include social welfare agencies, public health departments, correctional institutions, government offices, colleges, economic oppotunity offices, hospitals, rest homes, schools, parks and recreation agencies, etc.

As a research aid, there is *Human Service Organizations: A Book of Readings*, University of Michigan Press, 615 E. University, Ann Arbor, MI 48106. Deals with an

"I'm hoping to find something in a meaningful, humanist, outreach kind of bag, with flexible hours, non-sexist bosses, and fabulous fringes."

analysis of the structure of schools, employment agencies, mental health clinics, correctional institutions, welfare agencies and hospitals. If you're thinking about going to work in one of these human service organizations, this could help your research.

Thorough research on your part will often reveal other ways in which *funding can be found for positions not yet created if you know exactly what it is you want to do*, and find a person who knows something about *that*.

Honigsberg, Peter Jan, Kamoroff, Bernard, and Beatty, Jim, *We Own It: Starting and Managing Coops, Collectives, & Employee Owned Ventures*. Bell Springs Publishers, Box 640, Laytonville, CA 95454. 1982.

The Briarpatch Book: experiences in right livelihood and simple living. The Briarpatch Community, New Glide Publications, 330 Ellis St., San Francisco CA 94102. 1978.

5. IF YOU WANT TO MAKE YOUR LIVING BY WRITING AND GETTING PUBLISHED

I used to live in an apartment-complex, and as I walked through the courtyard each day, I could hear typewriters going incessantly, out of every open window. They couldn't *all* be part-time secretaries, working at home. Obviously, there are a lot of budding authors and authoresses in the land. For them, some helps:

Harry, M., *The Muckraker's Manual: How to Do Your Own Investigative Reporting*. Revised and expanded. Loompanics Unlimited, Box 1197, Port Townsend, WA 98368. 1984.

Powers, Melvin, *How to Self-Publish Your Book and Have the Fun and Excitement of Being a Best-Selling Author*. An expert's step-by-step guide to marketing your book successfully. Wilshire Book Co., 12015 Sherman Rd., North Hollywood, CA 91605. 213-875-1711/818-983-1105. 1984.

Boswell, John, *The Awful Truth about Publishing: Why They Always Reject Your Manuscript—and What You Can Do about It*. Warner Books, 666 5th Ave., New York, NY 10103.

Appelbaum, Judith, and Evans, Nancy, *How to Get Happily Published: A Complete and Candid Guide*. New American Library, 1633 Broadway, New York, NY 10019. 1978.

Schemenaur, P.J., and Brady, John, eds., *Writer's Market: Where to Sell What You Write*. Writer's Digest Books, 9933 Alliance Rd., Cincinnati, OH 45242. Hardcover. Issued annually.

Mainstream Access, Inc., *The Publishing Job Finder*. Prentice-Hall, Englewood Cliffs, NJ 07632. 1981.

6. IF YOU WANT TO MAKE YOUR LIVING THROUGH ARTS AND CRAFTS

If your creativity is not out of the left-hemisphere of your brain (words, words, words), but out of the right-hemisphere (pictures, art, crafts, and so forth), there are books for you too; issued annually:

Lapin, Lynne, ed., *Artist's Market*. Writer's Digest Books, 9933 Alliance Rd., Cincinnati, OH 45242.

———, ed., *Craftworker's Market*. Writer's Digest Books, 9933 Alliance Rd., Cincinnati, OH 45242.

Brohaugh, William, *Songwriter's Market*. Writer's Digest Books, 9933 Alliance Rd., Cincinnati, OH 45242.

Career Resources List for Visual Artists, Union of Independent Colleges of Art, Dean E. Tollefson, Executive Director, 4340 Oak St., Kansas City, MO 64111-1890. 1981.

7. IF YOU WANT TO GET A GOVERNMENT JOB

As with any other kind of job, you've got to decide *where* it is you want to work, what skills you want to be able to use, and what it is you want to do (in other words, chapters 5 and 6 in this book apply to you as much as to non-governmental workers).

If you are new to the idea of the government as your employer, you will of course suppose that researching them won't do you any good, because you are going to have to take a Civil Service examination of one kind or another. Well, eventually you probably *are* going to have to take that exam. But all the principles in chapter 7 apply just as much to government managers as they do to other employers. Government managers, too, are tired of hiring people ill-suited for the job. Civil service exams don't give these managers any better clues than resumes do for non-governmental employers. So if, in the course of your research, you happen to visit the government person who has the power to hire you, and if he or she takes a real liking to you, you can bet your bottom dollar they will do everything *they can* to guide you through the examination maze, so that you can end up in their office. Any government manager worth her or his salt knows how to manipulate—ah, excuse me, creatively use—standard operating procedures, so that it all works out to their best advantage.

When doing your research about salaries, once it's come down to that, it is helpful for you to know that unless you are up for an occupation for which there is an extremely limited supply of job-hunters, your government Personnel Officer will rarely have the authority to negotiate salary. If it *is* fixed, you can probably find it in the Temporary box, on a Federal SF-171. (Yes, I know you probably don't know what a Federal SF-171 is, at the moment; but you should know by the time you get to this stage of your research.)

Federal Yellow Book. An organizational directory of the top-level employees of the Federal departments and agencies. See your library.

The publisher (Washington Monitor, Inc., 1301 Pennsylvania Ave., NW, Washington DC 20004) also publishes *Congressional Yellow Book*, an up-to-date loose-leaf directory of members of Congress, their committees and their key aides.

Federal Research Service, Inc., *Federal Career Opportunities.* Federal Research Service, Inc., 370 Maple Ave. W., Box 1059, Vienna, VA 22180, 703-281-0200. Biweekly 64-page magazine. Six issues. Up-to-date listing of available federal jobs plus application instructions.

Lesko, Matthew, *Information U.S.A.*, Penguin Books, 625 Madison Ave., New York, NY 10022. 1983.

8. IF YOU WANT OVERSEAS WORK

Many people assume you find an overseas job by packing a bag, buying a ticket and passing out resumes at your foreign destination. But work permit requirements and high unemployment make finding jobs at foreign destinations difficult or impossible. The wiser approach is to conduct your overseas job search in the U.S. If you're hired in the U.S. by a company who'll send you overseas, they'll take care of the visa and work permit red tape, pick up your travel bill, and provide other lucrative benefits.

Every successful search for an overseas job starts with a resume and a source of information on "who's hiring now." Major metropolitan newspapers, professional association magazines, and "networking" will provide leads on current employers.

Beware of directories listing overseas employers. Many are out of date and tend to report on "who was hiring" versus "who's hiring now."

If you choose to do your own research about overseas work, how do you go about it? Well, first of all, talk to everyone you possibly can who has in fact been overseas, most especially to the country or countries that interest you. A nearby large university will probably have such faculty or students (ask). Companies in your city which have overseas branches (your library should be able to tell you which they are) should be able to lead you to people also—possibly to the names and addresses of personnel who are still "over there" to whom you can write for the information you are seeking. Alternatively, try asking every single person you meet for the next week (at the supermarket checkout, at your work, at home, at church or synagogue, etc.) if they know someone who used to live overseas and now is in your city or town. By doing research with such people, you will learn a great deal.

Talking to the consulate of the country in question (should you live in or near a major city) may also be very enlightening. Books from your local library or local bookstore in the travel section, if they are recent, may also tell you much.

As for the general facts about living overseas, books on this subject keep getting regularly published, regularly flourish for a season, and then regularly die. But currently these are:

The International Job Directory, Box 31, Claremont, CA 91711. Assists college students and graduates from around the world in finding employment in over fifty countries throughout the world. Send a self-addressed stamped envelope with all correspondence. Also provides new publications relating to overseas employment.

International Employment Hotline, Box 6170, McLean, VA 22106. Provides job search advice and names and addresses of employers hiring for international work in government, nonprofit organizations, and private companies.

Fenton, Thomas and Heffron, Mary, eds., *Third World Resource Directory: A Guide to Organizations and Publications*. Orbis Books, Maryknoll, NY 10545. 1984.

Casewit, Curtis W., *Foreign Jobs: The Most Popular Countries*. Monarch Press, a division of Simon and Schuster, Simon and Schuster Building, 1230 Avenue of the Americas, New York, NY 10020. 1984.

Wharton, John, *Jobs in Japan: The Complete Guide to Living and Working in the Land of Rising Opportunity*. Jobs in Japan, Box 31, Claremont, CA 91711. 1983.

Your library should also have books such as Angel, Juvenal, *Dictionary of American Firms Operating in Foreign Countries*. (World Trade Academy Press.)

And to research overseas public companies which sell stock in this country, the Securities Exchange Commission will have their Form 6-K, which they filed in order to be able to sell that stock.

In general, the principles found in Appendix C, in the section on how to research cities at a distance, will apply here with equal or greater force.

9. IF YOU WANT HELP WITH THE SPECIAL PROBLEMS OF WOMEN

> Books aimed at women in the world of work, appear faster than one can record them. Browse your local bookstore to see the full range of what's currently available, please.

Mendelsohn, Pam, *Happier By Degrees: A College Reentry Guide for Women*, Ten Speed Press, Box 7123, Berkeley, CA 94707. 1986.

Aslett, Don, *Who Says It's a Woman's Job to Clean?* Writer's Digest Books/North Light, 9933 Alliance Rd., Cincinnati, OH 45242. 1986.

LaRouche, Janice, and Ryan, Regina, *Strategies for Women at Work: Analyzing, Solving, and Overcoming Job Problems, Predicaments, Concerns, Complications, Obstacles, Tight Spots, Blocks, Hang-Ups, and Hazards.* Avon Books, a division of The Hearst Corporation, 1790 Broadway, New York, NY 10019. 1984.

Catalyst, *What to Do with the Rest of Your Life: The Catalyst Career Guide for Women in the '80s.* Simon and Schuster, 1230 Avenue of the Americas, New York, NY 10020. 1980.

If you are interested in sales positions, you will want to know about the National Association for Professional Saleswomen, Box 255708, Sacramento, CA 95865. They have chapters across the country, and they publish a newsletter, called *Successful Saleswoman.*

Harragan, Betty Lehan, *Games Mother Never Taught You: Corporate Gamesmanship for Women.* Warner Books, 666 Fifth Ave., New York, NY 10103. 1978, 1977. Detailing corporate politics as practiced by males, and how upwardly-mobile female executives can map their own game plan.

Ekstrom, Ruth B., Harris, Abigail M., and Lockheed, Marlaine E., *How To Get College Credit for What You Have Learned as a Homemaker and Volunteer.* 1977. Project HAVE SKILLS, Education Testing Service, Princeton, NJ 08541. They also publish the: *Have Skills Women's Workbook, Have Skills Counselor's Guide*, and *Have Skills Employer's Guide.* All of these include the famous "I CAN" lists, based upon the pioneering work, in the assessment of volunteer skills and knowledge, of the Council of National Organizations for Adult Education. Even for those not interested in college credit, but only in assessing the skills they picked up or sharpened as a volunteer or homemaker, this is an excellent resource. Classifies the skills under the various roles: administrator/manager, financial manager, personnel manager, trainer, advocate/change agent, public relations/communicator, problem surveyor, researcher, fund raiser, counselor, youth group leader, group leader for a serving organization, museum staff assistant (docent), tutor/teacher's aide, manager of home finances, home nutritionist, home child caretaker, home designer and maintainer, home clothing and textile specialist, and home horticulturist. *Very* helpful book, with accompanying aids.

The I CAN lists, incidentally, are also available from the National Center for Citizen Involvement's Volunteer Readership Service, Box 1807, Boulder, CO 80306.

10. IF YOU WANT HELP WITH THE SPECIAL PROBLEMS OF MINORITIES

Davis, George and Watson, Glegg, *Black Life in Corporate America: Swimming in the Mainstream.* Anchor Press/Doubleday, 245 Park Ave., New York, NY 10167. 1983.

The Black Resource Guide. Black Resource Guide, Inc., 501 Oneida Pl., NW, Washington, DC 20011. 1985. A comprehensive list of over 2,600 black resources or organizations in the U.S.

Johnson, Willis L., ed., *Directory of Special Programs for Minority Group Members: Career Information Services, Employment Skills Banks, Financial Aid Services*—Third Edition. Garrett Park Press, Garrett Park, MD 20766. 1980.

Wallace, Phyllis, with Datcher, Linda, and Malveaux, Julianne, *Black Women in the Labor Force.* The MIT Press, 28 Carleton St., Cambridge, MA 02142. 1980.

Cole, Katherine W., ed., *Minority Organizations: A National Directory.* Garrett Park Press, Garrett Park, MD 20766. 1978. An annotated directory of 2700 Black, Hispanic, Native, and Asian American organizations.

Financial Aid for Minority Students in: Allied Health, Business, Education, Engineering, Law, Mass Communications, Medicine, or Science. Available from Garrett Park Press, Garrett Park, MD 20766.

11. HELP WITH THE SPECIAL PROBLEMS OF HANDICAPPED JOB-HUNTERS

The National Library Service for the Blind and Physically Handicapped, Library of Congress, 1291 Taylor St. NW, Washington DC 20542 has many books on career planning and job-hunting (such as *Parachute*) on tape, which they will send, with special playback equipment, to your home and back, free, if you are able to prove a "print-handicap."

Recording for the Blind, Inc., 20 Roszel Rd., Princeton, NJ 08540 likewise has translated job-hunting books for the print-handicapped and visually-impaired.

Resources on Disabilities: McBurney Resource Center, 905 University Ave., Madison WI 53706. Access to Independence, Inc., 1954 E. Washington Ave., Madison, WI 53704. These resources help with psychological aspects of job-hunting.

Ryan, Colleen, *Job Search Workshop for Disabled, Dislocated and Discouraged Workers.* Adult Life Resource Center, Division of Continuing Education, The University of Kansas. 1985.

Rabby, Rami, *Locating, Recruiting, and Hiring the Disabled.* Pilot Books, 103 Cooper St., Babylon, NY 11702. 1981. Includes over 500 sources of information covering referral agencies, media lists and other points of contact for employers.

Bruck, Dr. Lilly, Producer, *The Assertive Jobseeker: A Telecommunications Conference of Nationally Prominent Experts.* In Touch Networks, 322 W. 48th St., New York, NY 10036. A three-cassette series, with speakers on such subjects as job-hunting and assertiveness, including *Parachute's* author.

"The So-Called 'Handicapped' Job-Hunter: Strategies for Helping Him or Her in Today's Job-Market," the November-December 1978 issue of the *Newsletter about life/work planning.* Single copies free if you send a self-addressed, stamped business envelope to: Newsletter, National Career Development Project, Box 379, Walnut Creek, CA 94596.

12. HELP WITH THE SPECIAL PROBLEMS OF EX-OFFENDERS

Federal/State Employment Offices often can be of particular assistance to ex-offenders. All offices can provide for bonding of ex-offenders, if needed to obtain employment. They also have information on tax-breaks for employers who hire ex-offenders. The larger offices even have Ex-Offender Specialists.

A general switchboard for ex-offenders is The Corrections Education Association, 1400 20th St. NW, Washington DC 20036. They will know what resources are available to help the job-hunting ex-offender.

You can obtain a "Pre-Employment Curriculum" from the American Correctional Association, 4321 Hartwick Rd., College Park, MD 20740. There is also: *A Survival Source Book for Offenders*, from Contacts, Inc., Box 81826, Lincoln, NB 68501.

Phil Young, who used to run a fine job-hunting program for offenders and ex-offenders, is now doing consultancy work in this field. You can contact him at 400 Linton, #7, Wilmington, OH 45177.

Prisoner's Yellow Pages, California Edition, 1985. Separated into two main sections, "In the Joint," and "On the Street," it lists names and addresses of organizations whose goods, services, or information can be obtained by mail by inmates. Primarily for those who live in the state of California, it has ideas which will be helpful to those living in other states. From: Prisoner's Yellow Pages, 484 Lake Park Ave., Box 221, Oakland, CA 94610.

13. HELP WITH THE SPECIAL PROBLEMS OF EXECUTIVES AND THE BUSINESS WORLD

Bard, Ray and Moody, Fran, *Breaking In*. The guide to over 500 top corporate training programs. A Stonesong Press Book, New York, NY. 1985.

Gordon, Judith R., *Human Resource Management. A Practical Approach*. Allyn and Bacon, Inc., 7 Wells Ave., Newton, MA 02159. 1986.

Naisbitt, John, and Aburdene, Patricia, *Re-inventing the Corporation: Transforming Your Job and Your Company for the New Information Society*. Warner Books, Inc., 75 Rockefeller Plaza, New York, NY 10019 1985.

Naisbitt, John and Aburdene, Patricia, *Re-inventing the Corporation*, Waldentapes, Box 1084, Stamford, CT 06904. Cassette, ISBN 0-87188-204-3.

Common Body of Knowledge for Management Consultants. The American Association of Consulting Management Engineers, Inc., 230 Park Ave., New York, NY 10017. If you are not at all familiar with the business world, and want a detailed breakdown of management functions and sub-functions, this is a very useful outline.

Figueroa, Oscar, and Winkler, Charles, *A Business Information Guidebook*, Amacom, 135 W. 50th St., New York, NY 10020. 1980.

Jablonski, Donna M., ed., *How to Find Information about Companies*, Washington Researchers, 918 16th St., NW, Washington DC 20006.

Albert, Kenneth J., ed., *The Handbook of Business Problem Solving*. McGraw-Hill Book Co., 1221 Avenue of the Americas, New York, NY 10020. 1980. For those who need a basic primer in understanding and solving problems in organizations.

How to Read a Financial Report. Merrill Lynch Pierce Fenner and Smith, Inc., 1 Liberty Plaza, New York, N.Y. 10080. If the organization you are interested in is large enough to have an annual financial report, that report *may* help you understand the organization better. And then again, it may not. Some (if not most) annual reports present their organizations only in *the most favorable* light possible. No warts, no pimples, no blemishes. You may also want to try: *What Else Can Financial State-*

ments Tell You? American Institute of Certified Public Accountants, 1211 Avenue of the Americas, New York, N.Y. 10036.

McCormack, Mark H., *What They Don't Teach You at Harvard Business School: Notes and Tips of a 'Street-smart' Executive.* Bantam Books, 666 Fifth Ave., New York, NY 10103. 1984.

Levering, Robert; Moskowitz, Milton; and Katz, Michael, *The 100 Best Companies to Work for in America.* Addison-Wesley Publishing Co., Reading, MA 01867. 1984. The problem is: is there any such animal as "the 100 best companies to work for," or are some companies excellent on the fifth floor, but poor down on the second floor? Nonetheless, this is a fascinating book, as is everything these authors have written.

Prashker, Marti, and Valiunas, S. Peter, *Money Jobs: Training Programs Run by Banking, Accounting, Insurance, and Brokerage Firms—and How to Get Into Them.* Crown Publishers, Inc., One Park Ave., New York, NY 10016. 1984.

Moskowitz, Milton; Katz, Michael; and Levering, Robert, eds. *Everybody's Business Scoreboard: Corporate America's Winners, Losers and Also-Rans.* Harper & Row, 10 E. 53rd St., New York, NY 10022. 1983. Who is the biggest, the best, the best-selling, the worst-selling. Who has triumphed, who's lost their shirt. Very fascinating book.

Peters, Thomas J., and Waterman, Jr., Robert H., *In Search of Excellence: Lessons from America's Best Run Companies.* Harper & Row, 10 E. 53rd St., New York, NY 10022. 1982. An instant classic. Well done. The title says it all.

Behn, Robert D., and Vaupel, James W., *Quick Analysis for Busy Decision Makers.* Basic Books, Inc., 10 E. 53rd St., New York, NY 10022. 1982. How to make perplexing decisions, when time is short and information is limited, through the use of a decision-tree, preference-probability factors, and the like. Very useful book, with loads of helpful examples.

Herzberg, Frederick, *The Managerial Choice: To Be Efficient and to Be Human.* Olympus Publishing Co., 1670 E. 13th S., Salt Lake City, UT 84105. 1982. By one of the pioneers in the whole field of jobs and motivation.

Haldane, Bernard, *Bernard Haldane's Career Satisfaction and Success: How to Know and Manage Your Strengths.* Revised and enlarged. Amacom, 135 W. 50th St., New York, NY 10020. By one of the pioneers in the creative job-hunting process.

Wood, Jr., Orrin G., *Your Hidden Assets: The Key to Getting Executive Jobs.* Dow Jones-Irwin, 1818 Ridge Rd., Homewood, IL 60430. 1981.

Campbell, David, *If I'm in Charge Here Why is Everybody Laughing?* Argus Communications, One DLM Pk., Allen, TX 75002. 1980.

Boll, Carl R., *Executive Jobs Unlimited.* Updated edition. Macmillan Publishing Co., Inc., 866 Third Ave., New York, NY 10022. 1979, 1965. The classic in the executive job-hunting field.

Kanter, Rosabeth Moss, *Men and Women of the Corporation.* Basic Books, Inc., Publishers, New York, NY. 1977. A thoroughgoing study of how a corporation works, and how it affects the lives of the women and men in it.

Drucker, Peter, *Management: Tasks, Responsibilities, Practices.* Harper & Row, Publishers, 10 E. 53rd St., New York, NY 10022. 1973. Should be absolutely required reading for anyone contemplating entering, changing to, or becoming a professional within the business world, or any organization.

14. HELP WITH THE SPECIAL PROBLEMS OF COUPLES

With more and more married women in the work-force, a body of literature has appeared concerning the problem of Both Partners Working:

Bastress, Frances, *The Relocating Spouse's Guide to Employment: Options and Strategies in the U.S. and Abroad*. Woodley Publications, 4620 Derussey Parkway, Chevy Chase, MD 20815.

Irish, Richard K., *How to Live Separately Together: A Guide for Working Couples*. Doubleday and Co., Inc., 245 Park Ave., New York, NY 10167. 1981.

Bird, Caroline, *The Two-Paycheck Marriage*. Pocket Books, 1230 Avenue of the Americas, New York, NY 10020. 1979.

Hall, Francine S., and Hall, Douglas T., *The Two-Career Couple*. Addison-Wesley, Jacob Way, Reading, MA 01867. 1979.

15. HELP WITH THE SPECIAL PROBLEMS OF THE CLERGY AND RELIGIOUS PEOPLE

Varner, Ruth, *Gifts Given to Us: A Children's Resource, Ages Four to Seven, for Vocation and Calling*. United Church Press, 132 W. 31st St., New York, NY 10001. 1985.

Anderson, Ruth M., *Being and Doing: A Children's Resource, Ages Eight to Twelve, for Vocation and Calling*. United Church Press, 132 W. 31st St., New York, NY 10001. 1985.

Imakyure, Carl and Miller, Audrey, *God, Is That You Calling?: A Youth Resource for Vocation and Calling*. United Church Press, 132 W. 31st St., New York, NY 10001. 1985.

Rinker, Richard N. and Eisentrout, Virginia, *Called to Be Gifted and Giving: An Adult Resource for Vocation and Calling*. United Church Press, 132 W. 31st St., New York, NY 10001. 1985.

Staub, Dick; Trautman, Jeff; and Cutshall, Mark, eds., *Intercristo's CAREER KIT: A Christian's Guide to Career Building*. Intercristo, Seattle 98133. 1985. Booklets (6) and cassette tapes (3) enclosed in binder.

Wehrheim, Carol and Cole-Turner, Ronald S., *Vocation and Calling. Introduction/ Hearing God's Call/Sharing Gifts: An Intergenerational Study Guide*. United Church Press, 132 W. 31 St., New York, NY 10001. 1985.

Moran, Pamela J., *The Christian Job Hunter*. Servant Publications, 840 Airport Blvd., Box 8617, Ann Arbor, MI 48107. 1984.

Mattson, Ralph, and Miller, Arthur, *Finding a Job You Can Love*. Thomas Nelson Publishers, Nelson Place at Elm Hill Pike, Nashville, TN 37214. 1982. Very helpful and useful book, written from the Christian perspective.

Farnsworth, Kirk, and Lawhead, Wendell, *Life Planning*. InterVarsity Press, 5206 Main St., Downers Grove, IL 60515. 1981.

Olson, Richard P., *Mid-Life: A Time to Discover, A Time to Decide: A Christian Perspective on Middle Age*. Judson Press, Valley Forge, PA 19481. 1980.

Zehring, John William, *Making Your Life Count*. Judson Press, Valley Forge, PA 19481. 1979.

If a book doesn't give you everything you need, there are some religious centers you can turn to. Probably no profession has developed, or had developed for it, so many resources to aid in career assessment as has the clerical profession. Many of them have broadened their services to include helping Church members, and not just clergy. Be warned however: clerical counselors are not perfect. Some are excellent, but some are not. They are, however, all sincere. Where you run into a clerical counselor who is sincere but inept, you will probably discover that the ineptness consists in an inadequate understanding of the distinction between career *assessment*—roughly comparable to taking a snapshot of people as they are in one frozen moment of time—vs. career *development*—which is roughly comparable to teaching people how to take their own motion pictures of themselves, from here on out.

Having issued this caution, however, we must go on to add that at some of these centers, listed below, are some simply excellent counselors who fully understand this distinction, and are well trained in that empowering of the client which is what career *development* is all about.

THE OFFICIAL INTERDENOMINATIONAL CAREER DEVELOPMENT CENTERS

The Career and Personal
Counseling Service
St. Andrews Presbyterian
College, Laurinburg,
NC 28352
919-276-3162
Also at: 725 Providence Rd.
Charlotte, NC 28207
704-376-4086
Elbert R. Patton, Director

The Career and Personal
Counseling Center
Eckerd College
St. Petersburg, FL 33733
813-867-1166, Ext. 356
John R. Sims, Director

The Center for Ministry
7804 Capwell Dr.
Oakland, CA 94621
415-635-4246
John R. Landgraf,
Director-Counselor

Clergy Career
Support System
3501 Campbell
Kansas City, MO 64109
816-931-2516
Eugene E. Timmons, Director

Lancaster Career
Development Center
561 College Ave.
Lancaster, PA 17603
717-397-7451
L. Guy Mehl, Director

North Central Career
Development Center
3000 Fifth St. NW
New Brighton, MN 55112
612-636-5120
Dr. John Davis, Director

Northeast Career
Development Center
291 Witherspoon St.
Princeton, NJ 08540
609-924-4814
Robert G. Foulkes,
Director

Career Development
Center of the Southeast
531 Kirk Rd.
Decatur, GA 30030
Robert M. Urie,
Director
404-371-0336

Midwest Career
Development Center
Box 7249
Westchester, IL 60153
312-343-6268
Ronald Brushwyler,
Associate Director

Southwest Career
Development Center
Box 5923
Arlington, TX 76011
817-265-5541
William M. Gould, Jr.,
Director-Counselor

Center for Career Development
and Ministry
70 Chase St.
Newton Centre, MA 02159
617-969-7750
Barton M. Lloyd, Associate Director
Harold D. Moore, Director

Midwest Career Development
Center, 2501 North Star Rd.,
Ste. 200
Columbus, OH 43221
614-486-0469
Ronald Brushwyler, Director

The centers listed above are all accredited and coordinated by the Career Development Council, Room 760, 475 Riverside Dr., New York, NY 10027. Some of them are accepting directors of Christian Education, ministers of music, and others in addition to clergy; some centers are open to all and not merely to church-related clients; some are open to high school students, as well as to adults.

ALSO DOING WORK IN THIS FIELD:

Mid-South Career Development Center, Box 120815, Acklen Station, Nashville, TN 37212, 615-327-9572. W. Scott Root, Director.

Career and Personal Counseling Center, 1904 Mt. Vernon St., Waynesboro, VA 22980, 703-943-9997. Lillian Pennell, Director.

The Episcopal Office of Pastoral Development, 116 Alhambra Circle, Ste. 210, Coral Gables, FL 33134, 305-448-8016. The Rt. Rev. David E. Richards.

Bernard Haldane, Wellness Education Council, 4502 54th NW, Seattle, WA 98105. 206-525-2205. A pioneer in the clergy career management and assessment field, Bernard teaches (totally independently of the agency which bears his name) seminars and training of volunteers (particularly in churches) to do job-finding counseling.

Life/Career Planning Center for Religious, 10526 W. Cermak Rd., Ste. 111, Westchester, IL 60153. 312-531-9228. Dolores Linhart, Director. Doing work with Roman Catholics.

16. HOW TO HANG ON TO YOUR PRESENT JOB

There is not enough said, generally, in job-hunting books about surviving after you get the job. The enemy is both within, and without. From within, the now-familiar problem of burnout. From without, various adversaries—both animate and inanimate.

Carnegie, Dale, *How to Enjoy Your Life and Your Job*, Pocket Books, 1230 Avenue of the Americas, New York, NY 10020. 1986.

Schwimmer, Larry, *Winning Your Next Promotion in One Year (Or Less!)*. Harper & Row, 10 E. 53rd St., New York, NY 10022. Published simultaneously in Canada by Fitzhenry & Whiteside, Ltd., Toronto. 1986.

Germann, Richard; Blumenson, Diane; and Arnold, Peter, *Working and Liking It*. Ballantine Books, a division of Random House, Inc., New York, NY. 1984.

De Mare, George, with Summerfield, Joanne, *101 Ways to Protect Your Job: A Handbook on How to Handle Your Most Valuable Single Asset, Your Job*. McGraw-Hill, 1221 Avenue of the Americas, New York, NY 10020. 1984. 297 pages. Has a good section on the key court cases from 1937 to 1982, as affecting the rights of employees; though readers should be aware there has been a good deal of ground-breaking litigation since that date.

Wachtel, S. Eric, *How to Hold on to Your Job*. M. Evans and Co., Inc., 216 E. 49th St., New York, NY 10017. 1983. 182 pages.

Viscott, M.D., David, *Taking Care of Business: A Psychiatrist's Guide for True Career Success*. William Morrow and Co., Inc., 105 Madison Ave., New York, NY 10016. 1985. 176 pages. How to handle people on the phone, in person, through letters, and the like.

Kennedy, Marilyn Moats, *Office Politics: Seizing Power, Wielding Clout*. Warner Books, 666 Fifth Ave., New York, NY 10103. 1981.

Kennedy, Marilyn Moats, *Career Knockouts: How to Battle Back*. New Century Publishers, Inc., 275 Old New Brunswick Rd., Piscataway, NJ 08854. 1980.

You will also find some *very* helpful words on this subject in *Where Do I Go From Here With My Life?* (Ten Speed Press, Box 7123, Berkeley, CA 94707, 1974), pages 241–245 ("Understanding the Nature of the World of Work"), and 150–160 ("How to Survive After You Get the Job").

17. HELP WITH BEING FIRED, REJECTED, RIFFED OR LAID-OFF

Avrutis, Raymond, *How to Collect Unemployment Benefits: Complete Information for All 50 States.* Prentice-Hall, Englewood Cliffs, NJ 07632. 1983. There is much mythology about unemployment—for example, that you cannot collect if you were fired. That's only true if you were fired for misconduct.

May, John, *The RIF Survival Handbook: How to Manage Your Money if You're Unemployed.* Tilden Press, 1737 DeSales St. NW, Ste. 300, Washington, DC 20036.

18. HELP WITH MID-LIFE, SECOND CAREERS, OR RETIREMENT

Kouri, Mary K., Ph.D., *Elderlife: A Time to Give—A Time to Receive.* A workbook for the elder adult who wants to put meaning and satisfaction into life after 55. Human Growth and Development Associates, 1675 Fillmore St., Denver, CO 80206. 303-320-0991. 1985.

Boyer, Richard, and Savageau, David, *Places Rated Retirement Guide: Finding the Best Places in America for Retirement Living.* Rand McNally and Co., Box 7600, Chicago, IL 60680. 1983.

Axford, Roger W., *Successful Recareering: How to Shift Gears Before You're Over the Hill.* Media Productions and Marketing, Inc. 344 N. 27th, Lincoln, NE 68503. 1983.

Bird, Caroline, *The Good Years: Your Life in the Twenty-First Century.* E. P. Dutton, Inc., 2 Park Ave., New York, NY 10016. 1983. Describes coming trends on a note of optimism, amidst the pervasive trend in our society of declining hope, among the young.

Odell, Louise Minter and Odell, Charles E., Sr., *You and the Senior Boom: New Challenges and Opportunities for All.*, Exposition Press, Inc., 900 S. Oyster Bay Rd., Hicksville, NY 11801. 1980.

Durkin, Jon, "Mid-Life Career Changes." Johnson O'Connor Research Foundation, Human Engineering Laboratory, 701 Sutter St., San Francisco, CA 94109.

19. HELP WITH GOING BACK TO SCHOOL OR GETTING AN EXTERNAL DEGREE

Haponski, William C., and McCabe, Charles E., *New Horizons: The Education and Career Planning Guide for Adults.* Peterson's Guides. 1985. Available from: ETC Associates, 507 Rider Rd., Clayville, NY 13322.

Haponski, William C., *Directory of External Degrees from Accredited Colleges and Universities.* ETC Associates, 507 Rider Rd., Clayville, NY 13322. 1985. 56 pages.

1985 Directory—Educational and Career Information Services for Adults, the National Center for Educational Brokering, 325 Ninth St., San Francisco, CA 94103 415-626-2378.

Bear, John, *How to Get the Degree You Want: Bear's Guide to Non-Traditional College Degrees.* Ten Speed Press, Box 7123, Berkeley, CA 94707. 280 pages.

To get equivalency examinations for the knowledge or experience you've already acquired out of life, write to CLEP (College-Level Examination Program), College Entrance Examination Board, Box 1822, Princeton, NJ 08541, or Box 1025, Berkeley CA 94701. It is a national standardized examination program for college credit.

Gross, Ronald, *The Independent Scholar's Handbook: How to Turn Your Interest in Any Subject into Expertise.* Addison-Wesley, General Books Division, Reading, MA 01867. 1982.

von Klemperer, Lily, *International Education: A Directory of Resource Materials on Comparative Education and Study in Another Country*. Garrett Park Press, Garrett Park, MD 20766.

20. HELP WITH THE SPECIAL PROBLEMS OF COLLEGE STUDENTS

Moore, Ph.D., Richard W., *Winning the Ph.D. Game: How to Get Into and Out of Graduate School with a Ph.D. and a Job*. Dodd, Mead & Co., 79 Madison Ave., New York, NY 10016. 1985. This seems to me to be an unusually helpful and well-researched book for Ph.D. graduates.

Hawes, Gene R., *The College Board Guide to Going to College While Working: Strategies for Success*. College Board Publications, Box 886, New York, NY 10101. 1985.

Careers and the MBA: 1984 Edition. Bob Adams Inc., 840 Summer St., South Boston, MA 02127. 1984.

Bernard, Susan, and Thompson, Gretchen, *Job Search Strategy for College Grads*. Bob Adams Inc., 840 Summer St., South Boston, MA 02127. 1984.

Gates, Anita, *90 Highest Paying Careers for the '80s*. Monarch Press, a division of Simon and Schuster, Inc., 1230 Avenue of the Americas, New York, NY 10020. 1984.

Moorpark College Counseling Staff, *Exercising Your Options: A Career Fitness Plan*. Gorsuch Scarisbrick, Publishers, 576 Central Ave., Dubuque, IA 52001. 1984.

Munschauer, John L., *Jobs for English Majors and Other Smart People*. Peterson's Guides, Inc., Box 2123, Princeton, NJ 08540. 1982.

"Business Week's Guide to Careers." Available on newsstands.

Goulet, Theresa, *Sell Yourself! The Career Handbook for Canadian University Students and Prospective Students*. Atgood Publications, Ltd., 401 Varsity Estates Bay NW, Calgary, Alberta, Canada T3B 2W7. 1982.

Kingstone, Brett, *The Student Entrepreneur's Guide*. Ten Speed Press, Box 7123, Berkeley, CA 94707. 1981. What college students are able to do as entrepreneurs, while still in college, has always staggered my imagination. One of them tells how it's done.

Figler, Howard E., *Path: A Career Workbook for Liberal Arts Students*. The Carroll Press Publishers, Box 8113, Cranston, RI 02920. 1979, 1975. Second edition, completely revised. Good stuff.

Our Canadian readers will want to know that their University and College Placement Association (43 Eglinton Ave. E., Suite 1003, Toronto, Ontario, M4P 1A2) puts out a number of publications for those related to the college scene. These include:

Career Planning Annual, 1983–1984. Published in either English or French.

McClure, Ross M., *Destiny: Career Planning Manual*. 1980. Also a counselor's guide to go with it.

Russell, Bonita I., *Heading Out. . . . A Job Search Workbook*. 1982, 1980.

Gaymer, Rosemary, *Teach Yourself How to Find a Job*. 1980, 1974.

Finding The Right Job For You. 1982.

The Resume. 1982.

The Interview. 1982.

Books on summer jobs are listed in
the next section.

21. HELP WITH THE SPECIAL PROBLEMS OF HIGH SCHOOL STUDENTS

Mosenfelder, Donn, *Vocabulary for the World of Work*. Educational Design, Inc., 47 W. 13th St., New York, NY 10014. 1985. The 300 words that people entering the work force most need to know.

Kimeldorf, Martin, *Job Search Education*. Educational Design, Inc., 47 W. 13th St., New York, NY 10014. 1985. Worksheets for the young job-hunter.

Otto, Ph.D., Luther B., *How to Help Your Child Choose a Career*. M. Evans and Co., Inc., 216 E. 49th St., New York, NY 10017. There is also an accompanying *Program Guide*.

Otto, Ph.D., Luther B., *Guide for Presenting Today's Youth and Tomorrow's Careers: A Seminar for Parents*. Boys Town, Father Flanagan's Boys' Home, Boys Town, NE 68010. 1984.

Douglas, Martha C., *Go For It: How to Get Your First Good Job*. Ten Speed Press, Box 7123, Berkeley, CA 94707. 1983. Based on Ms. Douglas' experience as coordinator of an industry training program for teenagers, at the *Contra Costa Times* newspaper in Walnut Creek, California.

O'Brien, Barbara, editor, *Summer Employment Directory of the United States*. Writer's Digest Books, 9933 Alliance Rd., Cincinnati, OH 45242. This book comes out each year. It lists 50,000 summer job openings at resorts, campuses, amusement parks, hotels, conferences and training centers, ranches, restaurants, national parks, etc. 1000 places, in all.

Woodworth, D. J., ed., *Overseas Summer Jobs: Where the Jobs Are and How to Get Them*. Writer's Digest Books, 9933 Alliance Rd., Cincinnati, OH 45242.

Henderson, Douglass, *Get Ready: Job-Hunters Kit* (for high school students). This package includes: *Get Ready, Teachers Manual; Get Ready, Students Manual*; and cassette. Get Ready, Inc., a subsidiary of Educational Motivation Inc., P.O. Box 18865, Philadelphia, PA 19119. 1980.

Career World—The Continuing Guide to Careers (a periodical), Joyce Lain Kennedy, Executive Editor. Curriculum Innovations, Inc. 501 Lake Forest Ave., Highwood, IL 60040.

22. HELP WITH GETTING A JOB IN EDUCATION

Teachers teach in schools. That has been the assumption that has dominated teacher-training for ages.

You would do well not to make this error. The range of places that use people with teaching skills is mind-boggling: but as just a sampling, there are—as experts like John Crystal point out—training academies (like fire and police); corporate training and education departments; local and state councils on higher education; designers and manufacturers of educational equipment; teachers associations; foundations; private research firms; regional and national associations of universities, etc.; state and congressional legislative committees on education; specialized educational publishing houses; professional and trade societies. An indication of some of the possibilities you may want to research, can be found in *Education Directory: Education Associations*. It's available in your local library, or from the Supt. of Documents, U.S. Govt. Printing Off., Washington, DC 20402.

Moreover, the range of jobs that are done under the broad umbrella of Education is multitudinous and varied; just for openers, there is: *teaching* (of course), *counseling* (an honorable teaching profession, where it isn't just used by a school system as the repository for teachers who couldn't 'cut it'), *general administration, adult education programs, public relations, ombudsman, training, human resource development,* and the like. If the latter—i.e., training and development—is of particular interest to you, you will find there is a very useful description of the particular competencies, skills, and knowledges needed in the training and development fields. You'll find it in *Training and Development Competencies*, Patricia A. McLagan, Volunteer Study Director. Published in 1983, it is available from the American Society for Training and Development. Also see: Stump, Robert W., *Your Career in Human Resource Development: A Guide to Information and Decision Making.* American Society for Training and Development, 1630 Duke St., Box 1443, Alexandria, VA 22313. 31 pages. 1985. Our Canadian friends, namely the Ontario Society for Training and Development, have put out also a helpful guide, entitled *Competency Analysis for Trainers: A Personal Planning Guide.* It is available from O.S.T.D., Box 537, Postal Station K, Toronto, M4P 2G9, Ontario, Canada. It outlines the kinds of skills which people who are entering this field ought to possess, and provides a checklist against which one can compare one's own skills.

All of which is to say, just because you have defined your dream of life for yourself as "teacher" doesn't mean you have even begun to narrow the territory down sufficiently for you to start looking for a job. You still have more research, and information gathering to do, before you have defined exactly *what kind* of teaching, *with what* kind of *groups, in what* kind of *place.* In other words, chapters 4 through 6 in this manual apply to you as much as, or even more than, anyone else.

If you decide to look elsewhere than teaching, there are aids produced for various teaching specialties, that you may want to seek out, e.g., for history majors there is: *Careers for Students of History*, from the American Historical Association, 400 A St. SE, Washington, DC 20003. 1977. While, for English majors, there is: *Aside from Teaching English, What in the World Can You Do?* by Dorothy K. Bestor, available from: University of Washington Press, Seattle, WA 98105. 1982, revised.

A more general guide for you, regardless of major, is: Bastress, Frances, *Teachers in New Careers: Stories of Successful Transitions.* The Carroll Press, Publishers, 43 Squantum St., Cranston, RI 02920. 1984. From: Career Development Services, Box 30301, Bethesda, MD 20814. See also:

Beard, Marna L. and McGahey, Michael J., *Alternative Careers for Teachers.* The complete job-changing handbook for educators. Arco Publishing, Inc., 215 Park Ave. S., New York, NY 10003. 1985.

23. HELP WITH ANALYSIS OF SKILLS

Smith, Bob R., *'86 Spring Catalog: Psychological and Educational Testing Materials for the Professional.* Psychological Assessment Resources, Inc., Box 98, Odessa, FL 33556. 1986.

Whitaker, Urban and Breen, Paul, *Bridging the Gap: A Learner's Guide to Transferable Skills.* The Learning Center, Box 27616, San Francisco, CA 94127. 415-334-3196. 1983.

Pearson, Henry G., *Your Hidden Skills: Clues to Careers and Future Pursuits.* Mowry Press, Box 405, Wayland, MA 01778. 1981.

Myers, Isabel Briggs and Peter, *Gifts Differing.* Consulting Psychologists Press, Inc., 577 College Ave., Palo Alto, CA 94306. 1980. Related to the increasingly-popular Myers-Briggs Test.

Figler, Howard E., *The Complete Job Search Handbook: Presenting the Skills You Need to Get Any Job, and Have a Good Time Doing It.* Holt, Rinehart and Winston, 521 Fifth Ave., New York, NY 10175. 1979. Deals with the skills actually used in the job-hunt process itself.

Scheele, Adele, *Skills For Success: A Guide to the Top for Men and Women.* Ballantine Books, 201 E. 50th St., New York, NY 10022. 1979.

Fine, Sidney A., *Functional Job Analysis Scales: A Desk Aid.* Methods for Manpower Analysis, No. 5. April 1973.

————, and Wiley, Wretha W., *An Introduction to Functional Job Analysis: A Scaling of Selected Tasks from the Social Welfare Field.* Methods for Manpower Analysis, No. 4. September 1971.

————, *A Systems Approach to New Careers: Two Papers.*, Methods for Manpower Analysis, No. 3. November 1969.

————, *Guidelines for the Design of New Careers.* September 1967.

The W.E. Upjohn Institute for Employment Research's *Studies on Functional Job Analysis and Career Design.*

The above pamphlets are available from The W. E. Upjohn Institute for Employment Research, 300 S. Westnedge Ave., Kalamazoo, MI 49007.

Fine, Sidney A., *Nature of Skill: Implication for Education and Training.* 1870 Wyoming Ave. NW, Washington, DC 20009. A superb summary of some recent thinking from the father of skills analysis in the Dictionary of Occupational Titles.

24. HELP WITH INTERVIEWING, SALARY NEGOTIATION, AND RESUMES

Parker, Yana, *The Damn Good Resume Guide.* Ten Speed Press, Box 7123, Berkeley, CA 94707. 1986. Describes how to write a *functional* resume.

Biegeleisen, J. I., *How to Write Your First Professional Resume.* The Putnam Publishing Group, 200 Madison Ave., New York, NY 10016.

Washington, Tom, *Resume Power: Selling Yourself on Paper.* Mount Vernon Press, 1121 112th NE, Bellevue, WA 98004. 1985.

Hellman, Paul, *Ready, Aim, You're Hired!: How to Job-Interview Successfully Anytime, Anywhere with Anyone*, AMACOM, 135 W. 50th St., New York, NY 10020. 1986.

Chapman, Jack, ed., *How to Make $1,000 a Minute*. Negotiating salaries and raises. JSC Publishing, 221 N. LaSalle, Box 1548, Chicago, IL 60601. 1985.

Robert Half on Hiring. Crown Publishers, Inc., One Park Ave., New York, NY 10016. 1985. 241 pages.

Keirsey, David and Bates, Marilyn, *Please Understand Me*. Prometheus Nemesis Books, Box 2082, Del Mar, CA 92014. 1978.

Zimbardo, Phillip G., *Shyness, What It Is, What to Do About It*. Jove Publications, 757 Third Ave., New York, NY 10017. 1977.

Granovetter, Mark S., *Getting a Job: A Study of Contacts and Careers*. Harvard University Press, c/o Uniserv Inc., 525 Great Road, Rt. 119, Littleton, MA 01460. 1974. *The* classic study of the importance of contacts for the job-hunt.

Lathrop, Richard, *Who's Hiring Who?* Ten Speed Press, Box 7123, Berkeley, CA 94707. 1977, updated 1980. The very best book on how to write a resume, or "qualifications brief," as the author prefers it be called.

Jackson, Tom, *The Perfect Resume*. Anchor Press/Doubleday. Garden City, NY 11530. 1981.

Teeple, Barbara, *Barbara Teeple's Guide through the Resume Workbook*. Rainbow Word Pros Ltd., 1002 Knottwood Rd. E., Edmonton, Alberta T6K 3R5, Canada. 1982.

Molloy, John T., *Dress for Success*. Warner Books, 666 Fifth Ave., New York, NY 10103. 1975. The classic in the "personal image consultancy" field: how to make a better impression through the way you dress.

Molloy, John T., *The Women's Dress for Success Book* (same publisher).

Supplement to Employment and Earnings, U.S. Department of Labor, Bureau of Labor Statistics. 1984. Order from: Supt. of Documents, U.S. Govt. Printing Off., Washington, DC 20402. Tells what different occupations pay.

Biegeleisen, J. I., *Make Your Job Interview a Success: A Guide for the Career-Minded Jobseeker*. Arco Publishing, Inc., 215 Park Ave. S., New York, NY 10003. 1984.

Biegeleisen, J. I., *Job Resumes: How to Write Them, How to Present Them, Preparing for Interviews*. Grosset & Dunlap, 51 Madison Ave., New York, NY 10010. 1982, revised. A classic in the field.

Williams, Eugene, *Getting the Job You Want With the Audiovisual Portfolio*. Comptex Associates, Inc., Box 6745, Washington, DC 20020. 1982. Manual for job-seekers and career changers in professions other than teaching.

The Catalyst Staff, *Marketing Yourself: The Catalyst Guide to Successful Resumes and Interviews*. Bantam Books, 666 Fifth Ave., New York, NY 10103. 1981.

Medley, H. Anthony, *Sweaty Palms: The Neglected Art of Being Interviewed*. Ten Speed Press, Box 7123, Berkeley, CA 94707. 1978. *The* classic on interviewing.

25. HELP WITH JOB-HUNTING IN GENERAL, AND PLACES TO LIVE

At the United Nations, when Swahili is being spoken, most people from other nations do not understand—until, over the earphones, the speech is translated into their own language. So, with job-hunting. Many do not understand the language of *Parachute*. Yet the same thoughts, spoken in another's style of writing, say Howard Figler's or Tom Jackson's, may suddenly hit home to those readers. There are over 20,000,000 different job hunters out there, in an average year. No one book will ever be understood by them all. Hence, we will always need many different books on job-hunting; and the more different 'styles' or 'languages,' the better.

Rockcastle, Madeline T., ed., *Where to Start: An Annotated Career Planning Bibliography*, 5th ed. 1985-1987. Cornell University Career Center. Peterson's Guides, Inc., Box 2123, Princeton, NJ 08540. 609-924-5338.

Porot, Daniel, *Comment Trouver Une Situation*. Les Editions d'Organisation, 5, rue Rousselet, F-75007 Paris, telephone (1) 567.18.40. 1985.

Bayless, Hugh, *The Best Towns in America: A Where-to-Go Guide for a Better Life*. Houghton-Mifflin Co., 2 Park St. Boston, MA 02108. 1983.

Noyes, Dan, *Raising Hell: A Citizen's Guide to the Fine Art of Investigation*. Revised. Foundation for National Progress, Mother Jones, 1663 Mission St., San Francisco, CA 94103. 1983.

Ullmann, John and Honeyman, Steve, eds., *The Reporter's Handbook: An Investigator's Guide to Documents and Techniques*. St. Martin's Press, Inc., 175 Fifth Ave., New York, NY 10010. 1983.

Mangum, Stephen I., *JOB SEARCH: A Review of the Literature*, Olympus Publishing Co., Box 9362, Salt Lake City, UT 84109. 1982.

Bowman, Thomas F.; Giuliana, George A.; and Minge, M. Ronald, *Finding Your Best Place to Live in America*. Red Lion Books, 609 Route 109, West Babylon, NY 11704. 1981.

Boyer, Richard, and Savageau, David, *Places Rated Almanac: Your Guide to Finding the Best Places to Live in America*. Rand McNally & Co. 1981.

Ruffner, James A., and Bair, Frank E., eds., *The Weather Almanac*. Avon Books, 1790 Broadway, New York, NY 10019. 1979.

Seavey, Bill, ed., *Greener Pastures Gazette*: a newsletter dedicated to the search for countryside Edens where the Good Life still exists. Published six times yearly. Relocation Research, Box 864, Bend, OR 97709. (They used to publish a newsletter called *Small Town, U.S.A.*, but this newsletter has supplanted it.)

Fiedler, J. Michael, ed., *Career Paths*. Bob Adams, Inc., 840 Summer St., Boston, MA 02127. 1984. Has interviews with forty professionals, salary and fringe benefits surveys, and reports on selected industries.

Anderson, Nancy, *Work With Passion: How to Do What You Love for a Living*. A copublication of Carroll & Graf Publishers, Inc., 260 Fifth Ave., New York, NY 10001, and Whatever Publishing, Inc., Box 137, Mill Valley, CA 94942. 1984. Good on how to establish contact with people.

Stevens, Paul, *Work Satisfaction: How to Plan for, Find, and Maintain It. A comprehensive guide to planning and managing your career*. William Brooks, 723 Elizabeth St., Waterloo, NSW 2017.

Feingold, S. Norman, and Winkler, Glenda, *Nine Hundred Thousand Plus Jobs Annually: Published Sources of Employment Listings*. Garrett Park Press, Garrett Park, MD 20896. Cites periodicals which list job announcements. 1982.

Feingold, S. Norman, and Nicholson, Avis, *The Professional and Trade Association Job Finder: A Directory of Employment Resources Offered by Associations and Other Organizations*. Garrett Park Press, Garrett Park, MD 20896.

Take Charge of Your Own Career—Job Search Card File. One hundred 4 × 6 job search cards, a set of index cards, and a portable filing case. Send order to Donna J. Moore, Box 723, Bainbridge Island, WA 98110. 206-842-2170.

Jackson, Tom, and Mayleas, Davidyne, *The Hidden Job Market for the Eighties*. Quadrangle/The New York Times Book Co., 3 Park Ave., New York, NY 10016. 1981.

Job Information and Seeking Training Program Instructor's Guide and Job Seekers Workbook. JIST, 1001 W. 10th St., Indianapolis, IN 46202. 1980.

Komar, John J., *The Great Escape from Your Dead-End Job*. Follett Publishing Co., Chicago, IL. 1980.

26. IF YOU ARE A CAREER COUNSELOR, OR WANT TO BE

Those just getting started in the field of career counseling (within or without academia) will, of course, want to read the current edition of *Parachute* from cover to cover, and then DO all the exercises within it, before they inflict them on their helpless students or clients. *Teaching is sharing, and Sharing should only follow Experiencing*.

Among the following listings, you will find a number of workbooks designed to help you with that Sharing.

Newsletter about life/work planning. Richard N. Bolles, editor. National Career Development Project, Box 379, Walnut Creek, CA 94596. Published six times a year, always written by the editor himself.

Career Planning & Adult Development Newsletter, published monthly by the Career Planning and Adult Development Network, 1190 S. Bascom Ave., Ste. 211, San Jose, CA 95128, 408-295-5461.

CNews: Career Opportunities News, Garrett Park Press, Garrett Park, MD 20896, 301-946-2553. Useful news for counselors (and job-hunters) about employment fields, fellowships, new books, etc.

Hodges, Robert T., ed., *The Career Planner's Letter*. Intended for career changers, job hunters, career consultants and counselors involved in career planning and development work. 6110 South Tabor St., Littleton, CO 80127.

The Vocational Guidance Quarterly, a professional journal concerned with research, theory, and practice in career development, career guidance, career resources, and career education. The official publication of the National Vocational Guidance Association, a division of the American Association for Counseling and Development, 5999 Stevenson Ave., Alexandria, VA 22304.

Wallach, Ellen J., with Fulford, Nancy, *Career Management: When Preparation Meets Opportunity. Leader's Guide*. AMA Film/Video, 85 Main St., Watertown, MA 02172. An excellent manual, designed to go with the film of the same title, in order to help you to use the film to serve a number of purposes: if you (as counselor) are trying to sell decision makers on the benefits of career management to their organization; or if you want to inform managers about the benefits of career management as part of an overall human resource system; or if you are working with HR professionals to assess organizational career management needs and/or to design a systems approach to career management; or if you want to give individual employees, their managers, or HR professionals an overview of career management; or if you are training personnel who are charged with career guidance responsibilities; or if you want to conduct a career management workshop; or if you are approached by an employee or manager seeking individual career counseling.

Knowdell, Richard L.; McDaniels, Carl; Hesser, Al; and Walz, Garry R., *Outplacement Counseling*. Eric Counseling and Personnel Services Clearinghouse, School of Education, University of Michigan, Ann Arbor, MI 48109. 1983. This is the area of career development, within the world of work, that is expanding the fastest these days. For counselors interested in this as a future field of endeavor, this overview.

Maze, Marilyn, and Cummings, Roger, *How to Select a Computer Assisted Career Guidance System*. EUREKA, 5625 Sutter Ave., Richmond, CA 94804. 1982. For schools, organizations and agencies thinking of acquiring one of the computerized systems now available. What they can do, what they can't do.

Wegmann, Robert, *How to Find a Job in Houston*. Ten Speed Press, Box 7123, Berkeley, CA 94707. 1983. Every counselor or workshop leader who teaches a course or leads a workshop on job-hunting should find this book very helpful. Professor Wegmann has for some years, now, taught a course, for credit, on job-hunting, at the University of Houston–Clear Lake City. This book is adapted from his curriculum, with supplementary research on the city of Houston. It illustrates how to dissect *any* city or geographical area, for the purposes of the job-hunter or career-changer. It has an appendix also on "Assisting Larger Groups of Unemployed Workers to Find New Employment," by Professor Wegmann; as well as an article, "The Loss of Values in Career Counseling," by Richard N. Bolles.

Making a Living Work is an eight-part television series about life/career planning. It features interviews with Richard Bolles and many others. For information, contact Elyzabeth Joffe, ITV Coordinator, Ohio University, Telecommunication Center, Athens, OH 45701. The series was produced by the Council for the Advancement of Experiential Learning (CAEL).

Lant, Dr. Jeffrey, *Tricks of the Trade: The Complete Guide to Succeeding in the Advice Business*. JLA Publications, 50 Follen St., Ste. 507, Cambridge, MA 02138. 617-547-6372. 1986.

Mencke, Reed, and Hummel, Ronald L., *Career Planning for the 80s*. Brooks/Cole Publishing Co., a Division of Wadsworth, Inc., 555 Abrego St., Monterey, CA 93940. 1984.

Borchard, David C., Kelly, John J., Weaver, Nancy Pat K., *Your Career: Choices, Chances, Changes*. Kendall/Hunt Publishing Co., 2460 Kerper Blvd., Dubuque, IA 52001. 1984.

Hopson, Dr. Barrie, and Scally, Mike, *Build Your Own Rainbow: A Workbook for Career and Life Management*. Lifeskills Assoc., Ashling, Back Church Le., Leeds LS16 8DN, England. 1984.

Career Planning for Office Workers: A Training Manual. Continuing Education Services, University of Wisconsin at Madison, 905 University Ave., Ste., 1, Madison, WI 53715. 1984. For workshop leaders and trainers, who work with office workers.

If you are going to want to do group work, or make group presentations—but the idea of getting up in front of a group fills you with trepidation—you may find some comfort and help in:

Nelson, Robert B., *Louder and Funnier: A Practical Guide for Overcoming Stagefright in Speechmaking*. Ten Speed Press, Box 7123, Berkeley, CA 94707. 1985. It has some very practical aids, such as your own personal "Fear Map," on which you can map out the precise areas where your fear lies.

Bloomfield, William M., *The Vocational Action Plan: Targeting Job Success; a Workbook*. William Bloomfield and Associates, Inc., 90 Park St., Ste. 22, Brookline, MA 02146. 1982.

Hagberg, Janet, and Leider, Richard, *The Inventurers: Excursions in Life and Career Renewal*. Addison-Wesley Publishing Co., Jacob Way, Reading, MA 01867. 1982.

Johnson, Miriam, *The State of the Art in Job Search Training*, Olympus Publishing Co., Box 9362, Salt Lake City, UT 84109. 1982.

Johnson, Miriam with Roberts, David, *Getting Youth on the Job Track*, Olympus Publishing Co., Box 9362, Salt Lake City, UT 84109. 1982.

Career & Job Search Instruction Made Easy, JIST Works, Inc., The Job Search People, 150 E. 14th St., Indianapolis, IN 46202. 1-800-648-JIST.

Leider, Richard J., and Harding, James S., *Taking Stock: A Daily Self-Management Journal*. Taking Stock, Box 8709, Portland, OR 97208. 1981.

Crites, John O., *Career Counseling: Models, Methods, and Materials*. McGraw-Hill, 1221 Avenue of the Americas, New York, NY 10020. 1981.

Pilder, Richard J., and William F., *How to Find Your Life's Work*. Prentice-Hall, Englewood Cliffs, NJ 07632. 1981.

Guide for Occupational Exploration. Supt. of Documents, U.S. Govt. Printing Off., Washington, DC 20402. 1979. Occupations organized by interest and job title.

Feldman, Beverly Neuer, *Jobs/Careers Serving Children and Youth* (including Supplement: Appendix C and Index–inserted into the book, but separate). Till Press, Box 27816, Los Angeles, CA 90027. 1978. Groups the jobs and careers according to how much education the job-hunter has had. For all those who want to work with youth or children.

Cosgrave, Gerald, *Career Planning: Search for a Future*. Guidance Centre/Faculty of Education/University of Toronto. 1973. Available from Customer Service, Teacher's College Press, 1234 Amsterdam Ave., New York, NY 10027; or from Consulting Psychologists' Press, 577 College Ave., Palo Alto, CA 94306. It relates to John L. Holland's six people-environments.

Hoppock, Robert, *Occupational Information: Where to Get It and How to Use It in Counseling and in Teaching*. Third edition. McGraw-Hill, New York, NY. 1976. A pioneer in this field.

Super, Donald E., et al., *Career Development: Self-Concept Theory. Essays in Vocational Development*. College Board Publication Orders, Box 2815, Princeton, NJ 08540. 1963. Another pioneer in the field.

27. PERSPECTIVES ON THE WORLD OF WORK TODAY

Collard, Betsy A., *The High-Tech Career Book: Finding Your Place in Today's Job Market*. William Kaufmann, Inc., 95 1st St., Los Altos, CA 94022. 1986.

Sukiennik, Diane; Raufman, Lisa; and Bendat, William, *The Career Fitness Program: Exercising Your Options*. Gorsuch Scarisbrick, 8233 Via Paseo Del Norte, Ste. E-400, Scottsdale, AZ 85258. 1986.

Wegmann, Robert; Chapman, Robert; and Johnson, Miriam, *Looking for Work in the New Economy*. Olympus Publishing Co., 1670 E. 1300 S., Salt Lake City, UT 84105. 1985.

Hallberg, Edmond; Levitt, Herbert; and Hallberg, Kaylene, *Getting into Overtime*. Ombudsman Press, Inc., 470 W. Highland Ave., Sierra Madre, CA 91024. 1984.

Caple, John, *Careercycles*. Prentice-Hall, Inc., Englewood Cliffs, NJ 07632. 1983

Cornish, Ed, ed., *Careers Tomorrow: The Outlook for Work in a Changing World*. World Future Society, 4916 St. Elmo Ave., Bethesda, MD 20814. 1983.

Feingold, S. Norman, and Miller, Norma Reno, *Emerging Careers: New Occupations for the Year 2000 and Beyond. Vol. I. The Newest of the New*. Garrett Park Press, Garrett Park, MD 20896. 1983.

Raines, John C.; Berson, Lenora E.; and Gracie, David McI., ed., *Community and Capital in Conflict: Plant Closings and Job Loss*. Temple University Press, Broad and Oxford Sts., Philadelphia, PA 19122. 1982.

Raelin, Joseph A., *Building a Career: The Effect of Initial Job Experiences and Related Work Attitudes on Later Employment*. W. E. Upjohn Institute for Employment Research, 300 S. Westnedge Ave., Kalamazoo, MI 49007. 1980.

U.S. Dept. of Labor, Bureau of Labor Statistics, *Handbook of Labor Statistics*. Supt. of Documents, U.S. Govt. Printing Off., Washington, DC 20402.

U.S. Dept. of Labor, Employment and Training Admin., *Selected Characteristics of Occupations Defined in the Dictionary of Occupational Titles*. Supt. of Documents, U.S. Govt. Printing Off., Washington, DC 20402. 1981.

U.S. Dept. of Labor, Employment and Training Admin., *Guide for Occupational Exploration*. Supt. of Documents, U.S. Govt. Printing Off., Washington, DC 20402. Stock #029-013-0080-2. 1979.

Bureau of Labor Statistics, *Occupational Outlook Handbook*, Supt. of Documents, U.S. Govt. Printing Off., Washington, DC 20402. 670-page encyclopedia of careers, covering hundreds of occupations and 35 major industries.

Edwards, Patsy B., *Leisure Counseling Techniques*. Constructive Leisure, 511 N. La Cienega Blvd., Los Angeles, CA 90048.

Lathrop, Richard, *The Job Market*. The National Center for Job-Market Studies, Box 3651, Washington, DC 20007. What would happen if we decreased the length of the job-hunt in America, and other iconoclastic ideas which are also eminently sensible.

28. PERSPECTIVES ON CREATIVITY AND THE BRAIN

Our whole vocational system is oriented toward people with high verbal, analytical, and logical skills—rather than toward people who have high picturing, intuitive and contextual skills. Those wishing to correct this imbalance, in themselves or others, will find it immensely helpful to know more about the brain. That organ's division into "left-mode" and "right-mode" has by now become familiar to most readers of airline magazines and other scholarly journals.

Books that can give you a broad overview of the subject, include the following:

Ornstein, Robert, *Multimind: A New Way of Looking at Human Behavior*, Houghton Mifflin Co., 2 Park St., Boston, MA 02108. 1986.

Von Oech, Roger, *A Kick In The Seat Of The Pants: Using Your Explorer, Artist, Judge and Warrior to Be More Creative*. Harper & Row, 10 E. 53rd St., New York, NY 10022. 1986.

Wonder, Jacquelyn, and Donovan, Priscilla, *Whole-Brain Thinking: Working from Both Sides of the Brain to Achieve Peak Job Performance*. William Morrow and Co., 105 Madison Ave., New York, NY 10016. 1984.

Lynch, Dudley, *Your High-Performance Business Brain: An Operator's Manual*. Brain Technologies Corporation, 414 Buckeye St., Fort Collins, CO 80524. 1984.

Von Oech, Roger, *A Whack on the Side of the Head: How to Unlock Your Mind for Innovation*. Warner Books, 666 Fifth Ave., New York, NY 10103. 1983. A very interesting and extremely popular book.

Segalowitz, Sid J., *Two Sides of the Brain: Brain Lateralization Explored*. Prentice-Hall, Englewood Cliffs, NJ 07632. 1983. One of the latest, and one of the best, on up-to-date findings concerning the two sides of the brain.

Durden-Smith, Jo, and DeSimone, Diane, *Sex and the Brain*. Arbor House, 235 E. 45th St., New York, NY 10017. 1983. Answers all those questions you have been just dying to ask, about how differences in the way the two sides of our brain actually function are related to sex differences between male and female.

Springer, Sally P., and Deutsch, Georg, *Left Brain, Right Brain*. W. H. Freeman and Co., 660 Market St., San Francisco, CA 94104. 1981.

Edwards, Betty, *Drawing on the Right Side of the Brain: A Course in Enhancing Creativity and Artistic Confidence*. J. P. Tarcher, Inc., 9110 Sunset Blvd., Los Angeles, CA 90069. 1979. Absolutely top-notch. On the surface, a book about drawing. Actually, a book about creativity in all its facets. Splendid.

For those of you who want to find out more about your own "left-brainedness" or "right-brainedness," there are two instruments—each quite different from the other—that are available:

Ned Herrmann has produced the "Herrmann Brain Dominance Instrument," for those of you who want to find out more about how "left-brained," "right-brained," or "double-dominant" you are. You can contact him at: Ned Hermann, 105 Laurel Dr., Lake Lure, NC 28746, for details as to how to get your hands on it.

Dudley Lynch, in Colorado, has produced a somewhat different kind of instrument, dealing more with styles of action, as related to the brain; it is called "The BrainMap." You can contact him at Brain Technologies Corporation, 414 Buckeye St., Fort Collins, CO 80524 for more details.

The kind of books listed earlier must, in the very nature of things, lag somewhat behind the fast-moving discoveries in this field. Ned Herrmann's corporation, therefore, has taken to publishing (twice yearly) a journal entitled, "The International Brain Dominance Review." It describes research, findings, and applications of brain dominance research to various fields and problems. Address: The International Brain Dominance Review, 105 Laurel Dr., Lake Lure, NC 28746.

There are two other periodicals which have *some* material on the latest research findings concerning the brain; but we would advise you to ask for a sample issue before making up your mind as to whether or not these will bring you the kind of information you are searching for. They devote much space to other subjects, reporting interesting developments in what can only be called "brain-related fields" (*everything* is a brain-related field, if you choose to call it so).

Brain/Mind Bulletin. Marilyn Ferguson, ed. Interface Press, Box 42211, Los Angeles, CA 90042.

Brain & Strategy. Dudley Lynch, ed. Brain Technologies Corp., 414 Buckeye St., Fort Collins, CO 80524.

Two are better than one;
    for if they fall,
the one will lift up his fellow;

but woe to him that is alone when he falleth,
and hath not another to lift him up.

Ecclesiastes

Appendix B

When Books Are Not Enough
and
You Want a Live Person
to Guide You:

Counselors and Other Resources

REQUIRED READING:
If You're Thinking of Hiring a Career Counselor to Help You

Okay, you're back here in this section either because you're just curious to know what it says, or because you're ready to admit you've just got to hire *somebody* to help you, with all this.

And you've decided you've got to find somebody to help you because either:

a) you *tried* doing the exercises in the book, and you just aren't getting anywhere; or

b) you've read the book—sections of it anyway—and without even trying the exercises, you know yourself well enough to know you need someone who will explain it all to you, step by step. You're an "ear" person, more than an "eye" person, and you do better when a human being is explaining something to you, than when you're trying to read it for yourself; OR

c) you've not read the book, nor tried any of the exercises, but you *have* counted the number of pages in the book, and the very thickness of it all was so intimidating, that you've decided to toss in the towel before you even begin. ("Help!")

You've turned to this section because you figure that back here must be some sort of "authorized list" of names: people who understand this whole job-hunting process thoroughly, know how to do all the exercises in this book, have been through some kind of careful credentialing process, and received the Parachute Seal of Approval.

Ah, dear reader, how I wish it were so. But, unhappily, there is no such list. First of all, while I do train people once a year, I haven't trained all that many, over the years. Moreover, I can't guarantee that simply because they've been through my hands, they truly understand. So, publishing a list of their names wouldn't necessarily give you the information you want.

Secondly, there are lots of people "out there" who understand the whole job-hunting process thoroughly and well, even though they've never been trained by me and may not even (necessarily) have read this book. In most cases, of course, I've never met them, and consequently I don't know who they are or where they are. I simply know *that* they are.

What this all adds up to, you've already guessed. Hunting for a decent person or place to help you is just like hunting for a job. You've got to do your own research, and your own interviewing, in your own area. Getting somebody else's opinion, in effect letting them do your research for you, isn't very effective. First of all, their information is often somewhat out-dated, and therefore questionable. Maybe the counselor or place they're telling you about is one they ran into a year ago. The counselor was excellent, at that time. But since then (unbeknownst to your friend) that counselor has been through a really rough time, personally: divorce, burnout, overwhelming fatigue—the works. It's affected their counseling, to say the least; they're no longer functioning at the top level they were a year ago. Your friend's recommendation is outdated—at least for the present. And, of course, it can be just the other way around. Your friend tells you someone is terrible, as a counselor, because when your friend ran into them, two or three years ago, it was true. But, that counselor has had dozens and dozens of clients since then, and learned a lot (most career counselors are trained by their clients, you know). That counselor is now very good. Your friend's "dis-recommendation" is now outdated.

Secondly, the three things you absolutely want from anyone you're paying good money to, are:

a) a firm grasp of the whole job-hunting process, at its most creative and effective level;

b) the ability to communicate that information lucidly and clearly to others;

c) rapport with you.

This last is a very difficult thing to pin down. Maybe this counselor is simply wonderful on the first two counts, but he reminds you of your Uncle Harry. You've always *hated* your Uncle Harry. No go. But how could anyone have known that, except you?

I repeat: no one can do this research about which job counselor is best, except you. Because the real question is not "Who is best?" but "Who is best for you?" Those last two words change everything.

What I want to do for you is:

1. Give you a brief crash course about this whole field of career counseling.

2. Tell you where to find some names with which *to start* your search for "who is best for you."

3. Give you some questions, that will help you separate the sheep from the goats, and make an intelligent decision.

Okay, here we go:

1. A CRASH COURSE ABOUT THIS WHOLE FIELD OF CAREER COUNSELING

In the whole big field of The Job Hunt, all professional help divides (one regrets to say) into the following three categories, so far as the job-hunter is concerned:

      1. Professionals who are sincere and skilled.

      2. Professionals who are sincere but inept.

      3. Professionals who are insincere and inept.

The problem we all face when we decide to seek help with our job-hunt, is: which is which. Or, who is who. We want a career counselor who falls into category No. 1; if he or she falls into the other two categories, which of the other two they fall into is really irrelevant: ineptness is ineptness, whether it is sincere or not.

The various clues which may at first occur to us, for identifying good career counselors, are upon more serious examination not terribly fruitful. Let us tick off some of them, and see why:

★ Clue No. 1: Perhaps we can tell who is sincere and skilled, by the name of the specialist or their agency. Difficulty: names vary greatly from one operation to another, even when the operations are similar. Among the names which some counselors or agencies bear, you will find: executive career counselors, executive career consultants, career management teams, vocational psychologists, executive consulting counselors, career guidance counselors, executive advisors, executive development specialists, executive job counselors, manpower experts, career advisors, employment specialists, executive recruitment consultants, professional career counselors, management consultants, placement specialists, executive search specialists, vocational counselors, life/work planners, etc. If, tomorrow, some legitimate counselor who is sincere and skilled takes on a new name, the day after that some counselor who is insincere and inept will copy the name directly. What it all comes down to, is this: Wolves need sheep's clothing. Names are sheep's clothing. Trouble is, hidden in there are some genuinely helpful people. We need another clue.

★ Clue No. 2: Perhaps we can tell who is sincere and skilled by reading everything that the agency or counselor has written. Difficulty: both good and bad counselors know the areas where the job-hunter feels exceedingly vulnerable. Consequently, there are "turn on" words which occur in almost everybody's advertisements, brochures, and books: we will give you help, say they, with evaluating your career history, in-depth analysis of your background, establishment of your job objective, in-depth analysis of your capabilities, writing an effective resume, names of companies, preparing

the covering letter, background materials on companies, interviewing techniques, salary negotiations, filling out forms, answering ads, aptitude tests, special problems—unemployment, age, too broad a background, too narrow a background, too many job changes, too few job changes, poor references, etc. We will, say they, open doors for you, tell you which companies are hiring, and so forth. Both the counselors who are skilled and those who are inept will never get anyone in their doors if they don't mention the areas that have put the job-hunter in Desperation City. So how they describe their services (real or alleged) doesn't separate the sheep from the goats, unfortunately. Next clue?

★ Clue No. 3: Perhaps we can tell who is sincere and skilled by the fee they charge? I mean, they wouldn't charge a high fee, would they, if they weren't skilled? Difficulty: as insiders say, low fees may mean well-intentioned but amateurish help. However, the reverse of this is *not* true. As we have already mentioned, the vacuum created by the chaotic condition of our job-hunting process has attracted both competent people *and* people who are determined to prey upon the acute state of anxiety that job-hunters are often in. And when the latter say "Let us prey" they *really* prey. And they *thrive.* They can charge anywhere between $2,000 and $10,000 (it's solely dependent on your previous salary) *up front,* before they've given you *any* services or help at all. And if you are later dissatisfied, your chances of getting your money back are remote, indeed—no matter what the contract said. (They've fashioned every legal loophole in the book, in order to keep your money.) P. T. Barnum knew what he was talking about.[1] Next.

★ Clue No. 4: Perhaps we can tell which professionals are both sincere and skilled, by talking to satisfied clients—or asking our friends to tell us who was helpful to them. If you stop to think about it, you will realize this most crucial truth: *all your friends can possibly speak to you about is the particular counselor or counselors that they worked with, at that agency, in that particular city.* Should you go to the same place, and get a different counselor, you might have a very different experience. One bad counselor in an agency that has say, six good ones, can cost you much money, time, and self-esteem, if *you* get that bad one as *your* counselor. The six good ones might as well be in Timbuktu, for all the good they'll do you. So should any of your friends offer (or should you solicit from them) advice about a place they went to, be sure to find out the counselor (or counselors) they worked with, there, *by name* so you will know who to ask for, if you decide to investigate or follow their lead.

Before we leave this clue, let us also observe that while most professional career counselors will show you letters from satisfied customers, or even give you (in some cases) their names to check out, it is impossible to find out what percentage of their total clientele these satisfied persons represent: 100%? 10? 1? .1? a fluke? If you want a clue, you may make what you

---

1. A sucker is born every minute. Or as the post office has updated it: "A sucker is shorn every minute."

will out of the fact that the top officers of the largest executive counseling firm, which allegedly did over 50% of the business in the industry before it declared bankruptcy in the fall of 1974 (namely, Frederick Chusid & Co.), gave testimony during a civil suit in a New York Federal district court which indicated that only three or four out of every ten clients had been successful in getting a new job, during a previous six-month period. More recently, another prominent executive counseling firm was reported by the Attorney General's Office of New York State to have placed only 38 out of 550 clients.[1] Are these figures average for the industry? Better than average? Worse? Nobody knows.

In any event, virtually no career counselor or career counseling firm will EVER show you letters from DISsatisfied clients. Were you to be given access to such letters (the files of many Better Business Bureaus, the Consumer Fraud division of your state or city Attorney General's office, not to mention the Federal Trade Commission, are loaded with such letters) you would find the complaints have certain recurrent themes: the career counseling firm being complained about, they say, did not do what they *verbally* promised to do, have the exclusive lists of job openings they claimed to have, nor the access to executive suites they claimed to have, nor the success rate they claimed, nor did they give the amount of time to the client they *verbally* promised in advance (sometimes it turned out to be as few as six hours). 'Job campaigns' for the clients were slow to start, usually not until the full advance fee was paid, promised lists were slow in being provided and often were outdated and full of errors, the friendly 'intake counselor' was actually a salesperson, and is never seen again once the contract is signed, the actual counselor was often difficult (or impossible) to get ahold of after a certain period of time (sometimes coinciding with the final payment by the client of the advance fee), the 'plan' was often no news at all to the client, the promised contact with employers on the client's behalf was not forthcoming, phone calls or letters of complaint were ignored, and the fee was not refunded in whole or in part, when the client was dissatisfied, despite implicit (or explicit) promises to the contrary. Whew!

Well, that's enough of a crash course on career counseling, and the pitfalls that await the unwary or the innocent. If you are dying to know more, and your local library has back files of magazines and newspapers (on microfiche, or otherwise), you can look up:

"Career-Counseling Industry Accused of Misrepresentation," *New York Times*, Sept. 30, 1982, p. C1.

"Consumer Law: Career Counselors and Employment Agencies" by Reed Brody, *New York Law Journal*, Feb. 26, 1982, p. 1. Reed was Assistant Attorney General of the State of New York, and more recently Deputy Chief of the Labor Bureau within that State's Department of Law; in this capacity he became the leading legal expert in the country, on career counseling malpractices. He has now, however, left this work, for a job in Cen-

---

1. "Career Counselors: Will They Lead You Down The Primrose Path?" by Lee Guthrie, in the December 1981 issue of *Savvy Magazine*, p. 60 ff.

tral America, so he is not available for the kind of helpful information he gave so many in the past.

"Career Counselors: Will They Lead You Down The Primrose Path?" by Lee Guthrie. *Savvy Magazine*, Dec., 1981, p. 60ff.

"Franklin Career Search Is Accused of Fraud In New York State Suit," *Wall Street Journal*, Jan. 29, 1981, p. 50.

"Job Counseling Firms Under Fire For Promising Much, Giving Little," *Wall Street Journal*, Jan. 27, 1981, p. 33.

Stuart Alan Rado has been waging a sort of "one man crusade" against career counseling firms which take advantage of the job-hunter. *His* advice, as the result of counseling many victims, is: don't go to *any* firm which requires the fee all in advance. If you are reading this too late, did pay some firm's fee all in advance, and feel you were ripped off, if you will send Mr. Rado a self-addressed stamped envelope, he will send you a one-page sheet of some actions you can take. His address is: 1500 23rd St., Sunset Island #3, Miami Beach, FL 33140. 305-532-2607. He is working to help bring about new state laws, which will make it at least a little more difficult for unconscionable career counseling firms to take advantage of the hapless job-hunter or career-changer. Some states, such as California, have already adopted such laws.

2. WHERE TO FIND SOME NAMES TO START YOUR SEARCH FOR WHO IS BEST FOR YOU

You start, of course, by asking everyone you know—family, friends, and people you've just met—if they know any really helpful career counselors.

You supplement this by looking in the Yellow Pages of your local telephone book. Possible headings to check out (they vary from phone book to phone book) are: vocational counselors, executive career counselors, career counselors, job counseling, guidance counselors, career consultants, employment counselors. Also any cross references that these lead you to.

I am printing in this Appendix a Sampler (only) of some of the kinds of places to be found around the country, including a number of private counselors who aren't very easy to stumble across. The sampler starts on page 258. This is not a complete directory of anything. Countless good people, agencies and places exist, which will not be found in this Sampler. Also, countless bad people, places and agencies. To list all such, would require an encyclopedia.

The listing of an organization, agency or person in this Sampler is NOT a recommendation or endorsement of that organization, agency or person: Likewise, the failure to list a particular organization, agency or person in this Sampler is NOT a condemnation of that organization, agency or person. It is what its name implies: a sample only. In any event, you MUST do your own comparison shopping, and ask some sharp questions. If you don't comparison shop, you will deserve whatever you get (or don't get).

There is *no way* this Sampler can stay up-to-date and accurate, for more than about two days. Places fold, almost weekly in this field. Places move. The staff changes. Their phone numbers and hours change. I apologize for any information or listing that proves to be inaccurate. You could be of great service by dropping us a line, if you find a place is no longer in existence, or impossible to get ahold of, or is—in your opinion—totally unhelpful. (Box 379, Walnut Creek, CA 94597)

3. SOME QUESTIONS, BY MEANS OF
WHICH YOU MAY BE ABLE TO SEPARATE
THE SHEEP FROM THE GOATS

Choose, from your friends' recommendations, from the phone book, from the Sampler attached hereto, at least THREE PLACES OR COUN-SELORS.

VISIT IN PERSON EACH OF THE THREE PLACES YOU HAVE CHOSEN. These are exploratory visits only. Leave your wallet and your checkbook home, please! You are only comparison shopping at this point, not decision reaching!!

Make this unmistakably clear, when you are setting up the appointment for the interview.

You will need a notebook. In this notebook, *before* you go to see each career counselor (or firm), you will need to write out the following questions. And, as you ask the questions at each place, take time to write down some notes (or direct quotes) of their answers. DON'T trust your memory.

You may prefer to make four columns across your notebook, so that it will be easier to compare the places, after you have visited all three:

At each place, with each counselor, ask every one of these questions— omitting none.

• *What is their program?* When all their gimmicks are set aside (and some have great ones, like rehearsing for interviews on closed circuit TV, or using video-tape or cassettes to record your skills or your resume, etc.) what are they offering: is it basically "the numbers game," *or* is it basically some variation of the creative minority's prescription?

• *Who will be doing it?* Do you get the feeling that you must do most of it, with their basically assuming the role of coach? (if so, three cheers); or do you get the feeling that everything (including decision making about what you do, where you do it, etc.) will be done for you (if so, three warning bells should go off in your head)?

• *What guarantee is there that it will work?* If they make it clear that they have had a good success rate, but if you fail to work hard at the whole process, then there is no guarantee you are going to find a job, give them three stars. On the other hand, if they practically guarantee you a job, and say they have never had a client that failed to find a job, no matter what, *watch out.* Pulmotor job-counseling is very suspect; lifeless bodies make poor employees.

• *Are you face-to-face, and talking, with the actual persons who will be working with you, should you decide to become a client?* It might help you to be aware

MY SEARCH FOR A GOOD CAREER COUNSELOR			
Questions	Answer from Counselor #1	Answer from Counselor #2	Answer from Counselor #3
1. What is their program?			
2. Who will be doing it?			
3. Guarantee?			
4. Who is the actual counselor?			

that some job-hunting or career counseling firms have professional sales-people who introduce you to the company, convince you of their 100% integrity and charm, secure your decision, get you to sign the contract—and then you never see them again. You work with someone entirely different (or a whole team). *Ask the person you are talking to, if they are the one (and the only one) you will be working with, should you eventually decide to become a client.* If they say No, ask to meet those who would be actually working with you—even if it's a whole battery of people. When you actually meet them, there are three considerations you should weigh:

(1) *Do you like the counselor?* Bad vibes can cause great difficulties, even if this person is extremely competent. Don't dismiss this factor!

(2) *How long has this counselor been doing this?* Ask them! And what training did they have for it? (Legitimate questions; if they get huffy, politely thank them for their time, and take your leave gently *but firmly.*) Some agencies hire former clients as new staff. Such new staff are sometimes given only "on the job training." Since you're paying for Expertise already acquired, you have a *right* to ask about this before making up your mind. Incidentally, beware of such phrases as "I've had eighteen years' experience in the business and career counseling world." What that may mean is: seventeen and a half years as a fertilizer salesman, and one half year doing

career counseling. Persist. "How long have you been doing formal career counseling, as you are now?"

(3) *How much time will they give you?* As a minimum? As a maximum? (There's got to be a maximum, no matter what they may at first claim. Every career counselor runs into extremely dependent types as clients, who would be there all day every day if the counselor or the firm didn't have some policy about time limits. *Press* to find out what it is, just so you'll know.) Over how long a period can you use their services? And, *will they put this in writing?* (That's the question that separates the men from the boys, and the women from the girls.)

● *What is the cost of their services? Is it paid hourly, as you go along, or must it all be paid "up front" before you even start?* You will discover that there are some career counselors or agencies that charge you an hourly rate, just as a therapist might. The fee normally ranges between $50–$85 an hour. Each time you keep an appointment, you pay them at the end of that hour (or hours) for their help. There is no written contract. You signed nothing. You can stop seeing them at any time, if you feel you are not getting the help you wish. Obviously, this sort of arrangement is very much to the advantage of the job-hunter. *However,* you will also discover that there are some career counselors or agencies that, by contrast, have a policy of requiring you to pay for the entire "program" before you start, —or shortly after you start. There is *always* a written contract. You *must* sign it. (If you are married, your spouse will usually be invited to come in, before the contract is signed; you may suspect this is to help "sell" them on the idea of the contract, so they then can sell you. You may be right.) The fee normally ranges between $600–$8,000.

The contract sometimes allows it to be paid in installments, but you *are* obligated to pay it, one way or the other. You are sometimes *verbally* told that you can get your money back, or a portion of it, at any time, should you be dissatisfied with the career counselor's services. This is often *not* in the written contract. (Verbal promises, without witnesses, are difficult if not impossible to enforce. The written contract takes precedence.) Sometimes the written contract will provide for a partial refund, up to a certain cut-off point in the program. (There is *always* a cut-off point; and many times it is calculated by the counselor or agency in a manner other than the way *you* are calculating it. Consequently you are beyond the cut-off point, and the possibility of any refund, before you know it. Or, you reach the cut-off point and allow it to pass because you are, up to that point, satisfied with their services, and you have been led to believe there is much more to come. Only, there isn't. Once the cut-off point is passed, the career counselor's time becomes harder and harder to get.)

Clearly this second financial arrangement (as opposed to the hourly) is to the advantage of the career counselor or agency, more than it is to the advantage of the job-hunter. There's nothing inherently meritorious about paying someone a whole lot of money before he (or she) has performed any of the services they say they are going to perform. If you should become increasingly dissatisfied with the counseling or "program" as it pro-

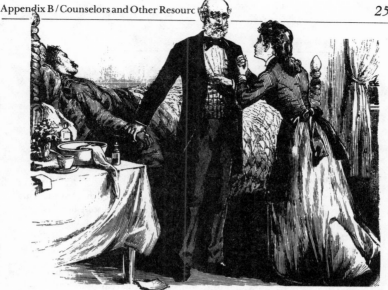

gresses, you may be "out" a lot of dough. With no legal recourse. And so, the moral of this tale:

Don't pay any fee that you can't afford to lose.

While you are still doing your information gathering on the three places, find out which of these two financial arrangements the counselor or agency requires. If a contract will be involved, ask for a copy of it, take it home, and show it to a good lawyer.

Having gotten the information *you* want, and therefore having accomplished *your* purpose for this particular visit, you politely thank them for their time and trouble, and depart. You then go on to two other places, and ask the very same questions, please! There ought to be no charges involved for such comparison-shopping visits as this, and if they subsequently bill you, inquire politely whether or not a mistake has been made by their accounting department (good thinking). If they persist in billing you, pay a visit to your local friendly Better Business Bureau, and lodge a nice unfriendly complaint against the firm in question. You'd be surprised at how many firms experience *instant repentance* when the Better Business Bureau phones them. They don't want a complaint on their BBB record.

BACK HOME NOW, after visiting the three places you chose for your comparison shopping, you have to decide: a) whether you want none of the three, or b) one of the three and if so, which one.

Look over your notes on all three places. Compare those places. Time for thought, maybe using some others as a sounding board: business friend, consultant friend, placement center, buddy, mate, or anyone whose judgment you trust.

Remember, you don't have to choose *any* of the three counselors. If you didn't really care for any of them, listen to your intuition. Choose three new counselors, dust off the notebook, and go out again. It may take a few more hours to find what you want. But, remember: the wallet or purse you will be saving is your own.

A Sampler

This Sampler Has Several Sections:
   I. Places Which Counsel Anyone
   II. Help for Women (Many of These Also Serve Men)
   III. Group Support for Those Who Are Unemployed
   IV. Directories of Career Counseling Services in Various Cities/States

If you are looking for a counselor in a particular state, check under all four categories, please. Even if a particular resource listed here is not what you are looking for, they may know of other places, not listed here.

The listing of a place here is NOT a recommendation of it. Many of these places are listed at their own request. On the other hand, we never *knowingly* list a place we know to be unhelpful.

If you have had a bad experience with any of them, you will help other readers by letting us know that (our address is in the rear of this book, on the UPDATE form). However, it is CRUCIAL that you read the preceding section two or three times, BEFORE you approach any of these sections. Often you could easily have discovered whether a particular counselor is competent or not, simply by asking the right questions. The just response to many a complaint is—as the Scots would say—"Ya dinna do your homework."

I. PLACES WHICH COUNSEL ANYONE

ALASKA

Gregory Professional Services, 709 W. Int'l Airport Rd., Ste. 205, Anchorage, AK 99502, 907-563-4612. Anne M. Grabowski, President.

ARIZONA

Phyllis Harper-Rispoli, 1845 S. Dobson Rd., Ste. 202, Mesa, AZ 85202, 602-820-0638.

Southwest Institute of Life Management, Theodore Donald Risch, Director, 2500 N. Pantano Rd., Ste. 120, Tucson, AZ 85715, 602-296-4764.

ARKANSAS

Cossatot Vocational Technical School, Box 746, DeQueen, AR 71832, 501-584-4471. Donald D. McKinney, Ed.D., Special Needs Career Counselor.

CALIFORNIA

Aware Advisory Center, YWCA, Second Floor, 2019 14th St. (near Pico Blvd.), Santa Monica, CA 90405, 213-452-3883.

Judy Kaplan Baron Associates, 7730 Herschel Ave., Ste. B, La Jolla, CA 92037, 619-456-1700. Judy Kaplan Baron, Director.

Beverly Brown, M.A., 1932 Overland Ave., #304, Los Angeles, CA 90025, 213-475-2503.

Branham & Associates, 2117 E. Brentford Ave., Orange, CA 92667, 714-637-4694.

Career Development Center, Moorpark College, 7075 Campus Rd., Moorpark, CA 93021, 805-529-2321.

Career Development Institute, 690 Market St., Ste. 404, San Francisco, CA 94104, 415-982-2636.

Career Development Life Planning, 2856 Cabrillo Dr., Ste. 201, Ventura, CA 93003, 805-644-0010 or 805-656-4866. Norma Zuber, M.S.C.

Career Dimensions, Box 7402, Stockton, CA 95207, 209-473-8255. Fran Abbott.

Career Renewal, 40 Museum Way, San Francisco, CA 94114. 415-626-2741. Kal Edwards, Director.

Constructive Leisure, Patsy B. Edwards, 511 N. La Cienega Blvd., Los Angeles, CA 90048, 213-652-7389.

Consultants Group, 3855 Avocado Blvd., Ste. 230, La Mesa, CA 92041, 619-466-7500. Philip J. Pekras, Director. Individual and group career counseling.

Criket Consultants, Box 323, Rancho Cordova, CA 95670, 916-363-4545.

De Lara & Associates, Inc., Citicorp Bldg., 1990 North California Blvd., Ste. 830, Walnut Creek, CA 94596, 415-932-7015. Joy De Lara, Director.

Margaret L. Eddie, Education and Promotions Consultant, Box 725, Solana Beach, CA 92075, 619-436-1516.

Effective Career Plans, 5767 Preston Dr., San Jose, CA 95124, 408-448-0123. M. Stoodley, M.S., Director.

El Chorro Employment Agency, 2040 Broad St., Ste. B, San Luis Obispo, CA 93401, 805-544-4858. Personalized job placement. Career counseling, resume writing. No registration fee. Other fees vary. Mon–Fri, 9–5.

Experience Unlimited, Mr. Herman L. Leopold, Coordinator, Employment Development Dept., 1225 4th Ave., Oakland, CA 94606, 415-464-1259/464-0659.

Beverly Neuer Feldman, Ed.D., 2656 Aberdeen Ave., Los Angeles, CA 90027. 213-665-7007.

G/S Consultants, Career Planning, 2910 Santa Rosa, Altadena, CA 91001, 818-791-1192.

Arthur M. Hugon, 9432 Gerald Ave., Sepulveda, CA 91343, 818-893-0098.

Life/Career Development, 4035 El Macero Dr., Davis, CA 95616, 916-648-1286. Russell A. Bruch, Director, Career consultant.

Life's Decisions, 2740 Fulton Ave. Sacramento, CA 95821, 916-481-1246. Joan E. Belshin, M.S.

MJC Career Counseling Agency, 1000 E. Walnut, Ste. 217, Pasadena, CA 91006, 818-584-0498. Marilyn Comouche, Director. Individual and group counseling.

Modern Career Decisions, 1811 Santa Rita Rd., Ste. 224, Pleasanton, CA 94566, 415-846-9071. Rod Meyer, Executive Director.

National University Career Center, 4007 Camino Del Rio S., San Diego, CA 92108, 619-563-7250.

New Ways to Work, 149 Ninth St., San Francisco, CA 94103. 415-552-1000. Monday–Friday, 10 a.m.–4 p.m. Free orientation session every Tuesday, 12 noon–1 p.m.

Project Joy (Job Opportunities for Youth), East Oakland Youth Development Center, 8200 E. 14th St., Oakland, CA 94621. 415-569-8088. Kathleen Sullivan, Director.

Fran Schwartz, 13219 Dobbins Pl., Los Angeles, CA 90049, 213-451-2755/778-1772.

Marion Bass Stevens, Ph.D., Career & Employment Counseling, 747 Mulberry Le., Davis, CA 95616, 916-756-0672.

Transitions, 171 N. Van Ness, Fresno, CA 93701, 209-233-7250. Margot E. Tepperman, L.C.S.W.

Turning Point Career Center, University YWCA, 2600 Bancroft Way, Berkeley, CA 94704, 415-848-6370. Marjorie Sywak, Ph.D., Director.

UCLA Extension Advisory Service, 10995 Le Conte Ave., Rm. 114, Los Angeles, CA 90024, 213-206-6201. Mon–Fri, 9 am–5 pm. College sponsored office. Educational and career counseling, continuing education courses. No fees.

YWCA Center for Career Development, 375 S. Third St., San Jose, CA 95112, 408-295-4011. Patricia Wilson, Director.

Joanne Young, Box 19273, Irvine, CA 92714, 714-552-7384.

COLORADO

Colorado Growth Center, Inc., 965 Humboldt St., Ste. 105, Denver, CO 80218, 303-831-9578. Arthur F. Smith, Jr., Counselor.

Samuel Kirk and Associates, Central Office, 1418 S. Race, Denver, CO 80210, 303-722-0717.

Training & Career Resource Services, 425 West Mulberry, Ste. 207, Fort Collins, CO 80521, 303-484-9810. Marilyn F. Pultz.

CONNECTICUT

Career Evaluation Services, 94 Rambling Rd., Vernon, CT 06066, 203-871-7832.

The Counseling Service of the Metropolitan Hartford YMCA, Inc., 160 Jewell St., Third Floor, Hartford, CT 06103, 203-522-4183.

Kathleen Gaughran, 625 Boston Post Rd., Guilford, CT 06437, 203-453-0522.

R. Ilise Gold, M.Ed., Career and Life Planning Specialist, 47 Strathmore Le., Westport, CT 06880, 203-866-4327.

People Management Inc., 10 Station St., Simsbury, CT 06070, 203-651-3581. Arthur F. Miller, Jr., President.

John H. Wiedenheft, M.A., Career Development, 38 Barker St., Hartford, CT 06114, 203-527-5523.

DELAWARE

Life/Career Planning, 2413 Brickton Rd., Wilmington, DE 19803, 302-478-7186. Minh-Nhat Tran, Consultant.

DISTRICT OF COLUMBIA

Georgetown University, School for Summer and Continuing Education, 37th and O. Sts. NW, Washington, DC 20057, 202-625-3003.

FLORIDA

The Career and Personal Counseling Center, Eckerd College, Box 12560, St. Petersburg, FL 33733, 813-867-1166, ext. 356. John R. Sims.

Center for Career Decisions, Atrium Plaza Ste. 300, 1515 N. Federal Hwy., Boca Raton, FL 33432, 305-392-4550. Individual/group counseling. Corporate outplacement. Seminars, workshops.

Ellen O. Jonassen, Ph.D., 901 Hercules Ave., Ste. G, Clearwater, FL 33575, 813-441-4579.

Life Designs, Inc., 7860 SW 55th Ave. #A, South Miami, FL 33143, 305-665-3212. Dulce I. Muccio and Deborah Tyson, co-founders.

Ruth A. Peters, Ph.D., Cypress View Professional Center, 2424 Enterprise Rd., Ste. A, Clearwater, FL 33575, 813-797-2512/799-0510.

GEORGIA

The Career Planning Center of Grace United Methodist Church, 458 Ponce de Leon Ave., Atlanta, GA 30308. Mark Canfield, Director.

Career Pursuit, Box 2313, Decatur, GA 30031, 404-636-1597. Estelle Ford Greene.

Charles W. Cates, Ph.D., Life Work Associates, Box 52, Decatur, GA 30030, 404-373-0336.

Judith L. Cole, M.Ed., Lenox Towers, 3390 Peachtree Rd., Atlanta, GA 30326, 404-233-0946.

Educational Information and Referral Service, Lenox Square Professional Concourse, 3393 Peachtree Road, North East, Atlanta, GA 30326, 404-233-7497. Christine G. Free, Executive Director.

IDAHO

Life/Work Planning Services, 1955 Wilmington Dr., Boise, ID 83704, 208-375-0742. Janet Atkinson Lawrence, M.Ed.

ILLINOIS

Career Directions, 5005 Newport Dr., Ste. 501, Rolling Meadows, IL 60008, 312-870-1290. Peggy Simonsen, Director.

Career Path, 3033 Ogden Ave., Ste. 203, Lisle, IL 60532, 312-369-3390. Hours by appt. Kristin Trom, Counselor.

Career Potential, 1318 E. State St., Rockford, IL 61108, 815-962-7666. Mary-Stuart Carruthers.

Career Workshops, 5431 W. Roscoe St., Chicago, IL 60641, 312-282-6859. Patricia Dietze.

Richard Gans, Career Counselor, 6057 W. Eddy St., Chicago, IL 60634.

David P. Helfand, Ed.D., 250 Ridge, Evanston, IL 60202, 312-328-2787.

Arlene S. Hirsch, M.A., 541 W. Arlington, Chicago, IL 60614, 312-528-2859.

Lansky Career Consultants, 676 N. St. Clair #1860, Chicago, IL 60611, 312-642-5738. Individual consultation and workshops. Sliding scale available.

Occupational Consultants, Paul J. Reibman, 1030 Indian Rd., Glenview, IL 60025, 312-729-2117.

The Professional Career Counselors' Network, 36 S. Wabash, Ste. 1202, Chicago, IL 60603, 312-332-2760. Jack Chapman, President.

Jane Shuman, Career Management Consultant, 122 Circle Dr., Springfield, IL 62703, 217-529-7220.

INDIANA

Career Consultants, 107 N. Pennsylvania St., Ste. 404, Indianapolis, IN 46204, 317-639-5601. Mike Kenney, Senior Partner.

John D. King, Career Counselor and Consultant, Graham Plaza, Ste. 312, 205 N. College Ave., Bloomington, IN 47401, 812-332-3888.

IOWA

Christian Business Support Center, 6102 1st Ave. NW, Cedar Rapids, IA 52405, 319-396-1963. Rob Robinson, Director.

Community Career Planning Center, Drake University, 25th and Carpenter, Des Moines, IA 50311, 515-271-2916.

KANSAS

Career Associates, Box 1368, Lawrence, KS 66044, 913-842-6527. Janice K. Friedman and Jackson D. Hawks.

KENTUCKY

P. Ronniger Associates, 101 North 7th Street, Louisville, KY 40202, 502-583-4115. Phillip Ronniger, President.

MAINE

Sojourn, Inc: Career Evaluation and Planning, Route 2, Box 5, Fairfield, ME 04937, 207-453-9756.

MARYLAND

Careerscope, Inc., Ste. 246, Wilde Lake Village Green, Columbia, MD 21044, 301-992-5042/596-1866. Virginia Matthias, Director.

Maryland New Directions, Inc., 2517 N. Charles St., Baltimore, MD 21218, 301-235-8800. Marjorie Rosensweig, Director.

Prince George's Community College, Career Assessment and Planning Center, 301 Largo Rd., Largo, MD 20772, 301-322-0886. David C. Borchard, Director.

D. Evan Wallick Associates, 1600 Angus Ct., Crofton, MD 21114, 301-261-6945. David E. Wallick, National Certified Counselor.

MASSACHUSETTS

Alewife Counseling Associates, 721 R. Pleasant St., Belmont, MA 02178, 617-484-8517. Jane Hynes. Available evenings and weekends.

Back Bay Resume Service, 115 Newbury St., Ste. 501, Boston, MA 02116, 617-266-4995. Don Gervich, Ed.D. Career counseling and resume preparation.

Career Development Consultant, Ellen J. Wallach, 8 Sherburne Rd., Lexington, MA 02173, 617-862-0997.

Career Resource Center, Worcester YWCA, 1 Salem Square, Worcester, MA 01608, 617-791-3181. Individual/group counseling, vocational testing, job placement, etc. Fees based on ability to pay. Day and evening hours by appointment.

Anne H. Doughty, Career Planning Consultant, 111 Holt St., Watertown, MA 02172, 617-484-5053.

David J. Giber, Ph.D., Career Counselor. 8 Westland Rd., Watertown, MA 02172, 617-924-2537.

New Beginnings Career Center, Assabet Center for Continuing Education, Fitchburg St., Marlboro, MA 01752. Susan Sock, Director, Career Services.

New England Career Center, 70 Chase St., Newton Centre, MA 02159. Barton M. Lloyd, Associate Director.

Carl Joseph Schneider, 9 Fairview Ave., Watertown, MA 02172, 617-924-2662.

Westford Psychological Services, The Gateway Bldg., 288 Littleton Rd., Westford, MA 01886, 617-692-6834. John W. Ried, Th.D., Director.

Widening Horizons, 120 Meriam Rd., Concord, MA 01742, 617-369-1626. Barbara SanClemente, M.Ed., Director.

MICHIGAN

Career Planning Services, 2777 Colony Rd., Ann Arbor, MI 48104, 313-973-9286. Catherine Schwarz.

Thibaudeaux Personnel of Grand Rapids, 820 Commerce Bldg., Grand Rapids, MI 49503, 616-459-8396. Donald D. Fink, Ed.D., Director of Career Counseling.

MINNESOTA

Assessment & Vocational Services, Inc., 6135 Kellogg Ave. S., Ste. 224, Edina, MN 55424, 612-922-4397 Robert D. Haskin, Director. Career/life planning, counseling.

Leider, Inc., 7101 York Ave. S., Minneapolis, MN 55435, 612-921-3334. Richard J. Leider, Career Development Specialist.

MISSISSIPPI

University of Southern Mississippi, Career Development Center and Adult Services Program, Southern Sta., Box 5112, Hattiesburg, MS 39406-5112, 601-266-4848. Charlotte E. Tullos, Director.

MISSOURI

Career Planning and Placement Center, Adult Evening Program, 110 Noyes Hall, University of Missouri, Columbia, MO 65211, 314-882-6803.

NEBRASKA

Career Information Center, Central Community College, Hastings Campus, Box 1024, Hastings, NE 68901, 402-463-9811. Monday–Friday, 8 am–4:30 pm. No fees.

Clemm C. Kessler III, Kessler, Kennedy & Associates, Executive Plaza, 6818 Grover St., Omaha, NE 68106, 402-397-9558.

NEW JERSEY

Arista Concepts Career Development Service. 41 Wittmer Ct., Princeton, NJ 08540, 609-921-0308. Kera Green Herzog, Counseling Psychologist.

Loree Collins, 3 Beechwood Rd., Summit, NJ 07901, 201-273-9219.

Sandra Grundfest, Princeton Professional Park, 601 Ewing St., Ste. C-1, Princeton, NJ 08540, 609-921-8400. Career and educational counseling. Job search strategies.

Simeon J. Touretzky, M.S. Career Counselor. 160 Evergreen Rd., 8-B, Edison, NJ 08837, 201-494-8291.

NEW YORK

The John C. Crystal Center, 111 E. 31st St., New York, NY 10016. Phone 212-889-8500. Our good friend, John Crystal, devotes himself exclusively to the work of the Crystal Center, of which he is Chairman (Nella G. Barkley is president), offering programs in New York and elsewhere in the country.

Career Management Resources, Inc., 6268 Jericho Turnpike, Ste. 1, Commack, NY 11725, 516-462-9388. Alfred R. Miller, President.

Career Services Center, Long Island University, C.W. Post Campus, Greenvale, NY 11548, 516-299-2251. Mince Kohler, Director.

LifeWork Associates, Lincoln Bldg., 60 East 42 St., Ste. 505, New York, NY 10165, 212-490-3335.

Life/Work Planning, Inc., 932 Genesee Park Blvd., Rochester, NY 14619, 716-328-4912. Randall E. Davis, Career Development Specialist.

On-Track, 342 Madison Ave., Ste. 2001, New York, NY 10017, 212-953-6445. Russell P. Bosworth, President.

NORTH CAROLINA

Thomas S. Baldwin, Ph.D., Licensed Practicing Psychologist, 87 S. Elliott Rd., Ste. 200, Chapel Hill, NC 27514, 919-929-0496.

OHIO

Adult Resource Center, The University of Akron, Buckingham Center for Continuing Education, Akron, OH 44325, 216-375-7448. Also has sites at: Akron-Summit County Public Library, 55 S. Main St., Akron, OH, and: Women's Network, People's Federal Bldg., 39 E. Market St., Akron, OH.

Bowling Green State University, College of Continuing Education, McFall Center, Bowling Green, OH 43403, 419-372-0181.

Career Resources, Third National Bank Bldg., 32 N. Main St., Ste. 1245, Dayton, OH 45402, 513-223-8000.

Career Shaping, 2801 Far Hills Ave., Dayton, OH 45419, 513-293-9675. Nancy Cook Cherry, Director.

J & K Associates, 539J Forest Park Ct., Dayton, OH 45405, 513-274-3630. Pat Kenney, Ph.D., President.

New Career, 931 Chelsea Drive, Dover, OH 44622, 216-343-8464. Marshall Karp, M.A., Owner/Operator.

Pathfinders, A Division of Special Edition, 3497 E. Livingston Ave., Columbus, OH 43227, 614-231-4088. Y. Hayon, Ph.D., Director.

Womonways, Inc., 503 McAlpin Ave., Box 20145, Cincinnati, OH 45220, 513-221-0579, 513-221-3358. Linda Keegan, Office Manager.

OREGON

The Employment Connection, 6318 SW Corbett, Portland, OR 97201, 503-244-1055. Pam Gross, Executive Director.

Sylvan Psychological and Counseling Services, 1012 SW King Ave., Portland, OR 97205, 503-224-3600. Joe Dubay, Founder.

PENNSYLVANIA

Barbara Bell, 450 Warick Rd., Wynnewood, PA 19096, 215-642-2183.

Center for the Study of Adult Development,
3910 Chestnut St., Philadelphia, PA 19104,
215-662-4080. Joy Matkowski, M.S.C., Staff
Counselor, Career Planning and
Outplacement Services Division. Also located
in King of Prussia, Allentown, Pennsylvania
as well as in Cherry Hill, New Jersey.

LaRoche College Career Center, 9000
Babcock Blvd., Pittsburgh, PA 15237, 412-
367-9300, ext. 144, 145 & 146. Kris
Rosenberg, Director.

Options, Inc., 215 S. Broad St., Philadelphia,
PA 19107, 215-735-2202. Marcia P. Kleiman,
Director.

Pennsburg Outreach Center, 643 Main St.,
Pennsburg, PA 18073, 215-679-5511.
Sponsored by Montgomery County
Community College, Blue Bell, PA 19422.

David C. Rich, United Ministries in Higher
Education, Pennsylvania Commission, 61
Cassatt Ave., Berwyn, PA 19312, 215-647-
8096. David C. Rich, Director.

TENNESSEE

Career Resources, 121 21st Ave., N., Ste.
200, Nashville, TN 37203, 615-327-0101.
Jane C. Hardy, President.

TEXAS

Adult Career Exploration Services (ACES),
300 E. Fifth St., Austin, TX 78768, 512-476-
2716. ACES is an open-door community
service provided by Austin Community
College.

Career Action Associates, Allied Bank Plaza,
Ste. 820, 12655 N. Central Expressway,
Dallas, TX 75243, 214-392-7337. Rebecca
Hayes and Neil Brasch.

Catalyst Career Consultants, 3906 N. Lamar
Blvd., Austin, TX 78756, 512-452-1229. Joia
Jitahidi, Senior Consultant.

Creative Careers, Jon Patrick Bourg. 34
Cromwell Dr., San Antonio, TX 78201, 512-
735-7287.

Counseling Services of Houston, Rosemary
C. Vienot, P.C., 1950 West Gray, Ste. 1,
Houston, TX 77019, 713-521-9391.

East Texas State University at Texarkana,
Career Planning & Placement Center, 2600
N. Robison Road, Texarkana, TX 75501,
214-838-6514. Tom Dart, Coordinator of
Placement and Career Counseling.

Life/Work Design, 3906 North Lamar Blvd.,
Ste. 202, Austin, TX 78756, 512-458-2844.
Jeanne Quereau, M.A.

UTAH

University of Utah, Center for Adult
Learning and Career Change, 1199 Annex
Bldg., Salt Lake City, UT 84112, 801-581-
3228.

VERMONT

Career Crossroads, 10 Linden St.,
Brattleboro, VT 05301, 802-257-7497, 802-
254-5114. Donald T. Baggs, Director.

VIRGINIA

Endependence Center of Northern Virginia,
4214 9th St. N., Arlington, VA 22203, 703-
525-3268.

Hollins College, Career Counseling Center,
Hollins, VA 24020, 703-362-6364. Peggy-
Ann Neumann, Director.

Life Management Services, Inc., 6825
Redmond Drive, McLean, VA 22101, 703-
356-2630. Hal and Marilyn Shook, President
and Vice President.

Psychological Consultants, Inc., 6724
Patterson Ave., Richmond, VA 23226, 804-
288-4125.

Swenholt Associates, Inc., 3414 Barger Dr.,
Falls Church, VA 22044, 703-256-2383.
Frankie P. Swenholt, President.

WASHINGTON

The Individual Development Center, Inc.,
1020 E. John, Seattle, WA 98102, 206-329-
0600. Mary Lou Hunt, Co-director. Tacoma
branch: 8404 27th St. W., Tacoma, WA
98466, 206-565-8818. Ruthann Reim,
Director.

WISCONSIN

David Swanson, Career Seminars and
Workshops, Inc., 11621 W. Blue Mound Rd.,
Milwaukee, WI 53226, 414-259-0265.

Madison Campus Ministry, 731 State St.,
Madison, WI 53706, 608-257-1039.

WYOMING

University of Wyoming, Counseling Center,
Box 3708, University Sta., Laramie, WY
82071, 307-766-2187.

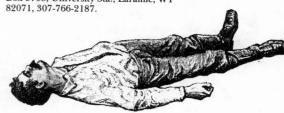

CANADA

Gilmore & Associates, Renaissance Plaza, 150 Bloor St. W., Ste. 340, Toronto, Ontario, M5S 2X9 Canada, 416-926-1944. Pat Gilbert, Director.

John Hamilton, Ed.D., 2161 Yonge St., Toronto, Ontario M45 3A6, Canada, 416-489-1221.

Barbara Teeple, 1002 Knottwood Rd. E., Edmonton, Alberta, T6K 3R5, Canada. 403-463-7759.

FOREIGN

Robert J. Bisdee & Associates, 22 Allenby Ave., Malvern E., Victoria, Australia 3145, 613-025-4716.

Raadgevend Bureau Claessens, Outplacement/Verandering Van Werkkring, Beneluxlaan 35, 3526 KK UTRECHT, Holland, 030-886530. Frans Claessens.

II. HELP FOR WOMEN
(MANY OF THESE ALSO SERVE MEN)

Resource centers for women are springing up all over the country, faster than we can record them. We are listing here *only a sampling* of same. If you have a favorite, not listed here, send us the pertinent information—in format similar to the next pages—and we'll list it in the next edition. (Don't, however, bother to send us college services which are available only to the students and alumnae of that college. We try not to list such places, since such a listing only frustrates non-alumnae. If, inadvertently, any such place thus restricted is already listed here, please let us know, and we'll gently remove it from the next edition.) Incidentally, the centers which are listed here will know (in all probability) what other centers or resources there are in your geographical area. Also, try your telephone book's yellow pages: "Women's Organizations and Services," or "Vocational Consultants."

In all of this you will remember, won't you, our earlier description (page 249) of all career counseling professionals, as falling into one of three groups: (1) Sincere and skilled; (2) Sincere but inept; and (3) Insincere and inept? Well, dear friend, groups or organizations or centers which have been organized specifically to help women job-hunters or career-changers are not—by that act—made immune to the above distinctions. Think about it, before you agree to put your (vocational) life into somebody else's hands. Remember, the numbers game (chapter 2), even if it is expressed in beautifully nonsexist language, is still the numbers game.

RESOURCES FOR WOMEN

ALABAMA

Enterprise State Junior College, Women's Center, Career Development Center, Highway 84 E., Box 1300, Enterprise, AL 36330, 205-347-7881 or 5431. Monday–Friday, 8 am–4:30 pm.

University of Alabama, Career Planning and Placement, 1300 8th Ave. S., Bldg. 5, Rm. 110, Birmingham, AL 35294, 205-934-4324 or 4470. Monday–Friday, 8:30 am–5 pm.

ALASKA

University of Alaska, Anchorage Education Opportunity Center, 3211 Providence Ave., Library Bldg., Rm. 103, Anchorage, AK 99504, 907-263-1525. Monday–Friday, 8 am–5 pm.

ARIZONA

University of Arizona, Student Counseling Service, Old Main, Tucson, AZ 85721, 602-626-2316. Monday–Friday, 8 am–noon and 1–5 pm; Tuesday and Wednesday, 5 pm–7 pm. Official college office. Educational and career counseling, and personal and marital counseling, continuing education courses. No fees.

CALIFORNIA

Advocates for Women, 414 Mason St., 4th Fl., San Francisco, CA 94102, 415-391-4870. Monday–Thursday, 9 am–4:30 pm; Tuesday, 9 am–7:30 pm. Independent nonprofit agency. Career counseling, job referral, placement. Offices also in Berkeley and Hayward.

Alumnae Resources, 660 Mission St., Ste. 201, San Francisco, CA 94105, 415-546-7220. Emphasis on Liberal Arts graduates. Offers workshops, seminars, individual counseling, and special events. Fees vary. Appointments necessary. Orientation Fridays at noon.

American River College, Student Services Bldg., 4700 College Oak Dr., Sacramento, CA 95841, 916-484-8391. Monday–Friday, 8 am–6 pm.

Career Design, An Affiliate of Ranny Riley & Associates, 2462 Broadway, San Francisco, CA 94115. 415-929-8150. Offers a variety of comprehensive workshops and intensive seminars, dealing with all aspects of the world of work. Fees vary.

Career Planning Center/Business Action Center, 1623 S. La Cienega Blvd., Los Angeles, CA 90813. 213-273-6633. Independent, non-profit agency. Offers career counseling, testing, workshops, and job information. Men welcome.

The Claremont Colleges, Special Academic Programs and Office for Continuing Education, Harper Hall 160, Claremont, CA 91711, 714-621-8000, ext. 8069. Monday–Friday, 9 am–5 pm. College sponsored office. Educational and career counseling, job referral, continuing education courses. Registration fee.

Crossroads Institute for Career Development, 2288 Fulton St., Berkeley, CA 94704, 415-848-0698. Monday–Friday, 9 am–5 pm.

Cypress College, Career Planning Center, 9200 Valley View St., Cypress, CA 90630, 714-826-2220, Ext. 221. Monday–Friday, 8 am–4:30 pm. Official college office. Educational and career counseling. No fees.

Susan W. Miller, M.A., 360 N. Bedford, Ste. 312, Beverly Hills, CA 90210, 213-837-7768. Career Counselor, Educational Consultant, private practice. Career counseling for individuals using a structured, action-oriented approach.

Resource Center for Women, 445 Sherman Ave., Palo Alto, CA 94306, 415-324-1710. Monday–Friday, 9 am–5 pm; Thursday, 9 am–9 pm. Independent nonprofit agency. Educational and career counseling, adult education courses, job referral. Fees for workshops.

Sacramento Women's Center, Women's Employment Services and Training, 2224 "J" St., Sacramento, CA 95816, 916-441-4207. Receives funding from the Job Training Partnership Act to help low-income women and single parents re-enter the job market. Also, primary resource in Sacramento for women interested in non-traditional employment.

San Jose State University, Re-Entry Advisory Program, Old Cafeteria Bldg., San Jose, CA 95192, 408-277-2188. Monday–Friday, 9 am–5 pm; Wednesday, 9 am–7 pm. Official college program. Educational and career counseling, referral to other services. No fees.

Caroline Voorsanger, Career Counselor for Women, 2000 Broadway, Ste. 1108, San Francisco, CA 94115, 415-567-0890. Career counseling, assistance with skills assessment and focusing.

Women at Work, 78 N. Marengo Ave., Pasadena, CA 91101, 818-796-6870. A career and job resource center. Includes workshops and individual counseling. Fees vary.

The Women's Opportunities Center, Univ. of California Extension, 2801 Main St., Irvine, CA 92714, 714-856-7128. Monday–Friday, 9 am–4 pm. College sponsored office. Educational and career counseling.

Women's World International, 400 N. Tustin, Ste. 410, Santa Ana, CA 92705, 714-547-7726. Assistance with interviewing techniques, communications skills, exploring career alternatives, and achieving a professional image.

YWCA, Counseling Services, 1000 Sir Francis Drake Blvd., San Anselmo, CA 94960, 415-456-0782. Monday–Friday, 9 am–5 pm.

COLORADO

Arapahoe Community College, Career Resource Center, 5900 S. Santa Fe Dr., Littleton, CO 80120, 303-794-1550. Monday–Friday, 8 am–5 pm. Educational, career, and personal counseling; variety of workshops and seminars; job search skills; community resources files; support groups; library; job referral and placement.

Career Development Center, 1650 Washington Street, Denver, CO 80203, 303-861-7254. Monday–Friday, 9 am–5 pm; evening services available. Independent nonprofit agency. A comprehensive combination of group and individual sessions for career counseling. Fees vary.

Women's Center, Red Rocks Community College, 12600 W. 6th Ave., Golden, CO 80401, 303-988-6160, ext. 213. Free career planning, resume help, job matching, brown bag lunches. Small fee for workshops, seminars.

Women's Resource Agency, 2340 Robinson St., Ste. 216, Colorado Springs, CO 80904, 303-471-3170. Monday–Friday, 8 am–5 pm.

CONNECTICUT

Fairfield University, Fairfield Adult Career & Educational Services (FACES), North Benson Rd., Julie Hall, Fairfield, CT 06430, 203-255-5411. Monday–Friday, 9 am–4 pm.

Norwalk Community College, Counseling Center, 333 Wilson Ave., Norwalk, CT 06854, 203-853-2040. Monday–Thursday, 9 am–7:30 pm, Friday 9 am–4 pm.

Vocational and Academic Counseling for Adults (VOCA), 115 Berrian Rd., Stamford, CT 06905, 203-329-1955. Monday–Friday, 9 am–5 pm; weekends and evenings by arrangement.

DELAWARE

University of Delaware, The Women's Center, State Office Bldg., 5th Fl., Wilmington, DE 19801, 302-571-2088. Monday–Friday, 8:15 am–2:15 pm. Official college office. Educational and career counseling, continuing education courses. No registration fee. Other fees vary.

Womanpower, A Program of the YWCA, 908 King St., Wilmington, DE 19801. 302-656-0592. An eleven-week classroom training program for economically disadvantaged women wanting nontraditional employment. Also have a weekly Job Junction for women who aren't employed. Contact: Evalee S. Hunter.

DISTRICT OF COLUMBIA

George Washington University, Continuing Education for Women, 801 22nd St. NW, Ste. T409, Washington, DC 20052, 202-676-7036. Monday–Friday, 9 am–5 pm. College sponsored. Educational and career counseling, continuing education courses, job referral. Fees vary.

FLORIDA

The Career Development Program, The Center for Climacteric Studies, University of Florida, The Professional Center, 901 NW 8th Ave., Ste. B-1, Gainesville, FL 32601. 904-392-3184 (3185). Monday–Friday, 8 am–5 pm. Evenings and Saturdays by appt. Help with the physical, psychological, and occupational concerns of women in their middle years (35–65 years of age). Fee.

The Center for the Continuing Education of Women, Miami-Dade Community College, 300 NE Second Ave., Miami, FL 33132, 305-577-6840. Monday–Friday, 8:30 am–5 pm. College sponsored office. Educational and career counseling, limited job referral, continuing education courses. Fees vary.

The Centre for Women, 305 S. Hyde Park Ave., Tampa, FL 33606, 813-251-8437. Lynn Hamilton Cole, President. The Centre offers job series classes, assessment and counseling, a referral system, Job Club. Registration fee of $20.

Challenge: The Displaced Homemaker, Florida Junior College at Jacksonville, 101 W. State St., Rm. 3070, Jacksonville, FL 32202, 904-633-8316. Elaine Richardson-Smith, Program Coordinator. Program geared specifically to the needs of the displaced homemaker—support, values clarification, vocational testing, goal setting, etc.

Council for Continuing Education for Women of Central Florida, Inc., Valencia Community College, 190 S. Orange Ave., 1st Fl., Box 3028, Orlando, FL 32802, 305-423-4813. Monday–Friday, 9 am–5 pm. Independent nonprofit agency. Educational and career counseling, adult education courses, testing.

Face Learning Center, Inc., 12945 Seminole Blvd., Bldg. 2, Ste. 8, Largo, FL 33544, 813-586-1110/585-8155. Monday–Friday, 9 am–5 pm and by appointment.

Stetson University Counseling Center, Campus Box 1365, North Woodland Blvd., De Land, FL 32720, 904-734-4121, Ext. 215. Monday–Friday, 8:30 am–4:30 pm.

ILLINOIS

Applied Potential, Box 585, Highland Park, IL 60035, 312-234-2130. Monday–Friday, 9 am–5 pm; evenings and Saturdays by arrangement. Nonprofit educational corporation. Professional counselors. Educational, career and personal counseling. No registration fee. Other fees vary.

Displaced Homemakers Program, Lincoln Land Community College, Shepherd Rd., Springfield, IL 62708, 217-786-2335. Educational and career counseling, job referral information. No fees.

Harper College Community Counseling Center, Palatine, IL 60067, 312-397-3000. Monday–Thursday, 8:30 am–4:30 pm and 6–10 pm; Friday, 8:30 am–4:30 pm. College sponsored office. Educational and career counseling. No registration fee. Other fees vary.

Jean Davis, Career Counseling, 500 Davis Center, Ste. 600, Evanston, IL 60201, 312-492-1002. Offers career assessment/design, resume and marketing strategies, job interview preparation, individual consultation and workshops.

Midwest Women's Center, 53 West Jackson Blvd., Ste. 1015, Chicago, IL 60604, 312-922-8530. Offers individual counseling, referrals, workshops, job-support groups, apprenticeship and skills training programs. The Center also has an extensive career library. Call for hours and fees.

Moraine Valley Community College, Career/Life Planning and Counseling, 10900 S. 88th Ave., Palos Hills, IL 60465, 312-974-4300. Monday–Thursday, 9 am–9 pm; Friday, 9 am–5 pm. Official college office. Fees vary.

Northwestern Illinois Career Guidance Center, 1515 S. 4th St., Dekalb, IL 60115, 815-758-7431. Monday–Friday, 8 am–4 pm.

Southern Illinois University, General Studies Division, Office of Continuing Education, Campus Box 48, Edwardsville, IL 62026, 618-692-3210. Monday–Friday, 8 am–5 pm. Official college office. Educational and career counseling, continuing education courses. No fees.

Southern Illinois University, Women's Programs Office, Woody Hall, B-244/245, Carbondale, IL 62901, 618-453-3655. Monday–Friday, 8 am–5 pm. Individual advising, group discussions. No appointment needed.

Thornton Community College, Counseling Center, 15800 S. State St., South Holland, IL 60473, 312-596-2000, Ext. 306. Monday–Thursday, 8 am–8:30 pm; Friday, 8 am–5 pm. Career Information Center.

University of Illinois Urbana-Champaign, Student Services Office for Married Students and Continuing Education for Women, 610 E. John St., Champaign, IL 61820, 217-333-3137. Monday–Friday, 8 am–5 pm. Official college office. Educational and career counseling. No fees.

INDIANA

Ball State University, Center for Student Employment and Career Information Services, Muncie, IN 47306, 317-285-5634. Monday–Friday, 8 am–5 pm.

Continuing Education Center for Women, Indiana University/Purdue University at Indianapolis, 1317 W. Mich River, Indianapolis, IN 46223, 317-264-4784. Monday–Friday, 8 am–5 pm. Official college office. Educational and career counseling, continuing education courses. Fees vary.

Fort Wayne Women's Bureau, Inc., 203 W. Wayne St., Fort Wayne, IN 46802, 219-424-7977/426-0023. Peer counseling, Monday–Friday, 10 am–2 pm. Not-for-profit agency. Career counseling, job search skills training, job opportunity book.

Indiana University, Continuing Education for Women, Owen Hall 201, Bloomington, IN 47405, 812-335-0225. Monday–Friday, 8 am–5 pm. Official college office. Educational and career counseling, continuing education courses. Fees vary.

University Center for Women, Counseling and Academic Development Division, Purdue University, 2101 Coliseum Blvd. East, Fort Wayne, IN 46805, 219-482-5393. Monday–Friday, 8 am–noon, 1 pm–5 pm. College sponsored office. Educational and career counseling, continuing education courses, job referral. Fees vary.

Women's Resource Center, YWCA, 802 N. Lafayette Blvd., South Bend., IN 46601, 219-233-9491. Monday–Friday, 9 am–5 pm.

IOWA

Division of Women's Programs, Drake University, 25th and Carpenter, Des Moines, IA 50311, 515-271-2916. Mon–Fri, 8 am–4:30 pm, Tues 8 am–8 pm. For adult students and the greater community. Workshops, information, referral, support services or issues related to career/life planning.

University Counseling Service, Iowa Memorial Union, University of Iowa, Iowa City, IA 52242, 319-353-4484. Monday–Friday, 8 am–5 pm. College sponsored office. Educational, vocational and personal counseling.

University of Iowa, Office of Career Planning and Placement, Iowa City, IA 52242, 319-353-3147. Monday–Friday, 8 am–5 pm. Official college office. Educational and career counseling, job referral, placement. Fee for job placement only.

KANSAS

University of Kansas, Adult Life Resource Center, Division of Continuing Education, 1246 Mississippi St., Annex A, Lawrence, KS 66045, 913-864-4794 or 800-532-6772 (toll free in Kansas). Monday–Friday, 8 am–noon and 1–5 pm. College sponsored. Educational and career counseling, continuing education, program for displaced homemakers. No registration fee. Other fees vary.

MAINE

The Women's Center, Westbrook College, Stevens Ave., Portland, ME 04103. 207-797-7261. Monday–Friday, mornings; and by appointment. Educational and career information resource, vocational testing, and workshops.

MARYLAND

Baltimore New Directions for Women, 2511 N. Charles St., Baltimore, MD 21218, 301-235-8800. Monday–Friday, 9 am–4:30 pm. Educational and career counseling, continuing education courses, job referral, placement. Information center.

College of Notre Dame of Maryland, Continuing Education Center, 4701 N. Charles St., Baltimore, MD 21210, 301-435-0100. Monday–Friday, 8:30 am–4:30 pm. College sponsored. Educational and career counseling, continuing education courses. Fees vary.

Goucher College, Goucher Center for Educational Resources, Towson, Baltimore, MD 21204, 301-337-6200. Monday–Friday, 9 am–4:30 pm. College sponsored. Counseling for women considering a return to school. Non-credit and credit courses for adults. Referrals for career and volunteer work.

MASSACHUSETTS

Career & Volunteer Advisory Service, Project Re-Entry, 14 Beacon St., Boston, MA 02108, 617-227-1762. Monday–Friday, 10 am–4 pm. Independent nonprofit agency. Career counseling, job information. Fee for consultation.

Continuum, Inc., 785 Centre St., Newton, MA 02158, 617-964-3322. Monday–Friday, 9 am–5 pm. A private, licensed school of career education. Internship programs for adults changing, advancing, or entering careers. Career counseling for men and women of all ages and for relocated spouses. Vocational testing available. Fees vary.

Radcliffe Career Services, 77 Brattle Street, Cambridge MA 02138. Fee for counseling session. Monday-Friday, 9 am–5 pm, evenings by appointment. Open to general public as well as Harvard and Radcliffe students and alumnae. Fees vary.

Resources Center for Educational Opportunities, 19 Fort Hill St., Hingham, MA 02043, 617-749-7445. Monday–Friday, 9:30 am–11:30 am and by appointment. Branch action project of American Association of University Women.

Smith College, Career Development Office, Pierce Hall, Northampton, MA 01063, 413-584-2700. Monday–Friday, 8:30 am–4:30 pm. Official college office. Educational and career counseling. No fees.

Widening Opportunity Research Center, Middlesex Community College, Box T, Bedford, MA 01730, 617-275-8910, Ext. 291. Monday–Friday, 9 am–2 pm. College sponsored office. Educational and career counseling, continuing education courses. Fees vary.

Women's Educational & Industrial Union, Career Services, 356 Boylston St., Boston, MA 02116, 617-536-5651. Monday–Friday, 9 am–5 pm. Independent nonprofit agency. Career counseling, job referral and placement. No registration fee. Placement fees vary.

Why Not? Program, YWCA, 1 Salem Sq., Worcester, MA 01608, 617-791-3181. Monday–Friday, 9 am–5 pm; evenings by appointment. Fees vary.

MICHIGAN

Every Woman's Place, 1433 Clinton, Muskegon, MI 49442, 616-726-4493. Monday–Friday, 9 am–5 pm.

Michigan Technological University, Division of Education and Public Services, Youth Programs, Rm. 208 Academic Offices Bldg., Houghton, MI 49931, 906/487-2219, Monday–Friday, 8 am–5 pm. Official College Office. Three, one-week, Women in Engineering Workshops. Career education and counseling.

Macomb County Community College, Community Resource Center, 14500 Twelve Mile Rd., K-332, Warren, MI 48093, 313-445-7417. Monday–Friday, 8:30 am–5 pm.

Montcalm Community College, Student Services Office, Sidney, MI 48885, 517-328-2111. Monday–Friday, 8 am–5 pm; evenings by appointment. College sponsored office. Education and career counseling. No fees.

C. S. Mott Community College, Guidance Services and Counseling Division, 1401 E. Court St., Flint, MI 48503, 313-762-0356. Monday–Thursday, 8 am–7 pm; Friday, 8 am–4:30 pm. Health counseling and vocational testing.

Northern Michigan University, Women's Center for Continuing Education, Marquette, MI 49855, 906-227-2101. Monday–Friday, 8:30 am–4:30 pm. Official college office. Educational and career counseling, job referral, continuing education courses. Fees vary.

Oakland University, Continuum Center for Adult Counseling and Leadership Training, Rochester, MI 48063, 313-377-3033. Monday–Friday, 8 am–5 pm. College affiliated. Personal, educational and career counseling, continuing education courses. Fees vary.

Schoolcraft College, Women's Resource Center, 18600 Haggerty Rd., Livonia, MI 48152, 313-591-6400, Ext. 430. Monday–Friday, 9 am–3 pm. Continuing Education Community Services; Educational and career counseling courses, workshops, referral to other agencies, and peer counseling. For widowed, displaced homemakers and re-entry women and men. Fees for courses and workshops only.

University of Michigan, Center for Continuing Education of Women, 350 S. Thayer St., Ann Arbor, MI 48109, 313-764-6555.

Western Michigan University, Center for Women's Services, Kalamazoo, MI 49008, 616-383-6097. Monday–Friday, 8 am–5 pm. Official college office. Educational and career counseling. Fees vary.

Women's Center, University of Michigan-Dearborn, Office of Student Affairs, 4901 Evergreen Rd., Dearborn, MI 48128, 313-593-5147. Discussions and information about employment trends, study skills, childcare, re-entry, scholarships, career planning, social interactions, marriage and divorce, legal issues, rape prevention, and health care. Fees vary.

Women's Resource Center, 252 State St., Grand Rapids, MI 49503, 616-458-5443. Monday and Wednesday, 9 am–8 pm; Tuesday and Thursday, 9 am–5 pm. Independent nonprofit agency. Educational and career counseling, job referral. Fees vary.

MINNESOTA

Chart, Wesley Temple Bldg., 123 E. Grant St., Minneapolis, MN 55403, 612-871-9100. By appointment. Career development and employment services to individuals and organizations. Fees vary.

Minnesota Women's Center, University of Minnesota, 5 Eddy Hall, Minneapolis, MN 55455, 612-373-3850. Monday–Friday, 8 am–4:30 pm. Offical college office. Informal advising and referral. No fees.

Southwest State University, Women's Resource Center, Marshall, MN 56258, 507-537-7160, September–May. Monday–Friday, 8 am–4:30 pm; evening schedule varies. Official college office. Educational and career counseling, job referral and placement, continuing education courses. Placement fee only.

Working Opportunities for Women, 2233 University Ave., Ste. 340, St. Paul, MN 55114, 612-647-9961. Monday–Friday, 8:30 am–5 pm. Complete career planning services for women.

MISSISSIPPI

Mississippi State University, Placement and Career Information Center, Drawer P, Mississippi State, MS 39762, 601-325-3344. Monday–Friday, 8 am–5 pm.

MISSOURI

New Directions Center, 806 N. Providence Rd., Columbia, MO 65201, 314-443-2421. Monday–Friday, 9 am–4 pm. Career planning, education referral and job placement center for women. Workshops and individual career counseling.

University of Missouri, St. Louis, Continuing Education-Extension, 313 Education Office Bldg., 8001 Natural Bridge Rd., St. Louis, MO 63121, 314-553-5511. Monday–Friday, 8 am–5 pm. Official college office. Educational and career counseling, adult education courses, limited job referral. Fees vary.

The Women's Center, University of Missouri, Kansas City, 5204 Rockhill Rd., Kansas City, MO 64110, 816-276-1638. Monday–Friday, 8 am–5 pm. Official college office. Educational and career counseling, job referral, continuing education courses. No fees.

MONTANA

Focus on Women, 9 Hamilton Hall, Montana State University, Bozeman, MT 59717, 406-994-4541. Monday–Friday, 8 am–5 pm. Workshops, seminars. Fee varies.

Women's Resource Center, Non-traditional Job Counselor, University of Montana, Missoula, MT 59801, 406-453-6691. Monday–Friday, 8 am–5 pm. Non-traditional career counseling, and job referral. No fee.

Women in Transition, Missoula YWCA, 1130 W. Broadway, Missoula, MT 59801, 406-543-6768. Monday–Friday, 8 am–5 pm. Job counseling, career counseling, job referral, resume preparation. Works with displaced homemakers.

NEW JERSEY

Adult Service Center, 112 Main Rd., Montville, NJ 07045, 201-575-0855, 335-4420. Monday, Tuesday, Thursday, Friday, 9 am–1 pm; Wednesday, 7 pm–10 pm.

Bergen Community College, Division of Community Services, 400 Paramus Rd., Paramus, NJ 07652, 201-447-1940. Monday–Friday, 9 am–5 pm. College sponsored office. Educational and career counseling, adult education courses. No fees.

Caldwell College, Career Development Center, Caldwell, NJ 07006, 201-228-4424, Ext. 307. Monday–Friday, 8:30 am–4:30 pm. College sponsored office. Educational and career counseling, limited job referral. No fees.

College Counseling and Education Center, 369 Forest Ave., Paramus, NJ 07652, 201-265-7729. Monday–Saturday, 9 am–9 pm.

Douglass College, Douglass Advisory Services for Women, Rutgers Women's Center, 132 George St., New Brunswick, NJ 08903, 201-932-9603. Monday–Friday, 9 am–2 pm. Educational and career counseling. No fees.

Fairleigh Dickinson University, Center for Women, Madison Ave., Madison, NJ 07940, 201-377-4700, Ext. 320. Monday–Friday, 9 am–5 pm. Official college office. Educational and career counseling, continuing education courses, job referral and placement. No fees.

Eve Adult Advisory Services, Kean College of New Jersey, Administration Bldg., Union, NJ 07083, 201-527-2210. Monday–Friday, 9 am–4:30 pm. College sponsored. Educational and career counseling. No registration fee. Other fees vary.

Jersey City State College, The Women's Center, 94 Audubon, Jersey City, NJ 07305, 201-547-3189. Monday–Friday, 9 am–4:30 pm. Official college office. Educational and career counseling, continuing education courses. No fees.

Jewish Vocational Service, 111 Prospect St., East Orange, NJ 07017, 201-674-6330. Five days, thirty-seven hours. Independent, nonprofit office. Educational and career counseling, job referral and placement. Fees vary.

Middlesex County College, Women's Career Information Center, Woodbridge Ave., West Hall Annex, Edison, NJ 08818, 201-548-6000, Ext. 411. Monday–Friday, 10 am–4 pm.

Montclair State College, Women's Center, Valley Rd., Upper Montclair, NJ 07043, 201-893-5106. Monday–Friday, 8:30 am–4:30 pm; evenings by appointment. College sponsored office. Educational and career counseling. No fees.

The Professional Roster, 171 Broadmead, Princeton, NJ 08609, 609-921-9561. Monday–Friday, 10 am–1 pm. Independent, nonprofit organization. Career counseling, job referral.

Reach, Inc., College of St. Elizabeth, O'Connor Hall, NJ 07961, 201-267-2530. Monday–Friday, 9:30 am–3 pm. Independent nonprofit office. Educational and career counseling, job referral. Fees vary.

NEW MEXICO

Young Women's Christian Association, Women's Resource Center, 316 Fourth St. SW, Albuquerque, NM 87102, 505-247-8841. Monday–Friday, 8 am–5 pm. Career counseling on a group basis. Classes, workshops, support groups, library. Fees on sliding scale: no one turned away for inability to pay.

NEW YORK

Academic Advisory Center for Adults, Turf Ave., Rye, NY 10580, 914-967-1653. Monday–Thursday, 9 am–4 pm, some evenings.

Hofstra University, Counseling Center, 240 Student Center, Hempstead, NY 11550, 516-560-6788. Monday–Friday, 9 am–5 pm; Monday, Thursday, 6–10 pm. Official college office. Educational and vocational counseling, testing, continuing education courses. Fees vary.

Kingsborough Community College, Office of Career Counseling and Placement, 2001 Oriental Blvd., Rm. C102, Brooklyn, NY 11235, 212-934-5115. Monday–Friday, 8 am–5 pm.

Janice La Rouche Assoc., Workshops for Women, 333 Central Park W., New York, NY 10025, 212-663-0970. Monday–Friday, 9 am–6 pm. Independent private agency. Career strategies counseling. Assertiveness training. No registration fee. Other fees vary.

Mercy College, Career Counseling and Placement Office, 555 Broadway, Dobbs Ferry, NY 10522, 914-693-4500, Ext. 215. Monday–Friday, 9 am–5 pm. Evenings by appointment. Official college office. Career counseling. Fees vary.

More for Women, 1435 Lexington Ave., New York, NY 10028, 212-534-0852. Monday–Friday, 9 am–9 pm; Saturday, 9 am–4 pm. Independent private agency. Educational and career counseling, workshops. Fees vary.

New Options, 960 Park Ave., New York, NY 10028, 212-535-1444. Monday–Friday, 9 am–5 pm. Evenings by appointment.

Orange County Community College, Office of Community Services, 115 South St., Middletown, NY 10940, 914-343-1121. Monday–Friday, 9 am–5 pm. Official college office. Educational counseling, continuing education courses. Fees vary.

Personnel Sciences Center, 341 Madison Ave., New York, NY 10017, 212-661-1870. Monday–Saturday, 9 am–5 pm. Independent private agency. Educational and career counseling. Fees vary.

Professional Skills Roster, 512 E. State St., Ithaca, NY 14850, 607-272-5533. Monday–Friday, 9:30 am–12:30 pm. Independent nonprofit agency. Job referral, limited educational and career counseling. No fees. Suggested donation.

Regional Learning Service of Central New York, 405 Oak St., Syracuse, NY 13203, 315-425-5252. Monday–Friday, 8:30 am–4:30 pm. Independent nonprofit agency. Educational and career counseling. Registration fees vary.

Ruth Shapiro Associates, 200 E. 30th St., New York, NY 10016, 212-889-4284, 212-679-9858. Monday–Saturday, 9:30 am–6 pm and evenings. By appointment only. Private agency. Career/assertiveness counseling, resume/letter writing. Fees vary.

SUNY at Buffalo, Career Planning Office, 252 Capen Hall, Buffalo, NY 14260, 716-636-2231. Monday–Friday, 8:30 am–5 pm. Official college office. Educational and career counseling, job referral and placement. No fees.

Vistas for Women, YWCA, 515 North St., White Plains, NY 10605, 914-949-6227. Monday–Thursday, 9 am–5 pm.

Women's Center for Continuing Education, Syracuse University College, 610 E. Fayette St., Syracuse, New York, 13202, 315-423-4116. Phyllis R. Chase, Director. Monday–Friday 9 am–5 am. Career and educational counseling. No fees.

Women's Career Center, Inc., 30 N. Clinton Ave., Rochester, NY 14604, 716-325-2274. Monday, Tuesday, Wednesday, Friday, 9 am–4 pm; Monday, Tuesday, 4:30 pm–8:30 pm.

NORTH CAROLINA

Duke University, Office of Continuing Education, 107 Bivins Bldg., Durham, NC 27708, 919-684-6259. Monday–Friday, 8:30 am–5 pm. Official college office. Educational and career counseling, continuing education courses, for men as well as women. Fees vary.

Fayetteville Family Life Center, 114 Highland Ave., Fayetteville, NC 28305. Monday–Thursday, 8:30 am–5 pm. Friday, 8:30 am–12 pm. Tuesdays and Thursdays in evening.

Salem College, Lifespan Center, Lehman Hall, Box 10548, Salem Station, Winston-Salem, NC 27108, 919-721-2807. Monday–Friday, 9 am–5 pm. College sponsored office. Lifespan planning, educational and vocational counseling. Fees vary.

OHIO

Baldwin-Wallace College, Experience CUE, Developmental Services, Administration Bldg. - No. 118, Berea, OH 44017, 216-826-2188. Monday–Friday, 8:30 am–5 pm; Tuesday and Thursday, 5:30 pm–9 pm.

Cleveland Jewish Vocational Service, 13878 Cedar Rd., University Heights, OH 44118, 216-321-1381. Monday–Friday, 8:30 am–5 pm; Thursday, 8:30 am–6 pm. Independent nonprofit agency. Educational and career counseling, job referral, placement.

Lifelong Learning/Women's Programs, Cuyahoga Community College, 2900 Community College Ave., Cleveland, OH 44115, 216-241-5966. Monday–Friday, 9 am–5 pm. Community service. College sponsored office. Individual educational and career counseling, no fee. Group series and programs, fees vary.

Ohio State University, Adult Career Services, Office of Continuing Education, 210 Sullivant Hall, 1813 N. High St., Columbus, OH 43210, 614-422-8860. Monday–Thursday, 8 am–7:30 pm. Friday 8 am–5 pm. Saturday 8 am–12 pm. Career services and programs for re-entry adult students and community adults—fees vary.

Pyramid, Inc., 1642 Cleveland Ave. NW, Canton, OH 44703, 216-453-3767. Monday–Friday, 8:30 am–4:30 pm.

Resource: Careers, 1258 Euclid Ave., Ste. 204, Cleveland, OH 44115, 216-579-1414. For professional development of women with one year of college or more. By appointment only. Fees vary.

University of Akron, Adult Resource Center, Akron, Ohio 44325. 216-375-7448. Monday–Friday, 8 am–5 pm. Career/life planning, job finding skills, educational guidance. Free individual appointments, minimal fees for workshops.

University of Toledo, Center for Women, 2801 W. Bancroft St., Toledo, OH 43606. 419-537-2058. Monday–Friday, 8 am–5 pm. Specialists in helping homemakers to enter the job market. Career counseling, workshops, seminars available. Fees based on ability to pay.

Wright State University, Women's Career Development Center, 140 E. Monument Ave., Dayton, OH 45402, 513-223-6041. Monday–Friday, 8:30 am–5 pm.

OREGON

Women's Programs, Division of Continuing Education, Oregon State System of Higher Education, 1633 SW Park Ave., (mail) Box 1491, Portland, OR 97207, 503-448-2219. Monday–Friday, 8:30 am–4:30 pm. Official college office. Educational and career counseling, continuing education courses. No registration fee. Other fees vary.

PENNSYLVANIA

Cedar Crest College, Women's Center, Allentown, PA 18104, 215-437-4471. Monday–Friday, 8:30 am–4:30 pm. Educational and career counseling, continuing education courses, career interest testing. Fees vary.

Indiana University of Pennsylvania, Transition Center, Uhler Hall, Indiana, PA 15705, 412-357-2227, Ext. 18. Monday–Friday, 8:30 am–4:30 pm. Educational counseling, workshops, continuing education. No fees.

Institute of Awareness, 401 S. Broad St., Philadelphia, PA 19147, 215-545-4400. Monday–Friday, 9 am–5 pm. Independent and nonprofit agency. Adult education courses, special workshops, training programs. Fees vary.

Job Advisory Service, 300 S. Craig St., Pittsburgh, PA 15213. 412-621-0940. Monday–Friday 9 a.m.–4:30 p.m. Saturday, 9 a.m.–1 p.m. Independent nonprofit career counseling center. Job counseling, vocational testing, resume writing, workshops. Second career internship program for re-entry women and teachers.

Lehigh County Community College, Alternatives for Women, 2370 Main St., Schnecksville, PA 18078, 215-799-2121, Ext. 177. Sponsored by college community service office. Workshops. Fees vary.

Temple University, Career Services, Mitten Hall, Philadelphia, PA 19122; or 1619 Walnut St., Philadelphia, PA, 215-787-1503. Monday—Friday, 9 am–5 pm. College sponsored offices: 215-787-7981. No registration fee.

University of Pennsylvania, Resources for Women, 1208 Blockley Hall/ sl, Philadelphia, PA 19104, 215-898-5537. Monday–Friday, 10 am–3 pm. University sponsored, continuing supportive career services, career and resume counseling, workshops, job referral and placement. Fees vary.

Villa Maria College, Counseling Services for Women, 2551 West Lake Rd., Erie, PA 16505, 814-838-1966. Monday–Friday, 9 am–4 pm. Official college office. Educational and career counseling, job referral, placement, adult education courses. No fees.

Villanova University, Office of Adult Services, 107 Vasey Hall, Villanova, PA 19085, 215-645-4310. Educational and career counseling. Fees vary.

Wilson College, Office of Career Services, Chambersburg, PA 17201, 717-264-4141. Monday–Friday, 8 am–5 pm. Official college office. Educational and career counseling, job referral and placement. No fees.

SOUTH CAROLINA

Converse College, Women's Center, Spartanburg, SC 29301, 803-585-6421, Ext. 340. Monday–Friday, 8 am–5 pm. Free to students and alumnae.

Greenville Technical College, Center for Continuing Education for Women, Greenville, SC 29606, 803-242-3170. Monday–Thursday, 8 am–8:30 pm; Friday, 8 am–4:30 pm.

Piedmont Technical College, Women's Center, P.O. Drawer 1467, Greenwood, SC 29648, 803-223-8357, ext 217. Hours are Monday–Friday, 8 am–4:30 pm or call Student Services at ext 247, 5 pm–8:30 pm.

SOUTH DAKOTA

Sioux Falls College, The Center for Women, Glidden Hall, Sioux Falls, SD 57101, 605-331-6697. Educational, personal and career counseling.

TENNESSEE

YWCA of Nashville, Career/Life Planning Center, 1608 Woodmont Blvd., Nashville, TN 37215, 615-385-3952. Monday–Friday, 8:30 am–4:30 pm.

TEXAS

Amarillo College, Women's Programs, Box 447, Amarillo, TX 79178, 806-376-5111, Ext. 2683. Monday–Friday, 8 am–5 pm.

Austin Women's Center, 1700 S. Lamar Blvd., Ste. 318, Austin, TX 78704, 512-447-9666. Job search workshops. Tuesdays 9:30 am and 5:30 pm. No income eligibility requirements.

Richard S. Citrin, Ph.D., Psychologist, 2516 Oakland Blvd., Ste. 6, Fort Worth, TX 76103, 817-535-1555. Continuing education classes, workshops, individual counseling. Fees vary.

Community Counseling, Everywoman Program, Richland College, 12800 Abrams Rd., Dallas, TX 75243, 214-238-6034. College-individual career and personal counseling, displaced homemakers center. No fee.

Vocational Guidance Service, Inc., 2525 San Jacinto, Houston, TX 77002, 713-659-1800. Monday–Thursday, 8:30 am–7 pm; Friday, 8:30 am–5 pm. Nonprofit organization. Educational and career counseling, job referral and placement. Fees based on sliding scale.

Women's Counseling Service, 1950 W. Gray, Ste. 1, Houston, TX 77019, 713-521-9391. Career development. Individual vocational, divorce adjustment and educational counseling.

The Women's Employment Network, Inc., 109 Lexington, Ste. 300, San Antonio, TX 78205. 512-224-3002. Group job search for women, with an "alumnae association" for graduates, to aid their job retention. Free to women on welfare and to single mothers.

Women's Resource Center, YWCA, 4621 Ross Ave., Dallas, TX 75204. 214-827-5600. Monday–Friday, 9 am–4 pm. Vocational testing, individual and group career counseling. Fees vary.

UTAH

The Phoenix Institute, 352 Denver St., Salt Lake City, UT 84111, 801-532-5080. Monday–Friday, 8 am–8 pm. Saturdays by appointment.

Women's Resource Center, 293 Union Bldg., University of Utah, Salt Lake City, UT 84112, 801-581-8030. Monday–Friday, 8 am–5 pm. Evening groups. Conferences, discussion programs, groups, personal and career counseling and referral information open to the community.

VIRGINIA

Educational Opportunity Center, 3830 Virginia Beach Blvd., Virginia Beach, VA 23452, 804-463-4810. Monday–Friday, 8 am–4:30 pm. Nonprofit agency. Educational, career, and financial aid counseling. No fees.

Hollins College, Career Counseling Center, Rose Hill House, Hollins College, VA 24020, 703-362-6364. Monday–Friday, 9 am–4:30 pm.

Mary Baldwin College, Offices of Career Services and Internships, Staunton, VA 24401, 703-887-7030. Monday–Friday, 8:30 am–4:30 pm. College affiliated office. Educational and career counseling. No fee.

Old Dominion University, Women's Center, 1521 W. 49th St., Norfolk, VA 23508. 804-440-4109. Monday–Friday, 8 a.m.–5 p.m. Call for appt. Continuing education courses and career counseling.

University of Richmond, Women's Resource Center, University College, VA 23173, 804-285-6319. Call for appointment.

Virginia Commonwealth University, University Advising Center, Rm. 114, 901 W. Franklin St., Richmond, VA 23284, 804-257-0200. Monday–Thursday, 8 am–7:30 pm; Friday, 8 am–4:30 pm; Saturday, 9 am–1 pm. Nancy B. Miller, Director. Official university office. Educational counseling, referral to university career and personal counseling services, continuing education courses.

Woman's Resource Center of Central Va., Inc., Houston Memorial Chapel, Randolph-Macon Woman's College, Lynchburg, VA 24503, 804-846-7392, ext. 320. Monday–Friday, 9 am–4:30 pm. Kathryn C. Mays, Executive Director. Specialize in helping displaced homemakers enter/re-enter job market. Career counseling, workshops, seminars. Fees vary.

WASHINGTON

Individual Development Center, Inc. (I.D. Center), Career and Life Planning, 1020 E. John St., Seattle, WA 98102, 206-329-0600. Monday–Friday, 9 am–4 pm. Evening counseling and appointments. Independent private agency. Career and life decision counseling, career development workshops for company and government agency employees, outplacement services and employee assistance programs. Partial scholarships available.

University of Washington, University Extension GH-21, Career/Life Planning, Seattle, WA 98195, 206-543-2300. Monday–Friday, 8 am–4:30 pm. Career counseling, testing, classes, workshops. Fees vary.

WISCONSIN

Employment Options, 2095 Winnebago St., Madison, WI 53704, 608-244-5181. Monday–Friday, 9 am–5 pm. Evening and weekend appointments arranged.

Waukesha County Technical Institute, Women's Development Center, 800 Main St., Pewaukee, WI 53072, 414-691-5400. Career and vocational counseling; free seminars and workshops on decision making, coping, career planning and job seeking skills. Special emphasis on nontraditional employment. All services free. Appointments and reservations advised. All services open to men also.

III. GROUP-SUPPORT FOR THOSE
WHO ARE UNEMPLOYED

Forty-Plus Clubs. Not a national organization, but a nationwide network of voluntary, autonomous non-profit clubs, manned by its unemployed members, paying no salaries, supported by initiation fees and monthly dues. Generally speaking (requirements vary from club to club), open only to those who are forty years of age or older, unemployed currently, seeking active employment, having made an average of between $25,000–$30,000 minimum annual salary previously. The minimum varies from club to club and has been lowered lately, so as not to discriminate against women (who are notoriously underpaid for their talents). The screening procedures again vary from club to club, and the process may take up to six weeks. It involves (usually) a personal interview, the checking out of your business references, and an informal meeting with representative active members. Insiders claim at least one-tenth leave without ever finding placement (sometimes due to their own lack of motivation), some try to hang around just for the sense of community (hence stays are often limited to six months, in some locations), and it takes the average successful member up to six months to find placement. While active in the club members must agree to give typically about sixteen hours a week, or two and one-half days, to club work. Fees and monthly dues vary from club to club. There have been clubs in the following cities: Toronto, Oakland, California, Los Angeles, Chicago, Denver, Honolulu, Philadelphia, Washington D.C., New York, Cleveland, and Winston-Salem. You will need to check if the club nearest you is still operating. The white pages of your phone book will have their address and phone number (they are all listed under the title of FORTY-PLUS).

Changes. 7 Woodbridge St., Cambridge, MA 02140, 617-876-5085. A group for unemployed professionals. Registration $6. Sessions $3 for unemployed, and $6 for the employed. Initial interview with the counselor is encouraged. Free. (Neither he nor the 100 or more fellow members of the Cambridge Psychotherapy Institute charge for the initial interview.) Carl J. Schneider, Counselor.

Talent Bank Associates, 475 Calkins Rd., Henrietta (near Rochester), NY 14467, 716-334-9676. An organized form of the "Job-Hunters Anonymous" idea. A non-profit organization comprised of unemployed persons of various professions and skills working together on a volunteer basis to find themselves meaningful, permanent employment. Free of charge. During a recent year, it served 350 people, 79% of whom found long-term employment through this program.

energy for employment, fourteen job-search groups in the Philadelphia area, providing both emotional and technical support for job-seekers through free weekly meetings. For information about locations, dates and times, contact: Laura C. Smith, Program Director, energy for employment, 311 S. Juniper St., Ste. 1002, Philadelphia, PA 19107, 215-985-1434.

Christian Employment Cooperative. A nonprofit ecumenical Christian effort to meet the needs of the unemployed, by using local congregations to bring together the unemployed, employers and support groups. For information, contact: Leon Bridges, Executive Director, Christian Employment Cooperative, 465 Boulevard, SE, Ste. 210, Atlanta, GA 30312, 404-622-2235.

Career Planning Center of Grace United Methodist Church. On two Saturdays per month, they run one-day workshops (9:30 am–4 pm). Fee: $25. Exercises must be completed prior to the workshop. For information contact: Mark Canfield, Director, 458 Ponce de Leon Ave., Atlanta, GA 30308, 404-876-2678.

St. Jude's Job Network Club, a non-denominational self-help support group meets every Monday at 7:30 pm at St. Jude's Catholic Church, 7171 Glenridge Dr., Sandy Springs, Georgia (near northern Atlanta).

Operation Job Search, 2844 South Calhoun St., Fort Wayne, IN 46807, 219-456-3542. A community-wide career assessment program, sponsored by the city; the only such program of its kind in the country, at this writing. For all residents of the city of Fort Wayne, who are unemployed or underemployed.

Chicago Career Clubs. Meets every other Tuesday evening (at this writing) from 6–8 pm at Three Arts Club, 1300 N. Dearborn, Chicago. $10 per session, payable at the door. Clubs also meet in Northbrook, Evanston, Oak Park and Glen Ellyn. Reservations are required: call 312-274-3169.

Career Planning and Placement Center, Adult Evening Program, 110 Noyes Hall, University of Missouri, Columbia, MO 65201, 314 882-6803. Tuesday and Thursday, 5–9 pm. Open to the public. Free. Drop-in for research. Schedule individual appointment. Help with goal clarification, resumes, interviews, job-seeking strategies, training opportunities. Job-seeking group.

Dublin Library Job Club, 7606 Amador Valley Blvd., Dublin CA. A weekly forum for all career changers and job seekers. Sponsored by Modern Career Decisions (Rod Meyer, Executive Director) as a community service. Each meeting focuses on a different subject from *Parachute.* Meets every Friday at 10 am. Free. 415-846-9071.

Experience Unlimited. An organization for unemployed professionals, based in California. Contact: Mr. Herman L. Leopold, Experience Unlimited Coordinator, Employment Development Dept., 1111 Jackson St., Rm. 1009, Oakland, CA 94607. Mailing address: 1225 4th Ave., Oakland, CA 94606, 415-464-0659/464-1259.

Civic Center Volunteers. Marin County Personnel Office, Administration Bldg., Civic Center, San Rafael, CA 94903, 415/499-6104. Placement in county jobs of volunteer re-entry women, career-experimenters and students wishing to gain experience. Volunteers sign a contract for each specific job, and receive supervision and evaluation. The purpose of this program is to give work experience in various jobs and provide a place to gain confidence in one's skills, new self-esteem, etc.

Additional groups spring up, monthly, including job clubs and other group activities. Many of these are listed in *National Business Employment Weekly,* on its pages called "Calendar of Events." Available on newsstands, $3 per issue; or, order directly from: National Business Employment Weekly, 420 Lexington Avenue, New York, NY 10170. 212-808-6792. You will have to pick and choose carefully.

IV. DIRECTORIES OF CAREER COUNSELING SERVICES IN VARIOUS CITIES/STATES

Enterprising souls are now putting together listings of counselors, agencies, resources and potential employers for individual cities or metropolitan areas. While such books, unless they are revised annually, are bound to become outdated rapidly (ah, how well I know) due to places moving, folding, or rising Phoenixlike from their own ashes in a different form, nonetheless these books offer at least a starting place if you are looking for help:

NATIONAL

Adams, Robert Lang, ed., *The National Job Bank*. Bob Adams, Inc., 840 Summer St., South Boston, MA 02127. 1983. $79.95, hardcover (add $1.75 for postage and handling, if ordering by mail). Lists employers, hospitals, universities, government agencies, as well as private employment agencies and services, for Metro New York, Boston, Chicago, D.C. and Baltimore, Atlanta, Texas, California, Pennsylvania, Colorado, Arizona, New Mexico and Utah. 10,000 entries, 1600 pages.

CALIFORNIA

Sweeney, Patricia; Olmsted, Daniel; Figueira, Hazel; and Marks, Linda, eds., *Looking For Work*: A Bay Area Guide to Employment Resources, New Ways to Work, 149 Ninth Street, San Francisco, CA 94103. 415-552-1000. 1986.

Fiedler, J. Michael, ed., The All-New, Second Edition of *The San Francisco Bay Area Job Bank*, Bob Adams, Inc., 840 Summer St., Boston, MA 02127. 1985.

Beach, Janet L., *How to Get a Job in the San Francisco Bay Area*. Contemporary Books, Inc., 180 North Michigan Ave., Chicago, IL 60601. 1983. $9.95, paper. An extremely well-done resource guide, describing the nature of the Bay Area, each major industry in that Area, the nature of that industry and key resources, job titles and salary ranges, insiders' advice, key companies or organizations, together with the name of the principal contact therein.

Adams, Robert Lang, ed., *The Northern California Job Bank*. Bob Adams, Inc., 840 Summer St., South Boston, MA 02127. 1982. $9.95, paper (add $1.75 for postage and handling, if ordering by mail). Lists employers, hospitals, universities, government agencies, as well as private employment agencies and services.

Visconti, Ron, *1983–1984 Bay Area Career Resource Directory*. Institute for Educational Improvement, 231 E. Millbrae Ave., Ste. 114, Millbrae, CA 94030. 1983. $6.50, paper (plus $1.25 postage and handling; California residents add $.42 tax). All orders must be prepaid.

Looking for Work .... A Bay Area Guide to Employment Resources. New Ways to Work, 149 Ninth St., San Francisco, CA 94103. 1983. $4.45, paper. Regular updates published, and included.

Adams, Robert Lang, ed., *The Southern California Job Bank*. Bob Adams, Inc., 840 Summer St., South Boston, MA 02127. 1981. $9.95, paper (add $1.75 for postage and handling, if ordering by mail). Lists employers, hospitals, universities, government agencies, as well as private employment agencies and services.

Camden, Thomas, and Greene, Freda, *How to Get a Job in Los Angeles*. Surrey Books, available (among other places) from B. Dalton, 131 N. La Cienega Blvd., Los Angeles, CA 90048. $13.95, paper.

DISTRICT OF COLUMBIA

Adams, Robert Lang, ed., *The Metropolitan Washington Job Bank*. Bob Adams, Inc., 840 Summer St., South Boston, MA 02127. 1983. $9.95, paper (add $1.75 for postage and handling, if ordering by mail). Lists employers, hospitals, universities, government agencies, as well as private employment agencies and services.

ILLINOIS

Camden, Thomas M. and Schwartz, Susan, *How to Get a Job in Chicago: The Insider's Guide*. Surrey Books, 500 N. Michigan Avenue, Suite 1940, Chicago, IL 60611 312-661-0050. 1986.

Adams, Robert Lang, ed., *The Greater Chicago Job Bank*. Bob Adams, Inc., 840 Summer St., South Boston, MA 02127. 1982. $9.95, paper (add $1.75 for postage and handling, if ordering by mail). Lists employers, hospitals, universities, government agencies, as well as private employment agencies and services.

MASSACHUSETTS

Boyd, Kathleen, and Ramsauer, Constance Arnold, and Senft, Ruth, *Career Connections: A Guide to Career Planning Services in Massachusetts*. Bob Adams, Inc., 840 Summer St., South Boston, MA 02127. 1983. $9.95, paper.

Adams, Robert Lang, ed., *The Boston Job Bank.* Bob Adams, Inc., 840 Summer St., South Boston, MA 02127. 1983, 1980 (all new second edition). $9.95, paper (add $1.75 for postage and handling, if ordering by mail). Lists employers, hospitals, universities, government agencies, as well as private employment agencies and services. Also has ads, of various services.

NEW YORK

Camden, Thomas, M. and Fleming-Holland, Susan, *How to Get a Job in New York: The Insider's Guide.* Surrey Books, 500 N. Michigan Ave., Suite 1940, Chicago, IL 60611 312-661-0050. 1986.

Adams, Robert Lang, ed., *The Metropolitan New York Job Bank.* Bob Adams, Inc., 840 Summer St., South Boston, MA 02127. 1983 (all new second edition) $9.95, paper (add $1.75 for postage and handling, if ordering by mail). Lists employers, hospitals, universities, government agencies, as well as private employment agencies and services.

PENNSYLVANIA

Adams, Robert Lang, ed., *The Pennsylvania Job Bank.* Bob Adams, Inc,. 840 Summer St., South Boston, MA 02127. 1982. $9.95, paper (add $1.75 for postage and handling, if ordering by mail). Lists employers, hospitals, universities, government agencies, as well as private employment agencies and services.

THE SOUTHWEST

Adams, Robert Lang, ed., *The Southwest Job Bank.* Bob Adams, Inc., 840 Summer St., South Boston, MA 02127. 1983. $9.95, paper (add $1.75 for postage and handling, if order-

ing by mail). In addition to primary employer listings, describes those positions with strong hiring outlooks, plus the basics of job-winning, as Adams sees it.

TEXAS

Adams, Robert Lang, ed., *The Texas Job Bank.* Bob Adams, Inc., 840 Summer St., South Boston, MA 02127. 1982. $9.95, paper (add $1.75 for postage and handling, if ordering by mail). Lists employers, hospitals, universities, government agencies, as well as private employment agencies and services.

Camden, Thomas M. and Bishop, Nancy, *How to Get a Job in Dallas/Ft. Worth—The Insider's Guide.* Surrey Books, Inc., 500 N. Michigan Ave., Suite 1940, Chicago, IL 60611. 1984. $13.95.

Wegmann, Robert, *How to Find a Job in Houston.* Ten Speed Press, Box 7123, Berkeley, CA 94707. 1983. $9.95, paper. Foreword and Appendix ("The Loss of Values in Career Counseling") by Richard N. Bolles. Appendix by the author on the subject "Assisting Larger Groups of Unemployed Workers to Find New Employment." Professor Wegmann teaches a class, for credit, on job choice, at the University of Houston–Clear Lake City. A large portion of this book, consequently, is devoted to the basic steps in the job-hunt process, as he teaches them in his excellent course.

Jitahidi, Joia, *Making Austin Work.* Tips to the hidden job market and a guide to Austin's employment resources. Catalyst Publications, Box 15785, Austin, TX 78761. Further information on workshops, seminars or individual consultations, call Catalyst Career Consultants 512-452-1129.

Appendix C

Special Problems

I. The World of Work: A Sampler

II. How to Do Job-Hunting While You Are Still Employed

III. How to Survey a Place Far Away

IV. How to Use a Computer to Aid in Prioritizing

The World of Work: A Sampler

Occupation	1. Leadership/persuasion	2. Helping/instructing others	3. Problem-solving/creativity	4. Initiative	5. Work as part of a team	6. Frequent public contact	7. Manual dexterity	8. Physical stamina	9. Hazardous	10. Outdoors	11. Confined	12. Geographically concentrated	13. Part-time	14. Earnings	15. Employment growth	16. Number of new jobs 1984–95 (in thousands)	17. Entry requirements
Executive, Administrative, & Managerial Occupations																	
Managers & Administrators																	
Bank officers & managers	•	•	•	•	•	•						•		H	H	119	H
Health services managers	•	•	•	•	•	•								H	H	147	H
Hotel managers & assistants	•	•	•	•	•	•								(1)	H	21	M
School principals & assistant principals	•	•	•	•	•	•								H	L	12	H
Management Support Occupations																	
Accountants & auditors		•	•		•	•						•		H	H	307	H
Construction & building inspectors		•	•	•	•		•			•				M	L	4	M
Inspectors & compliance officers, except construction		•	•	•	•		•			•				H	L	10	M
Personnel, training & labor relations specialists	•	•	•	•	•	•								H	M	34	H
Purchasing agents	•		•		•	•								H	M	36	H
Underwriters			•											H	H	17	H
Wholesale & retail buyers	•	•	•	•	•									M	M	28	H
Engineers, Surveyors, & Architects																	
Architects			•	•	•	•								H	H	25	H
Surveyors	•			•			•	•		•				M	M	6	M
Engineers																	
Aerospace engineers			•	•	•							•		H	H	14	H
Chemical engineers			•	•	•									H	H	13	H
Civil engineers			•	•	•									H	H	46	H
Electrical & electronics engineers			•	•	•									H	H	206	H
Industrial engineers			•	•	•									H	H	37	H
Mechanical engineers			•	•	•									H	H	81	H
Metallurgical, ceramics & materials engineers			•	•	•									H	H	4	H
Mining engineers			•	•	•									H	L	(2)	H
Nuclear engineers			•	•	•									H	L	1	H
Petroleum engineers			•	•	•							•		H	M	4	H

1. Estimates not available.
2. Less than 500.

L = Lowest   M = Middle   H = Highest

From *Occupational Outlook Quarterly*, Vol. 30, No. 3   Fall 1986.

Column legend (diagonal headers):

Job requirements: 1. Leadership/persuasion · 2. Helping/instructing others · 3. Problem-solving/creativity · 4. Initiative · 5. Work as part of a team · 6. Frequent public contact · 7. Manual dexterity · 8. Physical stamina · 9. Hazardous

Work environment: 10. Outdoors · 11. Confined · 12. Geographically concentrated · 13. Part-time

Occupational characteristics: 14. Earnings · 15. Employment growth · 16. Number of new jobs, 1984-95 (in thousands) · 17. Entry requirements

Occupation	1	2	3	4	5	6	7	8	9	10	11	12	13	14	15	16	17
Natural Scientists & Mathematicians																	
Computer & Mathematical Occupations																	
Actuaries			•	•								•	•	H	H	4	H
Computer systems analysts	•	•	•	•	•							•		H	H	212	H
Mathematicians			•	•										H	M	4	H
Statisticians			•	•										H	M	4	H
Physical Scientists			•	•										H	M		H
Chemists			•	•										H	L	9	H
Geologists & geophysicists			•	•	•					•		•		H	M	7	H
Meteorologists			•	•	•									H	M	1	H
Physicists & astronomers			•	•										H	L	2	H
Life Scientists																	
Agricultural scientists			•	•										(1)	M	3	H
Biological scientists			•	•										H	M	10	H
Foresters & conservation scientists		•	•	•	•			•	•	•				H	L	2	H
Social Scientists, Social Workers, Religious Workers, & Lawyers																	
Lawyers	•	•	•	•	•	•	•							H	H	174	H
Social Scientists & Urban Planners																	
Economists			•	•										H	M	7	H
Psychologists		•	•	•		•								H	H	21	H
Sociologists			•	•		•								H	L	(2)	H
Urban & regional planners	•		•	•	•	•								H	L	2	H
Social & Recreation Workers																	
Social workers	•	•	•	•	•	•								M	H	75	H
Recreation workers	•	•	•	•	•	•	•	•		•			•	L	H	26	M
Religious Workers																	
Protestant ministers	•	•	•	•	•	•								L	(1)	(1)	H
Rabbis	•	•	•	•	•	•								H	(1)	(1)	H
Roman Catholic priests	•	•	•	•	•	•								L	(1)	(1)	H

1. Estimates not available.
2. Less than 500.

	Job requirements								Work environment				Occupational characteristics			
	1. Leadership/persuasion	2. Helping/instructing others	3. Problem-solving/creativity	4. Initiative	5. Work as part of a team	6. Frequent public contact	7. Manual dexterity	8. Physical stamina	9. Hazardous	10. Outdoors	11. Confined	12. Geographically concentrated	13. Part-time	14. Earnings	15. Employment growth	16. Number of new jobs, 1984-95 (in thousands)	17. Entry requirements
Teachers, Counselors, Librarians, & Archivists																	
Kindergarten & elementary school teachers ..	●	●	●	●	●	●	●	●						M	H	281	H
Secondary school teachers	●	●	●	●	●	●		●						M	L	48	H
Adult & vocational education teachers......	●	●	●	●	●	●		●					●	M	M	48	H
College & university faculty	●	●	●	●	●	●		●					●	H	L	−77	H
Counselors........................	●	●	●	●	●	●								M	M	29	H
Librarians	●	●	●	●	●	●		●					●	M	L	16	H
Archivists & curators.................			●	●	●									M	L	1	H
Health Diagnosing & Treating Practitioners																	
Chiropractors......................	●	●	●	●	●	●	●							H	H	9	H
Dentists..........................	●	●	●	●	●	●	●							H	H	39	H
Optometrists	●	●	●	●	●	●	●							H	H	8	H
Physicians	●	●	●	●	●	●	●					●		H	H	109	H
Podiatrists........................	●	●	●	●	●	●	●							H	H	4	H
Veterinarians	●	●	●	●	●	●	●	●	●					H	H	9	H
Registered Nurses, Pharmacists, Dietitians, Therapists, & Physician Assistants																	
Dietitians & nutritionists	●	●	●	●	●	●								M	H	12	H
Occupational therapists	●	●	●	●	●	●	●	●						(1)	H	8	H
Pharmacists.......................	●	●	●	●	●	●						●		H	L	15	H
Physical therapists	●	●	●	●	●	●	●	●						M	H	25	H
Physician assistants	●	●	●	●	●	●	●							M	H	10	M
Recreational therapists	●	●	●	●	●	●	●	●			●			M	H	4	M
Registered nurses	●	●	●	●	●	●	●	●	●			●		M	H	452	M
Respiratory therapists	●	●	●	●	●	●	●							M	H	11	L
Speech pathologists & audiologists	●	●	●	●	●	●								M	M	8	H

1. Estimates not available.
2. Less than 500.

	Job requirements											Work environment		Occupational characteristics			
	1. Leadership/persuasion	2. Helping/instructing others	3. Problem-solving/creativity	4. Initiative	5. Work as part of a team	6. Frequent public contact	7. Manual dexterity	8. Physical stamina	9. Hazardous	10. Outdoors	11. Confined	12. Geographically concentrated	13. Part-time	14. Earnings	15. Employment growth	16. Number of new jobs, 1984-95 (in thousands)	17. Entry requirements
Health Technologists & Technicians																	
Clinical laboratory technologists & technicians		•		•		•			•					L	L	18	(3)
Dental hygienists		•		•	•	•	•						•	L	H	22	M
Dispensing opticians		•	•	•	•	•	•							M	H	10	M
Electrocardiograph technicians		•	•		•	•	•							(1)	M	3	M
Electroenceph. technologists & technicians		•	•		•	•								(1)	H	1	M
Emergency medical technicians	•	•	•		•	•	•	•	•					L	L	3	M
Licensed practical nurses		•			•	•	•	•	•				•	L	M	106	M
Medical record technicians					•							•		L	H	10	M
Radiologic technologists		•			•	•	•		•					L	H	27	M
Surgical technicians		•			•	•	•							L	M	5	M
Writers, Artists, & Entertainers																	
Communications Occupations																	
Public relations specialists	•		•	•	•	•								H	H	30	H
Radio & TV announcers & newscasters	•	•		•	•	•						•		L	M	6	H
Reporters & correspondents	•		•	•	•	•								(1)	M	13	H
Writers & editors	•		•	•	•							•		(1)		H	54	H
Visual Arts Occupations																	
Designers			•	•	•	•	•							H	H	46	H
Graphic & fine artists			•	•		•								H		60	M
Photographers & camera operators			•	•		•	•						•	M	H	29	M
Performing Arts Occupations																	
Actors, directors, & producers			•	•	•	•	•	•				•	•	L	H	11	M
Dancers & choreographers			•	•	•	•	•	•				•	•	L	H	2	M
Musicians			•	•	•	•	•	•				•	•	L	M	26	M
Technologists & Technicians Except Health																	
Engineering & Science Technicians																	
Drafters					•		•				•			M	M	39	M
Electrical & electronics technicians			•		•		•							M	H	202	M
Engineering technicians			•		•		•							M	H	90	M
Science technicians			•		•		•							M	M	40	M

1. Estimates not available.
2. Less than 500.
3. Vary, depending on job.

Job requirements | Work environment | Occupational characteristics

	1. Leadership/persuasion	2. Helping/instructing others	3. Problem-solving/creativity	4. Initiative	5. Work as part of a team	6. Frequent public contact	7. Manual dexterity	8. Physical stamina	9. Hazardous	10. Outdoors	11. Confined	12. Geographically concentrated	13. Part-time	14. Earnings	15. Employment growth	16. Number of new jobs 1984-95 (in thousands)	17. Entry requirements
Other Technicians																	
Air traffic controllers		●	●	●	●		●					●		H	L	(2)	H
Broadcast technicians			●		●		●					●		M	H	5	M
Computer programmers			●		●							●		H	H	245	H
Legal assistants				(3)	●	(3)								M	H	51	L
Library technicians		●		●	●	●							●	L	L	4	L
Tool programmers, numerical control			●				●	●						M	H	3	M
Marketing & Sales Occupations																	
Cashiers		●			●	●						●	●	L	H	566	L
Insurance sales workers	●	●	●	●		●							●	M	L	34	M
Manufacturers' sales workers	●	●	●	●		●								H	L	51	H
Real estate agents & brokers	●	●	●	●		●				●			●	M	M	52	M
Retail sales workers	●	●		●		●							●	L	M	583	L
Securities & financial services sales workers	●	●	●	●		●							●	H	H	32	H
Travel agents	●	●	●	●		●								(1)	H	32	M
Wholesale trade sales workers	●	●	●			●								M	H	369	M
Administrative Support Occupations, Including Clerical																	
Bank tellers					●	●						●	●	L	L	24	L
Bookkeepers & accounting clerks					●							●	●	L	L	118	L
Computer & peripheral equipment operators			●		●		●					●		L	H	143	M
Data entry keyers					●		●					●		L	L	10	L
Mail carriers					●	●	●	●		●				M	L	8	L
Postal clerks					●	●	●	●				●		M	L	−27	L
Receptionists & information clerks		●			●	●						●	●	L	M	83	L
Reservation & transportation ticket agents & travel clerks	●	●			●	●						●		M	L	7	L
Secretaries				●	●	●	●							L	L	268	L
Statistical clerks					●							●		L	L	−12	L
Stenographers				●	●	●	●							L	L	−96	L
Teacher aides	●	●			●	●	●	●					●	L	M	88	L
Telephone operators		●				●						●		L	M	89	L
Traffic, shipping, & receiving clerks			●	●	●									L	L	61	L
Typists							●					●	●	L	L	11	L

1. Estimates not available.
2. Less than 500.
3. Vary, depending on job.

Job requirements / Work environment / Occupational characteristics

Occupation	1. Leadership/persuasion	2. Helping/instructing others	3. Problem-solving/creativity	4. Initiative	5. Work as part of a team	6. Frequent public contact	7. Manual dexterity	8. Physical stamina	9. Hazardous	10. Outdoors	11. Confined	12. Geographically concentrated	13. Part-time	14. Earnings	15. Employment growth	16. Number of new jobs 1984-95 (in thousands)	17. Entry requirements
Service Occupations																	
Protective Service Occupations																	
Correction officers	•	•		•		•	•		•					M	H	45	L
Firefighting occupations		•	•		•	•	•	•	•	•			•	M	M	48	L
Guards					•	•	•	•				•	•	L	H	188	L
Police & detectives	•	•	•	•	•	•	•	•	•	•				M	M	66	L
Food & Bev. Preparation & Serv. Occupations																	
Bartenders			•		•	•	•				•		•	L	H	112	M
Chefs & cooks except short order			•			•	•				•		•	L	H	210	M
Waiters & waitresses			•		•	•	•						•	L	H	424	L
Health Service Occupations																	
Dental assistants		•			•	•	•	•					•	L	H	48	L
Medical assistants		•			•	•	•		•					L	H	79	L
Nursing aides		•			•	•	•	•	•				•	L	H	348	L
Psychiatric aides		•			•	•		•	•					L	L	5	L
Cleaning Service Occupations																	
Janitors & cleaners								•					•	L	M	443	L
Personal Service Occupations																	
Barbers						•	•	•			•		•	L	L	4	M
Childcare workers	•	•		•		•		•					•	L	L	55	L
Cosmetologists & related workers						•	•				•		•	L	H	150	M
Flight attendants		•				•	•	•						M	H	13	L
Agricultural, Forestry, & Fishing Occupations																	
Farm operators & managers	•	•	•	•	•		•	•			•			M	L	-62	L
Mechanics & Repairers																	
Vehicle & Mobile Equip. Mechanics & Repairers																	
Aircraft mechanics & engine specialists			•		•		•	•	•	•		•		H	M	18	M
Automotive & motorcycle mechanics			•			•	•	•	•		•			M	H	185	M
Automotive body repairers			•				•	•	•		•			M	M	32	M
Diesel mechanics			•		•		•	•	•		•			M	H	48	M
Farm equipment mechanics			•				•	•	•	•				M	L	2	M
Mobile heavy equipment mechanics			•				•	•	•		•			M	M	12	M

	Job requirements								Work environ-ment			Occupational characteristics				
	1. Leadership/persuasion	2. Helping/instructing others	3. Problem-solving/creativity	4. Initiative	5. Work as part of a team	6. Frequent public contact	7. Manual dexterity	8. Physical stamina	9. Hazardous	10. Outdoors	11. Confined	12. Geographically concentrated	13. Part-time	14. Earnings	15. Employment growth	16. Number of new jobs 1984-95 (in thousands)	17. Entry requirements
Electrical & Electronic Equipment Repairers																	
Commercial & electronic equipment repairers		●	●		●	●								L	M	8	M
Communications equipment mechanics		●	●		●	●								M	L	3	M
Computer service technicians		●	●		●	●								M	H	28	M
Electronic home entertainment equip. repairers		●	●		●	●		●				●		M	M	7	M
Home appliance & power tool repairers		●	●		●	●								L	M	9	M
Line installers & cable splicers		●		●		●	●	●	●					M	M	24	L
Telephone installers & repairers		●			●	●	●	●	●					M	L	– 19	L
Other Mechanics & Repairers																	
General maintenance mechanics		●				●		●						M	M	137	M
Heating, air-cond. & refrig. mechanics		●				●		●						M	M	29	M
Industrial machinery repairers		●				●	●	●						M	L	34	M
Millwrights		●				●		●						H	L	6	M
Musical instrument repairers & tuners						●								L	L	1	M
Office machine & cash register servicers		●	●	●		●								M	H	16	M
Vending machine servicers & repairers		●	●			●								(1)	M	5	M
Construction & Extractive Occupations																	
Construction Occupations																	
Bricklayers & stonemasons		●		●		●	●	●	●					M	M	15	M
Carpenters		●		●		●	●	●	●					M	M	101	M
Carpet installers		●		●	●	●	●	●						M	M	11	M
Concrete masons & terrazzo workers		●		●		●	●	●	●					M	M	17	M
Drywall workers & lathers		●		●		●	●	●						M	M	11	M
Electricians		●		●		●	●	●	●					H	M	88	M
Glaziers		●		●		●	●	●	●					M	H	8	M
Insulation workers		●		●		●	●	●						M	M	7	M
Painters & paperhangers		●		●	●	●	●	●	●					M	L	17	M
Plasterers		●		●		●	●	●				●		M	L	1	M
Plumbers & pipefitters		●		●	●	●	●	●	●					H	M	61	M
Roofers		●		●		●	●	●	●					L	M	16	M
Sheet-metal workers		●		●		●	●	●						M	M	16	M
Structural & reinforcing metal workers		●		●		●	●	●	●					H	M	16	M
Tilesetters		●		●		●	●							M	M	3	M
Extractive Occupations																	
Roustabouts				●		●	●	●	●			●		M	L	(2)	L

1. Estimates not available.
2. Less than 500.

	Job requirements									Work environment				Occupational characteristics			
	1. Leadership/persuasion	2. Helping/instructing others	3. Problem-solving/creativity	4. Initiative	5. Work as part of a team	6. Frequent public contact	7. Manual dexterity	8. Physical stamina	9. Hazardous	10. Outdoors	11. Confined	12. Geographically concentrated	13. Part-time	14. Earnings	15. Employment growth	16. Number of new jobs, 1984-95 (in thousands)	17. Entry requirements
Production Occupations																	
Blue-collar worker supervisors	●	●	●	●	●		●		●					M	L	85	M
Precision Production Occupations																	
Boilermakers			●				●		●					M	L	4	M
Bookbinding workers		●		●		●	●	●			●			L	M	14	M
Butchers and meatcutters					●	●	●	●			●			L	L	−9	M
Compositors & typesetters						●	●	●			●			L	M	14	M
Dental laboratory technicians							●				●			L	M	10	M
Jewelers	●	●	●	●	●	●	●				●	●		L	L	3	M
Lithographic & photoengraving workers		●	●			●	●	●			●			H	M	13	M
Machinists			●			●	●	●			●			M	L	37	M
Photographic process workers							●				●			L	H	14	L
Shoe & leather workers & repairers	●				●	●	●							L	L	−8	M
Tool-and-die makers			●			●	●	●			●	●		H	L	16	M
Upholsterers						●	●				●			L	L	6	M
Plant & System Operators																	
Stationary engineers			●			●	●	●						M	L	4	M
Water & sewage treatment plant operators			●	●		●			●	●				L	M	10	M
Machine Operators, Tenders, & Setup Workers																	
Metalworking & plastic-working mach. operators						●	●	●			●	●		L		3	L
Numerical-control machine-tool operators			●			●	●	●			●			M	H	17	M
Printing press operators	●	●		●		●	●	●			●			M	M	26	M
Fabricators, Assemblers & Handwrkg. Occup.																	
Precision assemblers			●			●	●				●			L	M	66	L
Transportation equipment painters						●	●	●			●			M	M	9	M
Welders & cutters						●	●	●	●					M	M	41	M
Transportation & Material Moving Occupations																	
Aircraft pilots		●	●	●		●					●			H	H	18	M
Busdrivers			●		●	●	●				●		●	M	M	77	M
Construction machinery operators				●		●	●	●	●	●	●			M	M	32	M
Industrial truck & tractor operators			●			●	●				●			M	L	−46	M
Truckdrivers			●			●	●				●			M	M	428	M
Handlers, Equip. Cleaners, Helpers & Laborers																	
Construction trades helpers			●			●	●	●	●	●				L	L	27	L

II.

HOW TO DO JOB-HUNTING WHILE YOU ARE STILL EMPLOYED

Many job-hunting books assume that you are unemployed, and hence have complete freedom as to how you allot your time. But what do you do about the job-hunt or career-change, if you are presently holding down a full-time job?

Good question. That is the case in which many find themselves. How many? Well, the government, bless its heart, did a study of job-hunting among employed workers about eight years ago, and discovered that in a typical month—it was May ten years ago—4.2% of all employed workers, or one out of every twenty, went looking for another job sometime during that month. In actual numbers, that represented 3,269,000 people who were job-hunting while still employed. If the same percentage obtains today, it means 4,500,000 are currently employed but job-hunting.

I would like to point out two things about this finding. First of all, it means that one-third of *all* job-hunters are conducting the search while they are still employed.

Secondly, they *must* be successful. There's a lot of movement going on, in the world of work. The *average* nonagricultural firm in this country has to hire—in a typical year—as many new people as it has employees. In other words, a firm with three employees will probably have to hire two or three employees each year. A firm with 100 employees will probably have to hire 90 new employees each year. That's on the average. If you want a more detailed breakdown, this is what the study turned up: the average retail firm with say 100 employees may have to hire 136 new people each year; the average firm dealing in services and having say 100 employees may have to hire 111 new employees each year; the average financial institution, 74; the average manufacturing firm, 65; the average transportation or public utilities company, 32; and the average construction company, a whopping 202 new employees for every 100 it currently has.

It is this job-hunting behavior on the part of employed workers which helps to create so many vacancies—thus increasing *every* job-hunter's chance of success so dramatically.

How do employed job-hunters go about their search? You guessed it: the same way unemployed job-hunters do. According to the government's study, 70% of all employed job-hunters contacted an employer directly. But, back to our original question: how do you find time to do the job-hunt if you are presently holding down a full-time job? We have asked employed job-hunters how they did it, and the sum of their advice to you—based on their experience—is:

(1) Determine to keep at it, with every spare hour you can find. Press evenings, weekends, lunch hours and the like, into the service of your job-hunt.

(2) Use evenings and weekends to do the original homework, figuring out what your skills are and what it is you want to do, as well as where you want to do it. Later on in your job-search, use evenings and the weekend also to write thank-you notes, send out letters, and the like.

(3) For the actual calling upon potential employers, if they are in the city where you presently work, press your lunch hours into service. If you "brown-bag it," you will have time to make and keep one appointment, particularly if your intent is to make the interview no longer than twenty minutes—a good idea, in any case, for the exploratory or information interview. People take lunch hours at all different times: 11:15 a.m., 11:45, 12 noon, 12:30, 1 p.m. While you are on your lunch hour, somebody you want to see hasn't gone to lunch yet, or has just come back. Sometimes you can move your lunch hour—if the place where you are presently working is flexible about that—to the 11 a.m.-12 noon time slot.

(4) Press late afternoons into service. Many people you will want to see are on an executive or management level, and they often do not get away from their offices promptly at 5. It is appropriate to estimate how long it will take you to get across town to them, and ask them if they could see you that long after your quitting time, on a particular day.

(5) Press holidays into service. Holidays fall into two classes: those which everyone observes, like Christmas and New Year's Day; and those which some people observe, like Washington's Birthday, etc. In the case of the latter kind of holiday, if you have it off, you will sometimes be able to visit the people you want to see, because they do not have it off.

(6) Press Saturdays into service. Sometimes the people you want to see work on Saturday, or are occasionally willing to set up appointments for Saturday.

(7) Press your sickleave into service. In some organizations, workers accumulate sickleave, and have the right to take it as time off. If that is the case with you, use such days off judiciously, to visit potential employers who interest you.

(8) Press your vacations into service. If you are dead-serious about the importance of your job-hunt or career-change, it is not too great a sacrifice to devote one year's vacation time to your job-hunt. This is especially important if you are trying to secure employment in a distant city. Schedule your vacation in that city, and make arrangements and appointments, by letter and phone, ahead of time (see chapter 6, on how to research a place at a distance).

(9) If you have sufficient savings, the following stratagem may be one you would like to consider in addition to all the above: If you have a whole list of people and places you need to visit, and you require a concentrated period of time in which to do this, and cannot wait until your vacation time, you have the right to ask your present employer if you can have a leave of absence without pay. So long as the time requested is no longer than a week or so, and so long as it is scheduled at the convenience of the employer (i.e., not in the week that they need you the most), this request will often be honored. You can give, as the reason, the simple truth: Personal Business.

Should you feel guilty about job-hunting while you are still employed? Well, sure, if you want to. But there is no need. One-third of all job-hunters are doing the same thing: it is a common practice in our economy. Nothing oddball about it. Moreover, remember these simple truths: Your employer has certain rights, including the right to fire you at any time, for sufficient cause; moreover, they have the right to prepare for this act of firing ahead of time, laying the groundwork, transferring part of your work to other colleagues, etc. You, as employee, likewise have certain rights, including the right to quit at any time, for sufficient cause; moreover, you have the right to prepare for this act of quitting ahead of time, laying the groundwork through interviewing and job-searching.

III.
HOW TO SURVEY A PLACE FAR AWAY

1. *If you are researching a far-away place, set down on paper which of the above informa-tion-searches you can do right where you are, and which ones you need others' help with, in the city or place of your choice.*

Your two lists will *probably* come out looking like this:

Searches I Can Do Here	Searches Others Must Do There
A- (in detail:)	
B- (in detail:)	the rest of
C- some detail	C-
D-	D-
E -	E- in detail
F- some	F-

2. *Figure out if there isn't **some way** in the near future that you could go visit the city or cities of your choice.*

You may be able to do this even if you are presently employed. Does a vacation fall within the time period you have between now and when you must finally have that job? Could you visit it on vacation? Could you take a summer job there? Go there on leave? Get sent to a convention there? Get appointed to a group or association that meets there? Think it through. You will *have* to go there, finally (in almost all cases) for the actual job interview(s). *If worst comes to worst,* go there a week or so ahead of that interview. Better late than never, to look over the scene in person, and do some on-site research.

3. *For the time being, regard the city or town where you presently are, as a replica of the city or town you are interested in going to (in some respects at least)—so that some of your research can be done where you are, and then its learnings transferred.*

You recall earlier we discussed the case of a man who loved psychiatry, and plants, and carpentry, and discovered that there was a branch of psychiatry which used plants in the treatment of deeply withdrawn patients. So, our man discovered an occupation where he could use his love of plants and his love of psychiatry together (and presumably use his carpentry to build the planters that would be needed). Suppose you were this man. Having found this out in the place where you live, you could then write to your target city or town to ask, What psychiatric facilities do you have *there,* and which ones—if any—use plants in their healing program?

Thus can you conduct your research where you are, and then transfer its learn-ings to the place where you want to go.

4. *Until you can physically go there, use every resource and contact you have, in order to explore the answers to C, D, E and F.*

✳ THE DAILY OR WEEKLY NEWSPAPER THERE.
Almost all papers will mail to subscribers anywhere in the world. So: subscribe, for a six-month period, or a year. You'd be surprised at what you can learn from the paper. Some of the answers to C, D, E and F will appear there. Additionally, from the ads and business news items, you will know which businesses are growing and expanding—hence, hiring—in that city.

✳ THE CHAMBER OF COMMERCE, AND CITY HALL
(OR THE TOWN HALL) THERE.
These are the places whose interest it is (in most cases) to attract newcomers, and to tell them what kinds of businesses there are in town—as well as some details about them. So: write and ask them, in the beginning, what information they have about the city or town in general. Then later, don't hesitate to write back to them with more specific questions, as your target organizations become clearer in your mind.

✳ THE LOCAL LIBRARY OR REFERENCE LIBRARIAN,
IF YOUR TARGET CITY/TOWN HAS ONE.
It is perfectly permissible for you to write to the library in your target city, asking for information that may be only there. If the librarian is too busy to answer, then use one of your contacts there to find out. "Bill (or Billie) I need some information that I'm afraid only the library in your town has. Specifically, I need to know about company x." Or whatever.

✳ YOUR CONTACTS.
Yes, of course, you know people in whatever city or town you're researching. For openers, write to your old high school and get the alumni list for your graduating class. If you went to college, ask for their alumni list also (for your class, at the very least). Subscribe to your college's alumni bulletin for further news, addresses, and hints. If you belong to a church or synagogue, write to the church or synagogue in your target city, and tell them that you're one of their own and you need some information. "I need to know who can tell me what nonprofit organizations there are in that city, that deal with x." "I need to know how I can find out what corporations in town have departments of mental hygiene." Or, whatever. To find further contacts, ask your family and relatives who *they* know in the target city or town of

your choice. You will find, upon patient and persistent exploration, that you know or can contact far more people in that city, who might help you, than you would originally think.

✴ THE APPROPRIATE STATE, COUNTY, AND LOCAL
GOVERNMENT AGENCIES, ASSOCIATIONS, ETC.
Ask your contacts to tell you what that appropriate agency might be, for the field or kinds of organizations (or jobs) that you are interested in.

FOR THAT FARAWAY CITY, SEND YOURSELF

It will ultimately be *essential* for you to visit the geographical area you want to work in—if it's not where you presently live.

If going into a strange new geographical area is a totally new experience for you, and you have no friends there in your chosen area, just remember there are various ways of meeting people, making friends, and developing contacts rather quickly with people who share some interest or enthusiasm of yours. There are athletic clubs, Ys, churches, charitable and community organizations, where you can present yourself and meet people, from the moment you walk in the doors. You will soon develop many acquaintances, and some beginning friendships, and the place won't seem so lonely after all.

Also, visit or write your high school before you set out for this new town and find out what graduates live in the area that you are going to be visiting for the first time: they are your friends already, because you went to the same school. As I indicated earlier, all of these acquaintances, friends and key individuals have one common name: contacts. Contacts, CONTACTS.

Once you get there, you will want to talk to key individuals *who can suggest other people you might talk to, as you try to find out what organizations interest you.* You will want to define these key individuals in your distant city ahead of time and let them know you are coming. Your list may include: friends, college alumni (if you attended college), high school pals, church or synagogue contacts, Chamber of Commerce executives, city manager, regional planning offices, appropriate county or state offices in your area of interest, the Mayor, and high level management in particular companies that look interesting from what you've read or heard about them.

When you "hit town," you will want to remember the City Directory, the Yellow Pages of your phone book, etc. You *may* want to put a modest-sized advertisement in the paper once you are in your chosen geographical area (or in the place where you currently live, if that is where you intend to do your job-hunting), saying you would like to meet with other people who are following the job-hunting techniques of *What Color Is Your Parachute?* That way you'll form a kind of 'job-hunters anonymous,' where you can mutually support one another in your hunt. With such help, or by yourself, you then set about the process. A job-hunter describes it:

"Suppose I arrived cold in some city, the one place in all the world I want to live—but with no idea of what that city might hold as a match and challenge for my 'personal-talent bank.' I have an economic survey to make, yes; but I also have an equally or more important personal survey to accomplish. Can this city meet my peculiarly personal needs? To find out, I meet Pastors, bankers, school principals, physicians, dentists, real estate operators, et al. I would be astonished if opportunities were not brought to my attention, together with numerous offers of personal introduction to key principals. All I would be doing is forging links (referrals) in a chain leading to my eventual targets. *The referral is the key.*"

HOW HARD SHOULD I
WORK AT THIS?

We kept score with one man's job-hunt. He was researching a distant place. While still at a distance, by means of diligent research he turned up 107 places that seemed interesting to him. Over a period of some time, he sent a total of 297 letters to them. He also made a total of 126 phone calls to that city. When he was finally able to go there in person, he had narrowed the original 107 that looked interesting, down to just 45. He visited all 45, while there. Having done his homework on himself thoroughly and well,—and having obviously conducted *this* part of his search in an extremely professional manner, he received 35 job offers. When he had finished his survey, he went back to the one job he most wanted—and accepted it.

No one can argue that you should be dealing with numbers of this magnitude. But this may at least give you some idea of *how hard you may need to work* at this. Certainly, we're not just talking about five letters and two phone calls. We're talking about rolling up your sleeves, and being *very thorough.*

IV.
HOW TO USE A COMPUTER
TO AID YOU IN
PRIORITIZING

If you are doing chapters 4 and 5 with thorough discipline, you will be using the Prioritizing Grid *a lot*. (I once used it 52 times in one weekend.) That's okay. Just stick it in a copy machine, and make as many copies as you need. Use it at every turn, in chapters 4 and 5—please. It will help you *immensely*.

But IF you have a computer, and IF you know how to type in a BASIC program, saving it to disk, here are three simple PRIORITIZING GRIDS for you to type and then load into your computer.

These programs are gifts to our readers, from fellow-readers, as noted.

What follows are actual printouts of the programs. Copy the appropriate one for your type of computer carefully, including each space or spaces. SAVE it to disk with whatever name you give it (say, "Prioritizing Grid"). Then, whenever you wish to use it, boot the disk, and once booted, type in the words: RUN PRIORITIZING GRID (or whatever name you chose).

No doubt some of you out there will think of some improvements to the program, and if you want to share them with our readers (and you don't add too many more lines to the listing) we'll be happy to print your ideas in next year's edition, with appropriate credit.

---

1. The Prioritizing Grid for
APPLE II COMPUTERS
Courtesy of our readers Peter Bagley, of Quincy, Illinois, and
Pete Boardman, of Groton, New York

```
50   HOME : PRINT "MODIFIED BY PET
     ER BAGLEY"
60   PRINT : PRINT : PRINT : PRINT
     : PRINT : PRINT : PRINT
70   PRINT "BY PETE BOARDMAN": PRINT
     : PRINT : PRINT : PRINT : PRINT

80   SPEED= 255: REM   BACK TO NORM
     AL SPEED
90   DIM ITEM(20),ITEM$(20)
92   REM : ESTABLISHED ADDED SPACE
     S FOR ITEM$(NBR)
95 SP$ = "
            "
100  REM    --WAIT FOR USER TO REA
     D--
110  FOR DL = 1 TO 3000: NEXT
120  HOME : REM   CLEAR SCREEN
130  PRINT "ENTER THE ITEMS"
131  PRINT : PRINT "YOU WANT TO":
      PRINT : PRINT "ONE AT A TIM
     E": PRINT : PRINT "PRESS <RE
     TURN> WHEN DONE."
135  PRINT "MAXIMUM LENGTH OF ITE
     M IS 23 SPACES"
140  PRINT : PRINT : PRINT : PRINT

143 NBR = NBR + 1
150  REM   MAKE SOUND
155  IF NBR > 20 THEN   GOTO 210
160  PRINT ""
170  PRINT   TAB( 6)NBR;")";
180  INPUT ITEM$(NBR)
190  IF ITEM$(NBR) = "" THEN   GOTO
     210
```

```
192 S =  LEN (ITEM$(NBR))
194  IF S < 23 THEN ITEM$(NBR) =
     ITEM$(NBR) +  LEFT$ (SP$,(23
     - S))
196  IF S > 23 THEN ITEM$(NBR) =
     LEFT$ (ITEM$(NBR),23)
200  GOTO 140
210 NBR = NBR - 1
220  IF NBR > 1 THEN  GOTO 500
230  HOME : PRINT "YOU MADE ONLY
     ONE ENTRY": PRINT "YOU WILL
     BE GIVEN ANOTHER CHANCE"
240  FOR DL = 1 TO 3000: NEXT : GOTO
     1506
500  REM   **EVALUATION ROUTINE**

510  FOR COMPARE = 1 TO NBR - 1
520  FOR OTHER = COMPARE + 1 TO N
     BR
530  HOME
550  PRINT "":
555  PRINT "1"
560  PRINT  TAB( 4)ITEM$(COMPARE)
     : PRINT : PRINT
561  PRINT "2"
562  PRINT  TAB( 4)ITEM$(OTHER): PRINT
     : PRINT
580  PRINT : PRINT : PRINT "CHOOS
     E 1 OR 2(HIT PROPER KEY, PLE
     ASE)"
581  PRINT : PRINT
590  GET KEY$
600  IF ( VAL (KEY$) < 1) OR ( VAL
     (KEY$) > 2) THEN 590
610  IF VAL (KEY$) = 2 THEN 640
620 ITEM(COMPARE) = ITEM(COMPARE)
     + 1
630  GOTO 650
640 ITEM(OTHER) = ITEM(OTHER) + 1

650  NEXT
```

```
 660   NEXT
 670   PRINT : PRINT : PRINT : PRINT
       : PRINT
 680   PRINT "WAIT, PLEASE": PRINT
       : PRINT : PRINT : PRINT
1000   REM   *SORT ROUTINE**
1005   FOR I = 1 TO NBR
1010   FOR J = 1 TO NBR - 1
1020   IF ITEM(J) <  = ITEM(J + 1)
       THEN 1090
1030 A = ITEM(J)
1040 A$ = ITEM$(J)
1050 ITEM(J) = ITEM(J + 1)
1060 ITEM$(J) = ITEM$(J + 1)
1070 ITEM(J + 1) = A
1080 ITEM$(J + 1) = A$
1090   NEXT : NEXT
1105   PRINT CHR$ (4);"PR# 1"
1120   FOR K = NBR TO 1 STEP  - 1
1130   PRINT ITEM$(K),ITEM(K)
1140 ITEM(K) = 0
1150   NEXT
1500   REM   **RESET PROGRAM**
1505   PRINT CHR$ (4);"PR# 0"
1506   HOME
1510   PRINT : PRINT : PRINT : PRINT
       : PRINT
1520   PRINT "PRESS 'Q' TO QUIT"
1530   PRINT "PRESS 'R' TO REEVALU
       ATE"
1540   PRINT "PRESS 'X'FOR NEXT PR
       IORITIZATION": PRINT : PRINT
       : PRINT
1550   GET KY$
1560   IF KY$ = "Q" OR KY$ = "q" THEN
       1601
1570   IF KY$ = "R" OR KY$ = "r" THEN
       510
1580 NBR = 0
1590   GOTO 120
1601   HOME
1610   END

]
```

---

2. The Prioritizing Grid for the
COMMODORE 128/64 COMPUTERS

Courtesy of Harold Bjornse, New Products Editor, and

Tim Walsh, Technical Editor of Run magazine

```
10 PRINT "C-128/C-64 VERSION BY TIM WALSH &
   HAROLD R. BJORNSEN - RUN MAGAZINE":
20 SPEED=255:
30 DIM ITEM(50),ITEM$(50)
40 FOR DL=1TO1500: NEXT
50 PRINT[CLR/HOME]
60 PRINT"ENTER 10 OR MORE ITEMS TO PRIORITIZE"
70 PRINT"PRESS RETURN WHEN DONE."
80 NBR=NBR+1
90 PRINT"":
100 PRINT TAB(6)NBR;
110 INPUT ITEM$(NBR)
120 IF ITEM$(NBR)=""THEN GOTO 140
130 GOTO 80
140 NBR=NBR-1
150 FOR COMPARE=1TONBR-1
160 FOR OTHER=COMPARE+1TONBR
170 PRINT [CLR/HOME]
180 PRINT "1";TAB(4)ITEM$(COMPARE)
190 PRINT "2";TAB(4)ITEM$(OTHER)
200 PRINT "CHOOSE 1 OR 2
210 GET KEY$:
220 IF (VAL(KEY$)<1) OR (VAL(KEY$)>2) THEN 210
230 IF VAL(KEY$)=2 THEN 260
240 ITEM(COMPARE)=ITEM(COMPARE)+1
250 GOTO 270
260 ITEM(OTHER)=ITEM(OTHER)+1
270 NEXT OTHER
280 NEXT COMPARE
290 PRINT "WAIT, PLEASE":
300 FORI=1TONBR
310 FORJ=1TONBR-1
320 IF ITEM(J)<=ITEM(J+1) THEN 390
330 A=ITEM(J)
```

```
340  A$=ITEM$(J)
350  ITEM(J)=ITEM(J+1)
360  ITEM$(J)=ITEM$(J+1)
370  ITEM(J+1)=A
380  ITEM$(J+1)=A$
390  NEXT J
400  NEXT I
405  PRINT"ITEM",,"PRIORITY
410  FORK=NBRTO1 STEP-1
420  PRINT ITEM$(K),,ITEM(K)
430  ITEM(K)=0
440  NEXT K
450  PRINT"PRESS Q TO QUIT, R TO RE-EVALUATE, OR
     X FOR NEXT PRIORITIZATION"
460  INPUT KY$
470  IF KY$="Q" THEN 510
480  IF KY$="R" THEN 150
490  NBR=0
500  GOTO 50
510  END

READY.
```

---

3. The Prioritizing Grid for
IBM COMPUTERS

(A universal form of BASIC that can be typed into
virtually any computer)
Courtesy of Dick Ainsworth of Ridgeway, Wisconsin

```
10 DIM W$(30): DIM W(30,30)
20 CLS: PRINT"Priority Calculator": PRINT
30 PRINT"Type the items you wish to prioritize"
40 PRINT"and press RETURN after each one.":PRINT
50 PRINT"Press RETURN twice after the last
   item.": PRINT
60 FOR L=1 TO 20
70 PRINT L;
80 INPUT W$(L)
90 IF W$(L)="" THEN GOTO 110
100 NEXT L
110 CLS: MAX=L-1
120 FOR M=1 TO (MAX*(MAX-1)/2)
130 X=INT(RND(1)*MAX)+1
140 Y=INT(RND(1)*MAX)+1
150 IF X=Y THEN GOTO 140
160 IF W(X,Y)=0 AND X<>Y THEN GOTO 200
170 IF Y<MAX THEN Y=Y+1: GOTO 160
180 IF X<MAX THEN X=X+1: Y=1: GOTO 160
190 X=1: Y=1: GOTO 160
200 CLS
210 PRINT "1: ";W$(X)
220 PRINT "2: ";W$(Y)
230 PRINT "0: (no preference)": PRINT
240 PRINT "Select (1-2-0)"
250 K$=INKEY$: IF K$="" THEN GOTO 250
260 IF K$="1" THEN W(X,Y)=2: W(Y,X)=-1
270 IF K$="2" THEN W(Y,X)=2: W(X,Y)=-1
280 IF K$="0" THEN W(X,Y)=1: W(Y,X)=1
290 NEXT M
300 FOR L=1 TO MAX
310 FOR M=1 TO MAX
320 T=T+W(L,M)
```

```
330  NEXT M
340  W(L,1)=T: T=0
350  CLS
360  NEXT L
370  PRINT"Print graph on printer? (Y-N)"
380  P$=INKEY$: IF P$="" GOTO 380
390  CLS: PRINT"Priority Calculator":PRINT
400  FOR M=1 TO MAX
410  X=1: G=-30
420  FOR L=1 TO MAX
430  IF W(L,1)>G THEN G=W(L,1): X=L
440  NEXT L
450  IF M=1 THEN MUL=39/G
460  PRINT G;W$(X)
470  IF P$="Y" OR P$="y" THEN LPRINT G;W$(X)
480  FOR A=1 TO MUL*G+1
490  PRINT "*";
500  IF P$="Y" OR P$="y" THEN LPRINT "*";
510  NEXT A: PRINT
520  IF P$="Y" OR P$="y" THEN LPRINT
530  W(X,1)=-30
540  NEXT M
```

A

Abbott Langer and Associates, 199
Absenteeism, employer fears about, 185, 189, 190
Accomplishments, diary of
  on the job, 205
  for skills identification, 101-2. *See also* Skills, identifying
Accuracy, importance of, 161
Acquaintances. *See* Contacts
Adult education, information sources, 234-35
Advertisements
  answering, 13, 17-20, 37
  clearinghouse of, 29-30, 33
  in journals, 33
  placing, 13, 21, 37
  skills level and, 72
  use and effectiveness (table), 37
  warnings about, 20
Agencies
  government
    as information sources, 294
    jobs with, 32, 223-24, 225
  nonprofit
    job registers, 33, 34
    jobs with, 219, 223-24
Alphabetized Occupations Finder, The (Holland), 214
Alternative patterns of work, information sources, 217-18
Alternative services jobs, information sources, 219, 223-24
Alumni bulletins, as research aids, 294
American Association of Consulting Management Engineers, Inc., 229

American Institute of Certified Public Accountants, 230
American Management Association, Inc. 15
American Men and Women of Science, 142
American Society of Training and Development Directory, 142
American Women's Development Corporation (AWED), 222
Anger
  letting go of, 44
  at the 'system,' 11-12
Animals, skills with, 77, 78, 84-85
Annual Reports
  help in reading, 229-30
  as research aid, 142, 159
    for salary information, 201
Appearance
  importance of, 180, 181, 182
  information sources, 239
Aptitude testing, 59
Art, in "What" phase, 56
Arts and crafts jobs, information sources, 224
Arts organization job registers, 33
Association of Executive Recruiting Consultants, 15
Associations, as salary information source, 198
Assumptions, avoiding, 48
Attitude
  toward enjoyment, 94-95, 99-100
  importance of, 65, 93
  stressing in interview, 187, 189
Audio materials, as job-hunting resource, 57-58
  for corporate jobs, 229
  for handicapped, 228
  Parachute overview, 215
Autobiography, for skill identification, 101-2

B

Benefits, value of, 203-4
*Bernard Haldane Associates' Job and Career
    Building* (Germann and
    Arnold), 215
Better Business Bureau, 142, 252, 257
Blacks, information sources, 228
Blind
    information sources, 228
    job register for, 32
Books
    availability of, 216-17
    as job-hunting resource, 57-58
    recommended titles, 214-15, *See also
        specific subjects*
Boredom, 64
Brain, workings of, information sources,
    244-45
"Broadcast letters," 16
Budgeting
    for determining salary needs, 125
    while unemployed, 234
Burnout, help in avoiding, 233
Business Information Sources, 142
Business school libraries, as organiza-
    tion information source, 142
Business Week, as information source,
    146, 235
Business world, information sources,
    229-30. *See also* World of work

C

California Manufacturers Register, 144
Calling-card, resume as, 169-71
Canada, job-hunting in, 144, 235, 237
Career, defined, 68
Career change
    See also Ideal job, researching
    exploring while employed, 290-96
    handicaps, 54
    looking for exceptions to rules, 45
    resources and information sources,
        57-60, 234, 240-41
    skills level and, 70
    skills prioritizing for, 98
    systematic view of options, 49-57
Career counseling
    on alternative work patterns, 218
    as career, information sources, 241-43

career assessment vs. career develop-
    ment, 231-32
    for clergy, 231-33
    at college placement offices, 25, 27
    at community colleges, 26, 58
    determining need for, 107
    for a fee, 59
        costs, 251, 256-57
    finding, xv, 247-78
        exploratory visits, 254-56
        identifying good career coun-
            selors, 250-52
        sample lists, by state, 258-64,
            277-78
    free sources of, 57-58
    general information sources, 240-41
    keeping your present job, 233
    National Career Development Proj-
        ect workshop, 324
    role of exercises in, 97-98
    sources, 58-60
    success rates, 251-52
    when not to use, 131
    for women, 222, 264-74
Career Development Council, 231
Career Guide to Professional Associations,
    142
Career Opportunities News, 199
Career planning
    audio-cassette on, 215
    books on, 214-15
        availability of, 216-17
    counseling for. *See* Career counseling
    exercises. *See* Exercises
    as life planning or life designing,
        104-5
Catalyst, 239
Chambers of Commerce
    as information sources, 142, 293
    job-clinics by, 58
Checklist, when things aren't going well,
    206-7
Chicago Tribune, 18
Child Care Personnel Clearinghouse, 33
Children, jobs with, 33, 243
Christian Placement Network, 32
Churches or synagogues
    See also Clergy
    jobs with, 32, 231-33
    as research aids, 60, 275-76
    support groups in, 60
Chusid, Frederick, & Co., 252
Cities, career counseling directories by,
    277-78

City or town halls, as information
    sources, 293
Civil Service examinations, 37, 225
Classified ads. *See* Advertisements
Clearinghouses or registers, 13, 27-35
CLEP (College-Level Examination
    Program), 234
Clergy
    See also Churches or synagogues
    career counseling resources, 60,
        231-33
    skills identification problems of, 104
College, going back to. *See* School,
    returning to
Colleges
    counseling offices, as research
        aids, 58
        at community colleges, 26, 58
    libraries, as organization information
        source, 142
    placement offices, 13, 25-27
        use and effectiveness (table), 37
    public service jobs with, 223-24
College graduates, help for, 58, 235
College-Level Examination Program
    (equivalency testing), 234
College Placement Council, 26
    salary surveys by, 198
College students, information sources
    for, 235, 236
Colorado Outward Bound School, "Jobs
    Clearing House" list by, 34
Commitment, importance of, 206, 207
Communications, as organization
    problem, 159
Community Careers Resource Center, 33
Community colleges
    placement offices at, 26, 27
    as research aids, 58
Community Jobs, 33
Community jobs, information sources,
    33, 219, *See also* Nonprofit
    agencies
Commute factors, 129
Competition
    as salary information source, 201
    skills levels and, 72-73
Complete Job Search Handbook, The
    (Figler), 215
Composite career option, 51, 117
Computer program, Prioritizing Grid,
    296-303

Computer-related jobs, information
    sources, 222
Computer resources, 222
    for career counselors, 242
*Consultants and Consulting Organizations
    Directory,* 142
Consulting, information sources, 142,
    219-22
Consumer Fraud Divisions, 252
Contacts
    being prepared for, 46
    establishing, 149, 240
    first approaches to, 141
    importance of, 48
    in Numbers Game, 13
    practice interviewing with, 132-33
    referrals from, 167, 171, 175-76
        to career counselors, 251, 253, 254
        in faraway locations, 294-95
        questions to ask, 167, 175
    as research aids
        for faraway locations, 173, 226,
            294-95
        names of organizations, 147-49
        power-to-hire, 152, 167
        problems of organization, 153,
            158, 159
        salary information, 201
    use and effectiveness (table), 37
*Contacts Influential: Commerce and Industry
    Directory,* 142-43
Contracts
    for career counseling, 256-57
    employment agreements, 204-5
    with private employment agencies, 22
Conventions, cultivating contacts at, 149
Corporate life problems, 154-55, 233
    for minorities, 228
    for women, 227
Corporate training programs, informa-
    tion sources, 229, 230
Corporations. *See* Employers
Costs
    of career counseling, 251, 256-57
    of clearinghouses or registers, 28
    of private employment agencies, 22
Counseling jobs, 237, 241-43
Courtesy, importance of, 48. *See also*
    Thank-you notes
Cover letters, "I" statements in, 75
Craftworkers, information sources, 224
Craftworker's Market. 224
Creativity and the brain, information
    sources, 244-45

Criminal justice job register, 33
Criminal record, help for job-hunters with, 229
Crystal, John
  on salary negotiation, 200, 203
  on teaching jobs, 237
  thanks to, xvii
  "written proposal" idea of, 175

D

Data, defined, 77
Database resources, 222
Data skills. *See* Information/Data skills
Diary
  of job accomplishments, 205
  for skills identification, 101-2
Dictionary of Holland Occupational Codes, 143, 214
Dictionary of Occupational Titles (D.O.T.)
  DOT numbers, 214
  as organization information source, 143
  skills lists from, 69-72
Directories
  career counseling, 277-78
  of college placement offices, 26
  of executive recruiters, 16
  for finding kinds of organizations, 142-46
  overseas job, cautions, 226
Directory of Career Planning and Placement Offices, 26
Directory of Corporate Affiliations, 143
Directory of Directories (Gale Research Company), 146
Directory of Executive Recruiters, 16
Directory of Information Resources in the United States, 143
Disabled workers, help for, 228
Disadvantaged groups, help for, 59
Dislocated or displaced workers, help for, 59, 228
DOT numbers. *See Dictionary of Occupational Titles*
Dreamers, realists vs., 111
Dress
  importance of, 46, 180, 181, 182
  information sources, 239
Dual-earner couples, special help for 231

Dun & Bradstreet's Middle Market Directory, 143
Dun & Bradstreet's Million Dollar Directory, 143
Dun & Bradstreet's Reference Book of Corporate Managements, 143
Dun's Review, 146
Dyer, Jim, resume by, 173-74

E

Education
  going back to school, 234-35
    credit for homemaking skills, 227
  international, directory, 235
  jobs in, 31, 139, 237-38
Educational and Career Information Services for Adults, 234
Educational Testing Service, I CAN lists from, 102, 227
Educational training opportunities, in organization, 159
Elderly, information sources, 234
Emerson, Ralph Waldo, on success, 211
Employed workers, job-hunting by, 290-96
Employees, problems of predecessor, 153, 157
Employers
  applying directly to, use and effectiveness, 37
  competing, as salary information source, 201
  contacting variety of, 46
  demonstrating skills to, 46-47, 177-78, 193-94
  fears of, 184-92
  getting in the door
    first approaches, 141
    personnel departments, 167-68
    using contacts, 167
  goals of, identifying, 120-24
  going face-to-face with, 46. *See also* Interviewing, by job-seeker
  information sources on, 140-46, 156-59
  job interviews with. *See* Interviewing, by employer

listening to, 156
narrowing down choice of, 108-63,
    146-47
    See also Ideal job, researching;
        "Where" phase
    goals of organization, 118, 120-24
    level of job, 124-25
    preferred geography factors, 125,
        129-30
    salary requirements, 124-25
    Special Knowledges, 115-18
    types of people worked with, 125,
        127-29
    working conditions, 125, 126-27
number of contacts required, 45
"problem child" type of, 140
problem-solving proposals for,
    177-78, 193-94
referrals by, 48
researching
    See also Interviewing, by job-
        seeker; Research
    accuracy concerns, 161
    goal of, 162-63
    in "How" phase, 52-53
    information sources, 140-46,
        156-59
    names of organizations, 146-49
    power-to-hire, 142-45, 152-61,
        167-68
    problems of organization, 149-61
    salary information, 197-202
    types of organizations, 139-46
    resume as memory jogger for, 169,
        171-72
return visits to, 48
small vs. large, 45, 139-40
    alternative work patterns and, 217
thank-you notes to, 48, 171, 193
volunteer work for, 48
worker pickup system, use and effec-
    tiveness (table), 37
Employment agencies
    clearinghouses or registers, 13
    college placement offices, 13, 25-27
    federal or state, 13, 24-25
        help for ex-offenders from, 229
        job-clinics by, 58
        as research aids, 58-59
        use and effectiveness (table), 37
    private, 13, 21-23
        Recruiters as, 16-17
        use and effectiveness (table), 37
Employment agreement, 204-5

Employment and Earnings (U.S. Depart-
    ment of Labor), as salary infor-
    mation source, 197
Encyclopedia of Associations, 143, 198
*Encyclopedia of Business Information
    Sources*, 143
Enjoyment
    identifying skills giving, 75
    importance of, 99, 100
    prioritizing skills by, 96-97
        on Tree diagram, 118
    Puritanical attitude toward, 99-100
Environmental Opportunities, 34
Environments, jobs as, 52. *See also*
        Working conditions
Equivalency examinations, 234
Exceptions to rules, searching for, 45
Executive Jobs Unlimited (Boll), 16n
Executive Manpower Directory, 35
Executive registers, 13
Executives, special help for, 229-30
Executive search firms, 13, 14-17
Exercises
    choosing a support person, 60
    interviewing practice, 132-33
    life planning as part of, 104-5
    narrowing down job market, 113-39
    "On the last day of my life . . ." 113
    for prioritizing skills, tree diagram,
        96-97
    shortcuts, 105-6
    skills identification, 73-85
        checking accuracy of, 103-5
        with diary, 101-2
        Puritanical attitude problems,
            99-100
        shortcuts, 105-6
        with stories, 75-76, 79, 103
    skills inventory, 79-85
    Tree diagram, 118
        goals of organization, 120-24
        level and salary desired, 124-25
        preferred geography factors,
            129-30
        prioritized skills, 96-97
        Special Knowledges, 115-17
        types of people worked with,
            127-29
        working conditions, 126-27
Ex-offenders, special help for, 229
External degree programs, information
    sources, 234-35

F

Family, help from, 60, 103. *See also*
    Contacts
Faraway locations, job-hunting in, 149,
    156-57, 292-96
    sending a resume, 172-75
    overseas jobs, 225-27, 236
Fears of interviewer, 184-92
Federal Career Opportunities, 32, 225
Federal employment agencies. *See*
    Employment agencies, federal
    or state
Federal jobs, information sources,
    25, 225
Federal Research Service, Inc., 32
Federal Trade Commission, 252
    on private employment agencies,
    22-23
Fields, careers vs., 68
Figler, Howard, xvii
Financial aid, for minority students, 228
Financial reports, help in reading,
    229-30. *See also* Annual
    Reports
Fine, Dr. Sidney A., xvii, 70
Firing
    anger after, 11, 43
    help after, 234
    possibility of, 11, 43
First job, help in finding, 236-37
Fitch Corporation Manuals, 143
Flex-time, information sources, 217-18
Forbes, as information source, 146
Fortune, as information source, 143, 146
Fortune's Plant and Product Directory, 143
Forty-Plus Clubs, 36, 275
Foundation Center, The, 221
Foundation Directory, The, 144, 221
Foundation grants, 221
Four-day work week, information
    sources, 217-18
France, job-hunting help in, 240
Franchises, information sources, 219-22
Frankl, Victor, on attitude, 64-65
Free professional help, 58-59
Friends, help from, 60, 103. *See also*
    Contacts
Fringe benefits, value of, 203-4
F & S Indexes, 143
Functional/transferable skills. *See* Skills,
    transferable
Funding
    for minority students, 228
    for self-employment, 220-21

G

Gale Research Company, *Directory of
    Directories,* 146
Geographical locations
    See also Faraway locations
    career counseling directories, by,
    227-78
    choosing, 129-30
    information sources, 240
        retirement planning, 240
    matching to names of organizations,
    146
    salary variations by, 198
Getting Yours (Lesko), 221
Gifts, *See* Skills
Goals of organizations
    identifying and prioritizing, 120-24
    matching to names of organizations,
    147
Goals of research, 162-63
Going back to school, information
    sources, 234-35
Government agencies
    grants from, 221
    as information sources, 294
    jobs with, 32, 223-24, 225
Grants, 221
Grooming, importance of, 46, 180, 181,
    182
Group support. *See* Support groups
Guerrilla Tactics in the Job Market
    (Jackson), 214
Guide to American Directories (Klein), 146

H

Haldane, Bernard, xvii, 205, 233
Handbook of Nonsexist Writing (Miller and
    Swift), xiv
Handicaps
    employer receptivity in spite of, 177
    help with special problems, 228
    listed, 54
    preparation as remedy for, 54-55
    ubiquity of, 48
Headhunters. *See* Executive search firms
Health, interview questions about, 190
Help, sources of. *See* Career counseling;
    Contacts; *specific problems*
Help Kids, 33
Herrmann, Ned, brain dominance
    instrument by, 245
High school students, information
    sources, 236-37

High-tech jobs, 243
Hiring
    decision making about, 186, 194-95
    employment agreement, 204-5
    fear of mistakes in, 184-92
Historical agencies, job registers, 33.
        See also Nonprofit agencies
"Holland code," 214
Holland, John L., xvii, 105, 243
Home-based businesses, information
        sources, 222
Homemakers, skills identification for,
        102, 227
Homework. *See* Exercises
Homeworking Mothers, 222
"How" phase, 52-53, 164-211
    luck vs. techniques in, 56, 106,
        208-10
How to Beat the Employment Game, 19
How to Choose and Change Careers (Bolles),
        215
How to Make a Habit of Success (Haldane),
        215
How to Reach Anyone Who's Anyone
        (Levine), 144
Human Engineering Laboratory
        (Johnson O'Connor), 59
Human resources management, as
        career, 237, 241-43
Human service agencies, jobs with,
        223-24

I

I CAN lists, 102, 227
I CAN program, 219
Ideal job, researching, 130-63
    See also Employers, narrowing down
            choice of; "Where" phase
    job registers for, 35
    interviewing practice, 132-33
    kinds of organizations, 139-46
    names of jobs, 134-38
    prioritizing skills for, 96-98
If You Don't Know Where You're Going . . .
        (Campbell), 215
Incorporation, information sources,
        221, 222
Individuality, importance of, 56
*Industrial Research Laboratories of the
        United States,* 144
Informational interviewing. *See*
        Interviewing, by job-seeker
Information/data
    defined, 77
    as goals of organizations, 123-24

Information/data skills
    identifying, 77, 78
    inventorying, 86-91
    levels of, 69
    prioritizing, 96 - 97
Information sources, 57-58
    See also Research; *specific subjects*
    books as, 57-58
        availability of, 216-17
        recommended titles, 214-15; *see
            also specific subjects*
    Chambers of Commerce as, 142, 293
    contacts as. *See* Contacts
    for faraway locations, 173, 226, 292-
            95; *see also* for overseas jobs
    general job-hunting guides, 214-15,
            238-41
    for high school students, 236-37
    interviewing techniques, 238-39
    journals as, 145
    librarians as. *See* Librarians
    magazines as, 146, 235
    for overseas jobs, 225-27, 236
    personnel offices as, 141
    power-to-hire. *See* Power-to-hire
    receptionists as, 141
    resumes, 238-39
    written material vs. people as, 140-42
Intercristo, 32
Interests testing, aptitude testing vs., 59
International education, directory, 235
International Employment Hotline,
        33, 226
International jobs, information sources,
        225-27, 236
Internships
    information sources, 219
    job registers, 33, 34
Inter-office politics, 154-55. *See also*
        Corporate life problems
Interviewing, by employer
    books on, 238-39
    employer decision making, 186,
            194-95
    fringe benefits, 203-4
    fundamental truths, 178-92
    getting feedback after, 207
    getting invitation to, 171
    hints about, 46-47, 48, 178-92
    making a good impression, 180-82
    preparing for, 176
    previous job questions, 189

purpose of interview
    for employer, 179, 182
    for job-seeker, 177-78, 179, 182
    questions by employer, 180-84
        fears behind, 184-92
    questions by job-seeker, 178
    raises or promotions, 204-5
    repeat, 195
    resume as agenda for, 169, 171
    resume as memory jogger after, 169,
        171-72
    salary negotiations, 195-205
        importance of timing, 182-84
    smoking vs. non-smoking during, 180
    thank-you notes after, 48, 171, 193
    time concerns
        for salary discussions, 182-84
        for speaking and listening, 184
    written proposal after, 193-94
Interviewing, by job-seeker
    on alternative patterns of work, 217
    books on, 238-39
    of career counselors, 254-56
    hints about, 48
    of "opposite number," 156, 157
    overcoming shyness, 132-33
    of people using same skills, 134-38
    for power-to-hire research, 167
    of predecessor, 157
    research before, 151-63
        importance of, 140-42
    responding to premature offers, 163
    of self-employed individuals, 220
    thank-you notes after, 48
Interviewing practice, 132-33
Investor, Banker, Broker Almanac, 144
"I" statements, 75

J

Jackson, Ellie, xvii
Jackson, Tom, xvii, 10, 48
Job, defined, 68
Job Banks, 24, 28-29
    directories of, 277-78
"Job beggar," "resource person" vs.,
    48, 55, 166
Job categories
    See also Skills, matching to jobs
    number of, 77
    public service jobs, 223
    researching, 134-38, 214
    skills vs., 77, 104

Job-clinics, 58
Job Clubs, 59, 276
"Job exchanges." *See* Clearinghouses or
    registers
Job Hunt, The (Sheppard and Belitsky), 13
Job-hunting. *See also* Job-hunting
    methods
    anger as reaction to, 11-12
    attitude toward, 44, 65
    books on, 214-15, 238-41. *See also
        specific types of jobs*
    checklist, 206-7
    commitment required for, 171
    competition in, skills levels and,
        72-73
    contacts and, 147-49. *See also* Contacts
    dreamers vs. realists, 111
    while employed, 290-96
    for first job, 236-37
    handicaps, 48, 54-55, 177
    inevitability of, 10-11, 43, 51
    as "job beggar" vs. "resource person,"
        48, 55, 166
    as job-training, 46, 131, 175, 238
    luck vs. techniques in, 56, 106, 208-10
    Map, 50-53
        ordering separate copy of, xiii
    Numbers Game, 12-38
    rejection shock, 9-10, 12
    research as part of. *See* Ideal job,
        researching; Research
    resources for, 57-60
    responding to premature offers, 163
    self-employment possibilities, 219-22
    self-esteem and, 12, 65-66
    self-management required for, 42-43
    skills level and, 70, 72-73
    skills prioritizing for, importance of,
        97-98
    successful vs. unsuccessful, 44
    the 'system,' 10-11
    systematic approach to, 56
    techniques. *See* Job-hunting methods
    thirty-five hints for, 43-48
    three phases of, 52-53. *See also specific
        phases*
    three requirements for, 56
    time required for, 43, 45, 46, 171,
        206, 207
    vacancies vs. dreams, 111
    World of Work sampler, 282-89
Job-hunting methods
    answering newspaper ads, 13, 17-20
    art required with, 56
    avoiding personnel departments,
        167-68

checklist, 206-7
college placement offices, 13, 25-27
commitment, 171
  while employed, 290-96
  for faraway locations. *See* Faraway
    locations
federal or state employment service,
    13, 24-25
going face-to-face, 171
information sources, 238-41
job interview. *See* Interviewing,
    by employer
job performance and, 46
luck vs. techniques, 56, 106, 208-10
Numbers Game, 12-38
off-beat, 36
placing newspaper ads, 13, 21
private employment agencies, 13,
    22-23
Recruiters, 13, 14-17
registers or clearinghouses, 27-35
resumes. *See* Resumes
thank-you notes, 48, 171, 193
use and effectiveness (table), 37
using contacts, 147-49, 171. *See also*
    Contacts
using a variety of, 45-46
Job interviews. *See* Interviewing,
    by employer
Job market
  books on, 243-44
  narrowing down, 113-39
  size of, 115
Job Market, The (Lathrop), 244
Job offers
  premature, 163
  salary issues 195-205
Job Opportunities for the Blind, 32
*Job Power: The Young People's Job Finding
    Guide* (Haldane, Haldane, and
    Martin), 215
Job requirements, World of Work
    sampler, 282-89
Job Search Companion, The (Wallach and
    Arnold), 214
"Job service," 24-25
"Jobs for people" vs. "people for jobs,"
    34-35
Job-sharing, information sources, 217-18
Job-support groups, 59
Job titles. *See* Job categories
Job Training Partnership Act, 59
Johnson O'Connor (Human Engineer-
    ing Laboratory), 59

Journals
  as information source, 145
  job listings in, 33
  placing ads in, 21
  use and effectiveness (table), 37

K

Klein's *Guide to American Directories,*
    146
Knowledge society, 162
Kookiness, as job-hunting method, 36

L

Laid-off workers, help for, 59, 234
Lesko, Matthew, on applying for grants,
    221
Letter of agreement, 204-5
Letters
  case history, for getting through
    screening process, 19
  "I" statements in, 75
Level of job, narrowing down, 124-25
Librarians, as research aids, 58, 146
  Dictionary of Occupational Titles
    (D.O.T.), 70
  for faraway locations, 294
  for finding books, 217
  on grants, 221
  information about organization, 142
  overseas jobs, 226, 227
  problems of organization, 158
  salary information, 197-98, 201
Library of Congress, National Referral
    Center, 145
Life planning, career planning as, 104-5
Listening, to employer's problems, 156
Los Angeles Times, ads in, 18
Low-income job-seekers, help for, 59
Luck
  techniques vs., 56, 106, 208-10
  ways of improving, 208-10
Lynch, Dudley, brain dominance instru-
    ment by, 245

M

MacRae's Blue Book, 144
Magazines, as research aids, 146, 235
Mail-order businesses, information
    sources, 222
Maister, David, 45, 104
Making Vocational Choices (Holland), 214

Management jobs, information sources,
    229-30
Manufacturers, registers of, 144
Map, Quick job-hunting, 50-53
    ordering separate copy of xiii
Maxi-geography, 129-30
Merrill Lynch Pierce Fenner and
    Smith, Inc., 229
Mid-life careers. *See* Career change
Miller, Arthur, xvii
Mini-geography, 129-30
Minorities, information sources, 228
Money. *See* Salary
Money management, while
    unemployed, 234
Moody's Industrial Manual, 144
Move In and Move Up (Butler), 15n
Multiple jobs, as option, 51, 52
    information sources, 217-18
Museum job registers, 33

N

Names of jobs. *See* Job categories; Skills,
    matching to jobs
Names of organizations, researching,
    146-49
National Association for Professional
    Saleswomen, 227
National Business Employment Weekly, 30
    "Calendar of Events," 276
    as salary information source, 199
National Career Development Project,
    xviii
    career development workshop by,
    325
    newsletter by, 323
National Center for Citizen Involve-
    ment, I CAN lists from, 102
*National Directory of Addresses and Tele-
    phone Numbers,* 144
National Education Service Center,
    NESC Jobs Newsletters, 31
National Employment Listing Service,
    NELS Monthly Bulletin, 33
National Federation for the Blind, job
    register, 32
*National Recreational Sporting and Hobby
    Organizations of the U.S.,* 144
*National Trade and Professional Associa-
    tions of the United States and
    Canada and Labor Unions,* 144
Natural Science for Youth Foundation,
    Opportunities, 34
NCES JOBSLETTER, 33

NELS Monthly Bulletin, 33
"Networking." *See* Contacts
Newsletters, help from, 241
    National Career Development
    Project, 323
Newspaper ads. *See* Advertisements
Newspapers, as information sources, in
    faraway locations, 293
New York Times
    ads in, 18
    on career counseling fraud, 252
900,000 Plus Jobs Annually (Feingold and
    Winkler), 33, 240
Nonprofit organizations
    job registers, 33, 34
    jobs with, 219, 223-24
Nonsexist writing techniques, xiv
Northeast Cultural Employment
    Services, *NCES
    JOBSLETTER,* 33
Numbers Game, 12-38
    See also Statistics
    answering newspaper ads, 13, 17-20
    college placement offices, 13, 25-27
    executive search firms, 13, 14-17
    federal or state employment services,
    13, 24-25
    placing ads, 13, 21
    private employment agencies,
    13, 22-23
    Recruiters; *see* executive search firms
    registers or clearinghouses, 27-35
    resume-in-a-book, 35
    using to advantage, 13-28
    use and effectiveness (table), 37

O

Occupational characteristics, World of
    Work sampler, 282-89
Occupational Outlook Handbook, 144, 244
    as salary information source, 198
*Occupational Outlook Handbook for College
    Graduates,* 144
Occupational Outlook Quarterly, 37
    World of Work sampler from, 282-89
Occupational titles. *See* Job categories
Occupations Finder, 214
Off-beat job-hunting methods, 36
Offers. *See* Job offers
Ombudsman jobs, 237
On-the-job training programs, informa-
    tion sources, 219, 229, 230
Opportunities, 34

"Opposite number"
    of person with power-to-hire, 156-57
    of predecessor, 157
Organizations, as job search aid, 37.
        See also Employers
Outdoor jobs, 34
Outward Bound, job register, 34
Overseas jobs, information sources,
        225-27, 236

P

Part-time jobs
    as alternative, 51, 52
    information sources, 219-22
    multiple, 51, 52
        information sources, 217-18
    Tree diagrams for, 117
Party metaphor, 73-74
People, defined, 77
People environments, narrowing down
        choice of, 127-29. *See also*
        Working conditions
People skills
    hierarchy of, 69, 71-72
    identifying, 77, 78
    inventorying, 80-85
    prioritizing, 96-97
Periodicals, as research aids, 146, 235
    on brain research, 245
Personal contacts, 13. *See also* Contacts
Personnel offices, 167-68
    as information sources, 141
Physical appearance, importance of,
        180, 181, 182
Physically handicapped workers, infor-
        mation sources, 229
Pick Your Job and Land It (Edlund and
        Edlund), 215
Plan Purchasing Directory, 144
Porot, Daniel, xvii, 240
Power-to-hire
    in committee, 152
    finding person with, 42-45, 52-53,
        167-68
    finding problems of person with,
        152-61
        language concerns, 160-61
        by talking to opposite number,
            156-57
    getting in to see, 175-76
    government jobs, 225
Practice, in doing research 132-33

Predecessor
    discovering problems of, 153
    as information source, 157
Present job, keeping, 233
    job-hunting while, 290-96
Previous job, interview questions about,
        189
"Principles of exclusion." *See* Employers,
        narrowing down choice of
Prioritizing Grid, 116
    computer program for, 296-303
    for geographical locations, 129-30
    for information or data choices,
        123-24
    for people environments, 127-29
    for products choices, 120-22
    for services choices, 122-23
    for Special Knowledges, 116-17
    for working conditions, 126-27
Prioritizing skills, 96-98, 116-18
    enjoyment problems, 99-100
    importance of, 97-98, 103-4
    on Tree diagram, 117, 118
Prisoner's Yellow Pages, 229
Private employment agencies, 21
Problem-solving proposals
    importance of problem identifica-
        tion before, 154-55
    importance of skills, 46
    language issues, 179
    sending after employment interview,
        193-94
Problems of organization
    accuracy concerns, 161
    language concerns, 160-61
    researching, 149-61
Products
    as goals of organizations, 120-22
    matching to names of organizations,
        146-47
Professional groups, as salary informa-
        tion source, 198
Professional journals, placing ads in, 21
    use and effectiveness (table), 37
Professionals, career counseling
        resources, 60
Professors, referrals from, 37
Promotions, in salary negotiation, 204-5
Proposals, sending after first interview,
        193-94
Prospective employer, doing volunteer
        work for, 48
Publications, placing ads in, 21
Public relations jobs, 237

Public relations officers, as information sources, 141
Public service careers, information sources, 223-24
Publishing jobs, information sources, 224
Puritanical attitudes, 99-100

Q

"Qualifications brief"
  "I" statements in, 75
  resume vs., 175
Quality of work, importance of, 46

R

Rado, Stuart Alan, career counseling fraud crusade by, 253
Raises, in salary negotiation, 204-5
  diary of accomplishments to support, 205
  help with, 239
Realists, dreamers vs., 111
Receptionists
  as information sources, 141
  thank-you notes to, 48, 193
Recruiters (executive search firms), 13, 14-17
Referrals, by employers, 48. See also Contacts
Registers or clearinghouses, 13, 27-35
Rejection Shock, 9-10, 12
  avoiding, 48
  feedback after, 207
  help after, 234
Relatives, use and effectiveness (table), 37
Religious jobs, 231-33. See also Churches or synagogues; Clergy
Relocation, information sources, 231, 240
Research
  See also Information sources
  accuracy of information, 161
  clearinghouses or registers for, 35
  at a distance, 156-57, 292-94
  for exceptions to rules, 45
  goal of, 166, 167
  on grants, 221
  importance of, 131, 207
  impression on employer with, 176
  kinds of organizations, 139-46
  in knowledge society, 162
  names of jobs, 134-38

names of organizations, 146-49
  practice exercise, 132-33
  problems of organization, 149-61
  salary, 97-202
    on range, 200-203
    on self-employment, 220, 221
Research Centers Directory, 144
"Resource person," "job beggar" vs., 48, 55, 166
Resumes
  as agendas for interview, 169, 171
  answering newspaper ads with, 17-19
  "broadcast letters," 16
  effectiveness of, 12-13, 18
  employer visits vs., 46
  as extended calling cards, 169-71
  four functions of, 169
  getting through the screening process, 19
  guidance in writing, 175
  help with, 238-39
  "I" statements in, 75
  as memory joggers, 169, 171-72
  in Numbers Game, 12-13
  for overseas jobs, 226
  "qualifications brief," 175
  as self-inventories, 169, 171
  sending, 16, 17-19, 169-70
    in a book, 35
    to faraway locations, 172-75
    after interview, 171, 194
    to Recruiters, 16-17
  "written proposal," 175
Retirement, information sources, 234
Retraining
  as folly, 68
  as option, 51, 52
Riffed, help after being, 234
Rockport Institute, 59
Rules, finding exceptions to, 45

S

Salary
  average, by occupation, 199
  determining requirements, 124-25
  fringe benefits, 203-4
  negotiations, 195-205
    fringe benefits as part of, 203-4
    information sources, 197-98, 201, 238-39
    raises or promotions as part of, 204-5
  premature discussions of, 19, 196

range, 200-203
regional variations in, 198
researching, 197-202
for women, 204
Sales jobs, for women, 227
School, returning to
credit for homemaking skills, 227
information sources, 234-35
retraining as folly, 68
retraining as option, 51, 52
School administration jobs, 237
School placement offices. *See* College
placement offices
Science jobs, 34
Scientific Manpower Commission, as
salary information source, 199
Screening process, for resumes, 12-13, 16
getting through, 19
Second careers. *See* Career change
Secretaries, thank-you notes to, 48, 193
Securities Exchange Commission, as
overseas job information
source, 226
Self, as job-hunting resource, 57
Self-Directed Search instrument, 214
Self-employment option, 51, 52
information sources, 219-22
Self-esteem
erosion of, 12, 169-70
through knowing what you want,
65-66
Self-inventories, resumes as, 169, 171
Self-management skills/traits, job hunting requires, 42-43, 127-29
Services, as goals of organizations,
122-23
matching to names, 146-47
people environments, 127-29
Shapero, Albert, 108, 164
Shortcuts, for skills identification, 105-6
Shyness, help with, 239
Skills
analyzing, help in, 238
categories of, 69
creativity studies, 244-45
deciding where to use. *See* "Where"
phase
defined, 68
demonstrating to employers, 46-47,
177-78, 193-94
enjoyable, on Tree diagram, 118
functional/transferable; *see*
transferable

hierarchy of, 69-72
identifying, 73-95
as art, 56
checking accuracy of, 103-5
exercises, 101-2
help in, 238
for homemakers, 102, 227
importance of, 65-66, 67
shortcuts, 105-6
special problems, 99-104
with stories, 75-76, 79, 103
in volunteer work, 219, 227
in "What" phase, 52
with information or data
hierarchy of, 69, 78
identifying, 77, 78
inventorying, 86-91
prioritizing, 96-97
interview questions about, 187-88
inventorying, 79-95
even while working, 53
in "What" phase, 52
job-hunting, as job training, 131, 238
job titles vs., 77, 104
levels of
competition for jobs and, 72-73
job advertisements and, 72
listed, 69, 71-72
matching to jobs, 134-38
See also Job categories
for homemakers or volunteers,
102, 227
information sources, 214, 215, 238
in interview, 178, 179, 180, 187-88
World of Work sampler, 282-89
matching to names of organizations,
146-49
matching to problems of organization, 149-61
with people
hierarchy of, 69, 71-72, 78
identifying, 77, 78
inventorying, 80-85
prioritizing, 96-97
prioritizing, 96-98
computer program for, 296-303
by enjoyment, 99-100, 118
importance of, 97-98, 103-4
Prioritizing Grid, 116
Special Knowledges, 116-18
on Tree diagram, 117, 118
self-management skills/traits, job-
hunting requires, 42-43,
127-29

Special Knowledges
    identifying, 115-16
    prioritizing, 116-18
testing, sources for, 59
with things
    hierarchy of, 69, 78
    identifying, 77, 78
    inventorying, 92-95
    prioritizing, 96-97
three types of, 69. *See also specific types*
transferable
    as answer to interviewer's fears,
        188
    defined, 52
    finding jobs using, 134-38
    identifying and inventorying, 52,
        73-95
    on Tree diagram, 118
    verbs used for, 74-75
volunteer, identifying, 219, 227
Small businesses
    advantages of, 45, 140, 201
    openness to alternative work
        patterns, 217
    self-employment options, 219-22
    women owners of, 222
Social change jobs, 219, 223-24
Social service jobs, 223-24
Songwriter's Market, 224
Special Knowledges
    identifying, 115-16
    prioritizing, 116-18
Staff turnover, as problem of
    organization, 159
Standard and Poor's Corporation Records,
    145
Standard and Poor's Industrial Index, 145
Standard and Poor's Listed Stock Reports,
    145
*Standard and Poor's Register of Corpora-
    tions, Directors and Executives*,
    145
State employment agencies. *See* Employ-
    ment agencies, federal or state
States, career counseling resources
    listed by, 258-64, 277-78
    for women, 264-74
Statistics
    See also Numbers game
    career counseling successes, 251-52
    effectiveness of resumes, 12-13, 18,
        169
    hiring through want ads, 18

job attrition rate, 137
job-hunting while still employed, 290
multiple part-time jobs, 217
Numbers Game problem, 14
private employment agency
    effectiveness, 22-23
self-employment successes and
    failures, 219
"underemployment," 111
USES effectiveness, 25
want ad responses, 18
Staub, Dick, 32
Stories, for skill identification, 75-76,
    79, 103
Students, information sources for,
    235-37
Success, Emerson's view of, 211
Summer jobs, information sources, 236
Support groups, 59
    for unemployed, 275-76
Support person, importance of, 60
Swift, Kate, xiv
Systematic Approach, importance o, 56

T

Talents. *See* Skills
Tasks. *See* Skills
Teachers, referrals from, use and effec-
    tiveness (table) 37
Teaching jobs, 31, 139, 237-38
    career counseling jobs as, 241-43
Techniques. *See* Job-hunting methods
Telephone Contacts for Data Users. 145
Television, career counseling series for,
    242
Temporary jobs, information sources,
    217-18
TGIF, 64
Thank-you notes, 48, 171, 193
Things, defined, 77
Things skills
    hierarchy of, 69
    identifying, 77, 78
    inventorying, 92-95
    prioritizing, 96-97
*Thomas' Register of American
    Manufacturers*, 145
Time requirement, 43, 45, 46, 206, 207
    luck and, 209
Timing, in salary negotiations, 182-84
Town or city halls, as information
    sources, 293

Trade association journals
    as information sources, 145
    placing ads in, 21
Trade journals
    as information sources, 145
    use and effectiveness (table) 37
*Training and Development Organizations
        Directory,* 145
Training jobs, information sources,
        237-38
Training opportunities, once employed,
        159
Transferable skills
    as answer to interviewer's fears, 188
    defined, 52
    finding jobs using, 134-38
    identifying and inventorying, 52,
        73-95
    on Tree diagram, 118
    verbs used for, 74-75
Tree diagram, 118-19
"Trioing," 103
Truth About You, The (Miller and
        Mattson), 215
"Trying on jobs," 134-38
Turnover of staff, as problem of
        organization, 159

U

"Underemployment," 111, 191
Unemployment
    group support resources, 275-76
    information sources, 234
    interview questions about, 190
Union hiring hall, use and effectiveness
        (table), 37
United Ministries in Education, National
        Career Development Project,
        xviii, 325
United States Department of Labor,
        Bureau of Labor Statistics, 239
    job register for blind, 32
United States Employment Service
        (USES), 24-25
    job attrition rate, 137
United States Government Manual, 145
University of Michigan, on pride in
        work, 46

V

Vacancies, dreams vs., 111
Vacations, job-hunting during, 291
Value Line Investment Survey, 145

Values
    increasing consciousness of, 104-5
    as job interview issue, 179, 180
    types of people worked with and,
        127-29
Visual arts jobs, information sources, 224
Visual materials, as job-hunting
        resource, 57-58
Vocational testing, sources for, 59
Volunteer work
    information sources, 219
    job skills identification, 227
    as option, 51, 52
    for prospective employer, 48

W

*Walker's Manual of Far Western Corpora-
        tions and Securities,* 145
Wall Street Journal
    ads in, 18, 21, 30
    on career counseling fraud, 253
    as information source, 146
Weaknesses, interview questions about,
        191
Welfare recipients, job-hunting help for,
        59
"What" phase, 63-107
    art required in, 56
    identifying skills, 73-85
Where Do I Go From Here With My Life?
        (Crystal and Bolles), 203, 214
    diary exercise in, 101
    on keeping a job, 233
    "trioing" described in, 103
"Where" phase, 52, 108-63
    See also Employers, narrowing down
        choice of
    exercises for, 113-39
    goals of organization, 120-24
    level and salary desired, 124-25
    narrowing down job market, 113-39
    narrowing down personal choices,
        115-30
        goals of organization, 120-24
        level and salary desired, 124-25
        preferred geography factors, 125,
            129-30
        Special Knowledges, 115-17
        types of people worked with,
            127-29
        working conditions, 125, 126-27
    preferred geography factors, 125,
        129-30

researching ideal job, 130-63
  interviewing practice, 132-33
  job registers for, 35
  kinds of organizations, 139-46
  names of jobs, 134-38
  prioritizing skills, 96-98
Special Knowledges, 115-17
techniques required in, 56
Tree diagram, 118-19
types of people worked with, 125,
  127-29
values and, 104-5
working conditions, 125, 126-27
Who's Hiring Who? (Lathrop), 145, 175,
  214
WIN recipients, "job clubs" for, 59
Women
  black, 228
  career counseling resources for,
    264-74
  as homemakers, job skills identifica-
    tion, 102, 227
  information sources, 227
  salary issues for, 204
  sales jobs for, 227
  as small-business owners, 222
  special help for, 227
    dual-earner couples, 231
  working mothers, information
    sources, 222
Work experience programs, information
  sources, 219

Working conditions
  matching to names of organizations,
    146-47
  narrowing down choice of, 126-27
    for people worked with, 127-29
  World of Work sampler, 282-89
Work satisfaction, help in finding, 240
Work times, alternative patterns of,
  217-18
World of work
  See also Business world
  attitude toward, 65
  boredom in, 64
  information sources, 243-44
  sampler, 282-89
  vocabulary guide, 236
Writer's Market, 224
Writing jobs, 224
"Written proposal," resume vs., 175

Y

Yellow Pages, as research aid, 253, 254,
  264
  for faraway locations, 295
Young, Phil, ex-offenders help from, 229
Youth
  job-hunting help for, 59
  jobs with, 33, 34, 243

Z

Zehring, John William, 33n

Author Index

A

Aburdene, P., 229
Adams, R. L., 235, 277
Albert, K. J., 229
American Historical
    Association, 237
Anderson, N., 240
Anderson, R. M., 231
Angel, J., 226
Appelbaum, J., 224
Arnold, P., 214, 215, 233
Aslett, D., 227
Avrutis, R., 234
Axford, R. W., 234

B

Bair, F. E., 240
Bard, R., 229
Bastress, F., 231, 238
Bates, M., 239
Bayless, H., 240
Beach, J. L., 277
Bear, J., 234
Beard, M. L., 238
Beatty, J., 224
Behn, R. D., 230
Behr, M., 222
Belitsky, A. Harvey, 13
Bemard, S., 235
Bendat, W., 243
Berson, L. E., 244
Bestor, D. K., 237
Biegeleisen, J., I., 238, 239
Bird, C., 231, 234
Bishop, N., 278
Bloomfield, W. M., 243
Blumenson, D., 233
Boll, C. R., 16n, 230
Bolles, R. N., 214, 215, 241
Borchard, D. C., 242
Boswell, J., 224
Bowman, T. F., 240
Boyd, K., 277
Boyer, R., 234, 240
Brabec, B., 222
Brady, J., 224
Breen, P., 238
Briarpatch Community,
    224

Brody, R., 252
Brohaugh, W., 224
Bruck, Dr. L., 228
Butler, L. A., 15n

C

Camden, T. M., 277, 278
Campbell, D. P., 215, 230
Caple, J., 244
Career Planning and
    Adult Development
    Network, 241
Carnegie, D., 233
Casewit, C. W., 226
Catalyst, 227
Chapman, J., 239
Chapman, R., 243
Cole, K. W., 228
Cole-Turner, R. S., 231
Collard, B. A., 243
Cook, B. E., 221
Cornish, E., 244
Cosgrave, G., 243
Council for the Advance-
    ment of Experiential
    Learning (CAEL), 242
Crites, J. O., 243
Crystal, J., 214
Cummings, R., 242
Cutshall, M., 231

D

Daniels, L. M., 142
Datcher, L., 228
Davis, G., 228
DeMare, G., 233
DeSimone, D., 245
Deutsch, G., 245
Donovan, P., 245
Douglas, M. C., 236
Drucker, P. F., 222, 230
Durden-Smith, J., 245
Durkin, J., 234

E

Edlund, M., 215
Edlund, S., 215
Edwards, B., 245
Edwards, P., 222

Edwards, P. B., 244
Edwards, S., 222
Eisentrout, V., 231
Ekstrom, R. B., 227
Esperti, R. A., 221
Evans, N., 224

F

Farnsworth, K., 231
Federal Research
    Service, Inc., 225
Feingold, S. N., 33, 240,
    244
Feldman, B. N., 222, 243
Fenton, T., 226
Ferguson, M., 245
Fiedler, J. M., 240, 277
Figler, H. E., 215, 235, 238
Figueira, H., 277
Figueroa, O., 229
Fine, S. A., 238
Fleming-Holland, S., 277
Fulford, N., 241-42

G

Gates, A., 235
Gaymer, R., 235
Germann, R., 215, 233
Giuliana, G. A., 240
Gordon, J. R., 229
Gottfredson, G. D., 214
Goulet, T., 235
Gracie, D. M., 244
Granovetter, M. S., 239
Gross, R., 234
Guthrie, L., 253

H

Hagberg, J., 243
Haldane, B., 215, 230
Haldane, J., 215
Half, R., 239
Hall, D. T., 231
Hall, F. S., 231
Hallberg, E., 243
Hallberg, K., 243
Hansard-Winkler, G. A.,
    33, 240
Haponski, W. C., 234

Harding, J. S., 243
Harragan, B. L., 227
Harris, A. M., 227
Harry, M., 224
Hawes, G. R., 235
Heffron, M., 226
Hellman, P., 239
Henderson, D., 236-37
Herrmann, N., 245
Herzberg, F., 230
Hesser, A., 242
Hodges, R. T., 241
Hoge, C. C., Sr., 222
Holland, J. L., 214
Honeyman, S., 240
Honigsberg, P. J., 224
Hoppock, R., 243
Hopson, Dr. B., 242
Hughes, K., 219
Hulse, L. S., 219
Hummel, R. L., 242

I

Imakyure, C., 231
Irish, R. K., 231

J

Jablonski, D. M., 229
Jackson, T., 214, 239, 241
Jitahidi, J., 278
Job Information and
    Seeking Training Pro-
    gram (JIST), 241, 243
Johnson, M., 243
Johnson, W. L., 228

K

Kamoroff, B., 221, 224
Kamil, A., 219
Kanter, R. M., 230
Katz, M., 222, 230
Keirsey, D., 239
Kelly, J. J., 242
Kennedy, J. L., 237
Kennedy, M. M., 233
Kiam, V., 221
Kimeldorf, M., 236
Kingstone, B., 235
Knowdell, R. L., 242
Komar, J. J., 241
Kouri, M. K., 234

L

Lant, Dr. J. L., 221, 242
Lapin, L., 224
LaRouche, J., 227
Lathrop, R., 175, 214,
    239, 244
Lawhead, W., 231
Lazar, W., 222
Lee, P., 217
Leider, R. J., 243
Lesko, M., 222, 225
Levering, R., 222, 230
Levine, M., 144
Levinson, J. C., 217, 221
Levitt, H., 243
Lockheed, M. E., 227
Lynch, D., 245

M

McCabe, C. E., 234
McClure, R. M., 235
McCormack, M. H., 230
McDaniels, C., 242
McGahey, M. J., 238
McLagan, P. A., 237
Mainstream Access, Inc.,
    224
Malveaux, J., 228
Mangum, S. I., 240
Marks, L., 277
Martin, L., 215
Mattson, R. T., 215, 231
May, J., 234
Mayall, D., 217
Mayleas, D., 241
Maze, M., 242
Medley, H. A., 239
Mencke, R., 242
Mendelsohn, P., 227
Miller, A., 231
Miller, A. F., 215
Miller, C., xiv
Miller, N. R., 244
Minge, M. R., 240
Molloy, J. T., 239
Moody, F., 229
Moore, D. J., 241
Moore, R. W., 235
Moorpark College Coun-
    seling Staff, 235
Moran, P. J., 231
Mosenfelder, D., 236
Moskowitz, M., 222, 230
Mother's Home Business
    Network, 222

Munschauer, J. L., 235
Myers, I. B., 238
Myers, P., 238

N

Naisbitt, J., 229
National Vocational
    Guidance Assn., 241
Nelson, K., 217
Nelson, R. B., 243
New Ways to Work, 277
Nicholas, T., 222
Nicholson, A., 240
Noer, D., 19
Noyes, D., 240

O

O'Brien, B., 236
Odell, C. D., Sr., 234
Odell, L. M., 234
Ogawa, D. K., 214
Olmstead, B., 217
Olmsted, D., 277
Olson, R. P., 231
Olympus Research
    Corporation, 19
Ontario Society for
    Training and
    Development, 237
Ornstein, R., 245
Otto, L. B., 236

P

Parker, Y., 238
Pearson, H. G., 238
Peters, T. J., 230
Peterson, R. L., 221
Pilder, R. J., 243
Pilder, W. F., 243
Pinchot, G., III, 221
Porot, D., 240
Powers, M., 224
Prashker, M., 230

R

Rabby, R., 228
Raelin, J. A., 244
Raines, J. C., 244
Ramsauer, C. A., 277
Raufman, L., 243
Rinker, R. N., 231
Roberts, D., 243
Rockcastle, M. T., 240
Rothberg, D. S., 221

Ruffner, J. A., 240
Russell, B. I., 235
Ryan, C., 228
Ryan, R., 227

S

Savageau, D., 234, 240
Scally, M., 242
Scheele, A., 238
Schemenaur, P. J., 224
Schwartz, S., 277
Schwimmer, L., 233
Seavey, B., 240
Segalowitz, S. J., 245
Senft, R., 277
Shenk, E. J., 219
Sheppard, H. L., 13
Smith, B. R., 238
Smith, S., 217
Springer, S. P., 245
Stanton, T., 219
Staub, D., 231
Stevens, 240
Stump, R. W., 237
Sukiennik, D., 243
Summerfield, J., 233
Super, D. E., 243
Sweeney, P., 277

T

Teeple, B., 239
Thompson, G., 235
Trautman, J., 231

U

Ullmann, J., 240
U.S. Dept. of Labor,
    197, 244
U.S. Government Print-
    ing Office, 243
University of Wisconsin
    Continuing Education
    Service, 242
Upjohn, W. E., Institute
    for Employment
    Research, 238

V

Valiunas, S. P., 230
Varner, R., 231
Vaupel, J. W., 230
Visconti, R., 277
Viscott, D., M.D., 233
von Klemperer, L., 235
Von Oech, R., 245

W

Wachtel, S. E., 233
Wallace, P., 228
Wallach, E. J., 214, 241-42
Walz, G. R., 242
Washington, T., 238
Waterman, R. H., Jr., 230
Watson, G., 228
Weaver, N. P. K., 242
Wegmann, R., 242, 243,
    278
Wehrheim, C., 231
Wharton, J., 226
Whitaker, U., 238
Wiley, W. W., 238
Williams, E., 239
Winkler, C., 229
Winkler, G. *See*
    Hansard-Winkler, G. A.
Wonder, J., 245
Wood, O. G., 230
Woodworth, D. J., 236

Z

Zehring, J. W., 231
Zimbardo, P. G., 239

Mailing List
& Newsletter '87

The author of *Parachute*, Richard Bolles, is the Director of the National Career Development Project headquartered in Walnut Creek, California (26 minutes due East of San Francisco).

The Project maintains a mailing list. If you wish to be on the mailing list, please fill out the form below, and enclose a check for $15 payable to "National Career Development Project." People on the mailing list receive notification of new books or other creations from the pen of Richard Bolles, as well as of his annual two-week workshop.

You will also receive a Newsletter, published at widely separated intervals, but published a total of six times during the year, written and edited by him, containing his latest thoughts on various subjects. It contains articles about special problems that job-hunters or career changers are encountering; plus descriptions of new research or publications; plus more of Bolles' philosophy; plus news of the Project, and what we are up to lately (three new books are currently wending their way toward a 1988 publication date).

TO: Mailing List & Newsletter '87
     NCDP
     P.O. Box 379
     Walnut Creek, CA 94597

Dear Folks:

Please add me to your mailing list for the next six issues of your Newsletter, so that I may receive periodic announcements of your newly-published works, your workshop, etc. My check for $15, U.S., is enclosed, payable to: "National Career Development Project." ($30, U.S., if this is for two years.)

Name _____

Address _____

City, State, Zip _____

Organization (optional) _____

Life/Work Planning
at the Inn of The Seventh Mountain

Many readers write to ask if Richard Bolles ever does any teaching that is open to the public. The answer is that while he spends most of the year writing, he does do one training workshop a year,—the proceeds of which go entirely to the support of the National Career Development Project of United Ministries in Education.

This workshop is open to job-hunters, career-changers and career-counselors, and is held annually, beginning on the first Friday in August, at the Inn of the Seventh Mountain in Bend, Oregon. The workshop is fourteen days in length, and features over 100 hours of instruction. Dick Bolles and his famous European friend and colleague, Daniel Porot of Geneva, Switzerland, are normally the sole instructors throughout the two weeks.

The tuition is $10 per hour of instruction. Room and board at the Inn is additional. This latter cost varies, depending on the type of accommodations desired, but generally runs around $72 a day. The Inn of the Seventh Mountain is a first-class resort set in the high mountain air, on the flank of Mount Bachelor, with warm sunny days, and such varied activities as swimming, sauna, water-slide, hiking, roller-skating, tennis, mopeds, white-water rafting, horseback riding and the like. The food is outstanding. Most lunches and dinners are served outdoors. Participants in previous years have raved about this setting for the workshop.

The dates in 1987 are August 7–21, and the 1988 dates are August 5–19.

If you are interested in this training, please write to:

Registrar, Two-Week Workshop,
National Career Development Project
    of United Ministries in Education
P.O. Box 379
Walnut Creek, CA 94597

Update for 1988

To: PARACHUTE
P.O. Box 379
Walnut Creek, CA 94597

☐ I think that the information in the '87 edition needs to be changed, in your next revision, regarding (or, the following resource should be added):

_____

_____

_____

_____

_____

_____

☐ I cannot find the following resource, listed on page _____ :

_____

_____

_____

_____

_____

_____

Name _____

Address _____

_____

(Please submit this before June 30, 1987. Thank You.)

Other Books by Richard N. Bolles

THE THREE BOXES OF LIFE
And How To Get Out Of Them

"Parachute" has reshaped the way people think about jobs and how to find them. *The Three Boxes of Life* calls for as much change in the way we think about school, work, and retirement.

" . . . a rich and rewarding guidebook that provides literally hundreds of resources and opportunities for growth."—*Library Journal.* "Why aren't learning, working, and playing, lifelong—simultaneous—activities rather than boxes or blocks of times as we traditionally have been taught they must be?"—*American School Board Journal.* " . . . truly a monumental work which provides a wealth of information."—*Journal of College Placement.* " . . . an eloquent plea for the restructuring of our work lives."—*Career Planning and Adult Development Newsletter.*

Contains hundreds of resources, exercises, charts, illustrations and the complete *Beginning Quick Job-Hunting Map.* 6 x 9 inches, 480 pages, $9.95 paper. $14.95 cloth

WHERE DO I GO FROM HERE WITH MY LIFE?
by John C. Crystal and Richard N. Bolles

Here is *the workbook* for the self-motivated individual, student, professional or anyone who has an interest in a systematic approach to job-hunting and career mobility, bringing together two of the leading people in the field. "A master work in career literature." *Washington Star-News.* 9 x 7 inches, 272 pages, $9.95 paper

THE NEW QUICK JOB-HUNTING MAP
Advanced Version

A practical book of exercises designed to give job seekers detailed help in analyzing their skills, finding the right career field, and knowing how to find job openings and get hired. This is a 48-page version, 8½ x 11 inches, of the exercises printed in this book, $1.95 paper.

THE QUICK JOB-HUNTING MAP FOR BEGINNERS
Offers special help to new job seekers and others looking for their first jobs. 8½ x 11 inches, 32 pages, $1.25 paper

TEA LEAVES:
A New Look At Resumes

Richard Bolles describes how well resumes work, or don't work, and why. Also what you can do about it. 6 x 9 inches, 24 pages, $.50

Available at your local book store, or when ordering direct from the publisher please include $.75 additional per clothbound copy for postage and handling, or $.50 additional per paperback copy for postage and handling.

1☺ TEN SPEED PRESS • Box 7123, Berkeley, California 94707